HOLBEIN
at the Tudor Court

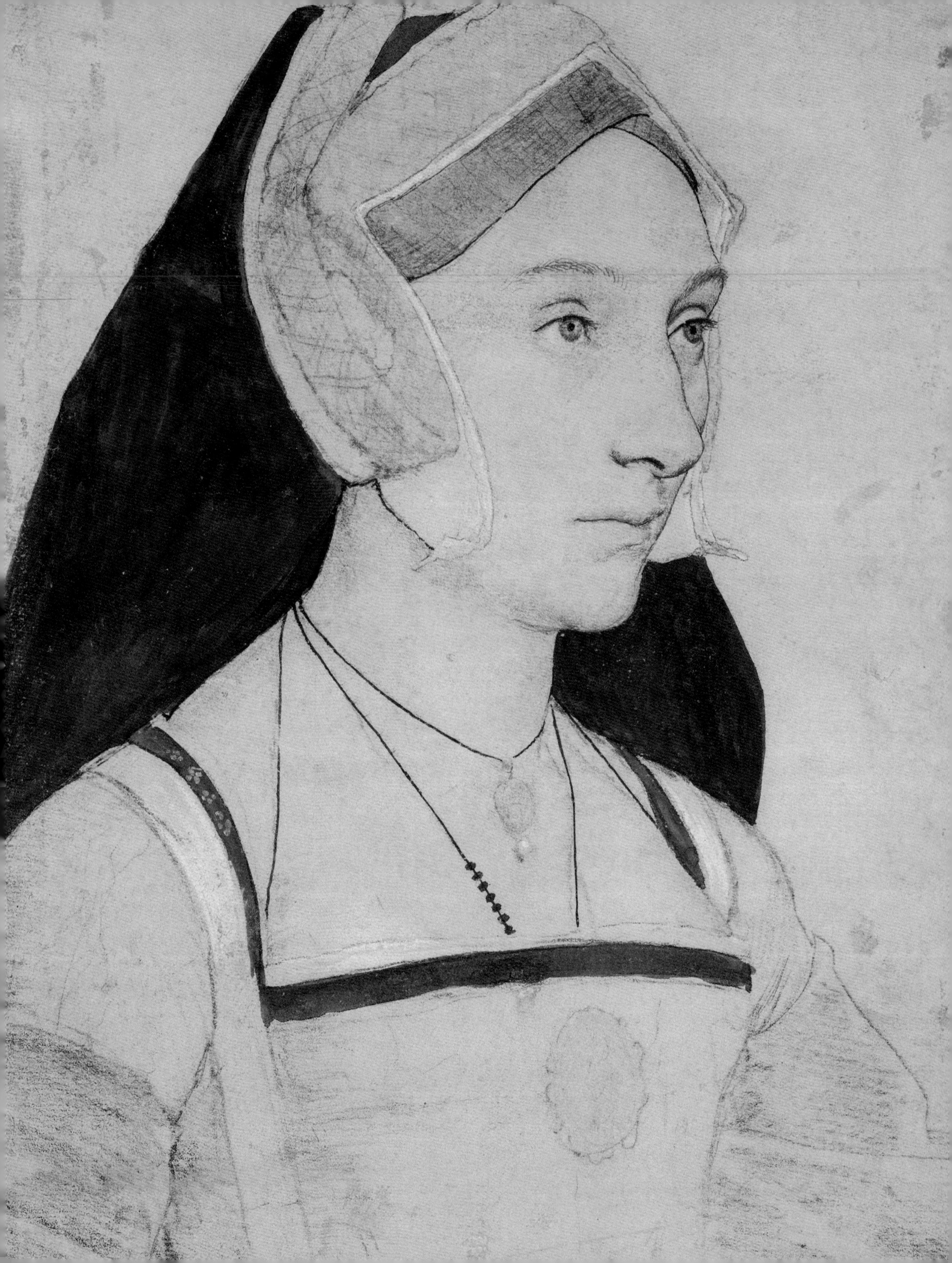

HOLBEIN
at the Tudor Court

Kate Heard

ROYAL COLLECTION TRUST

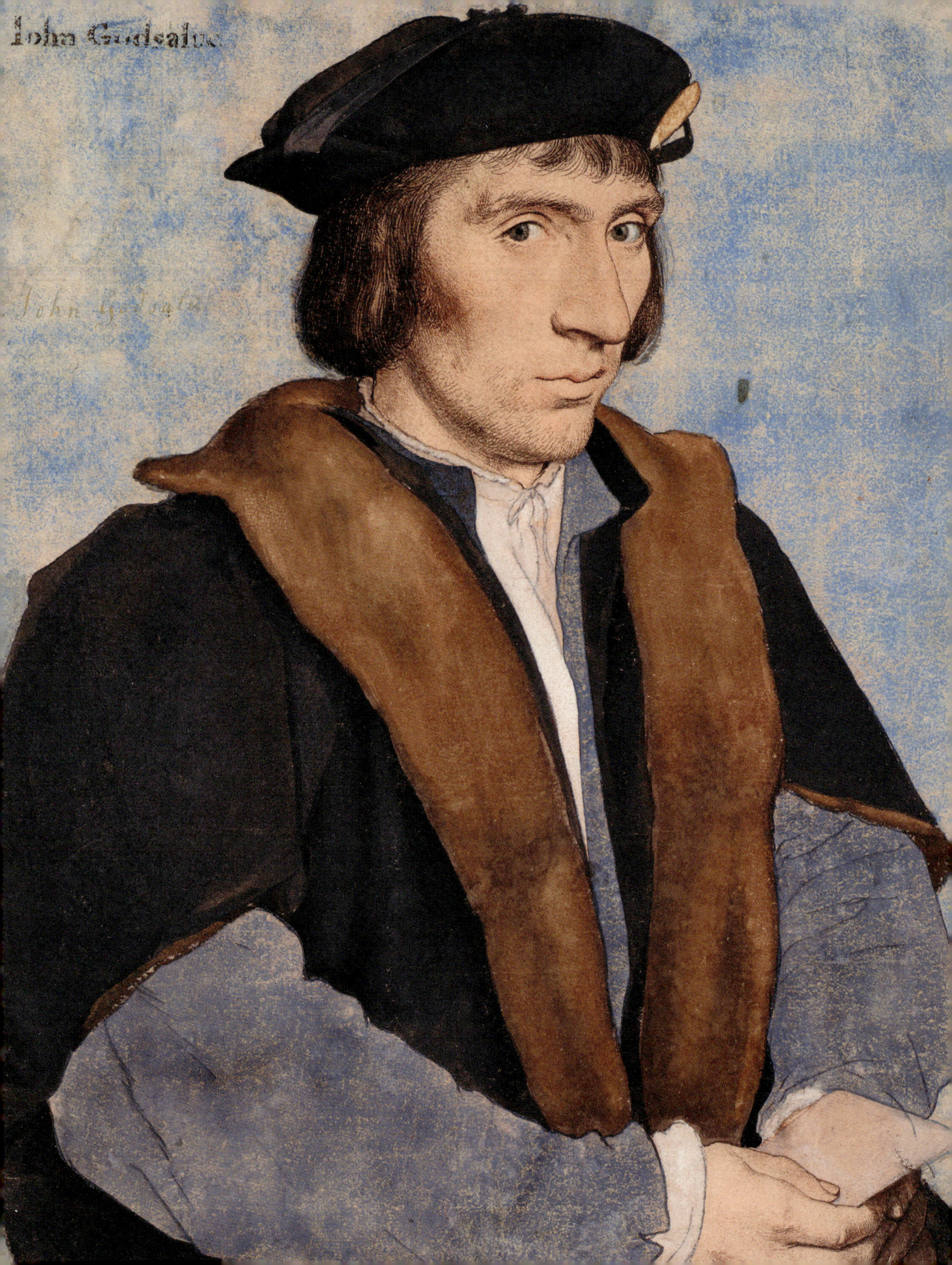
Iohn Godsalue

Contents

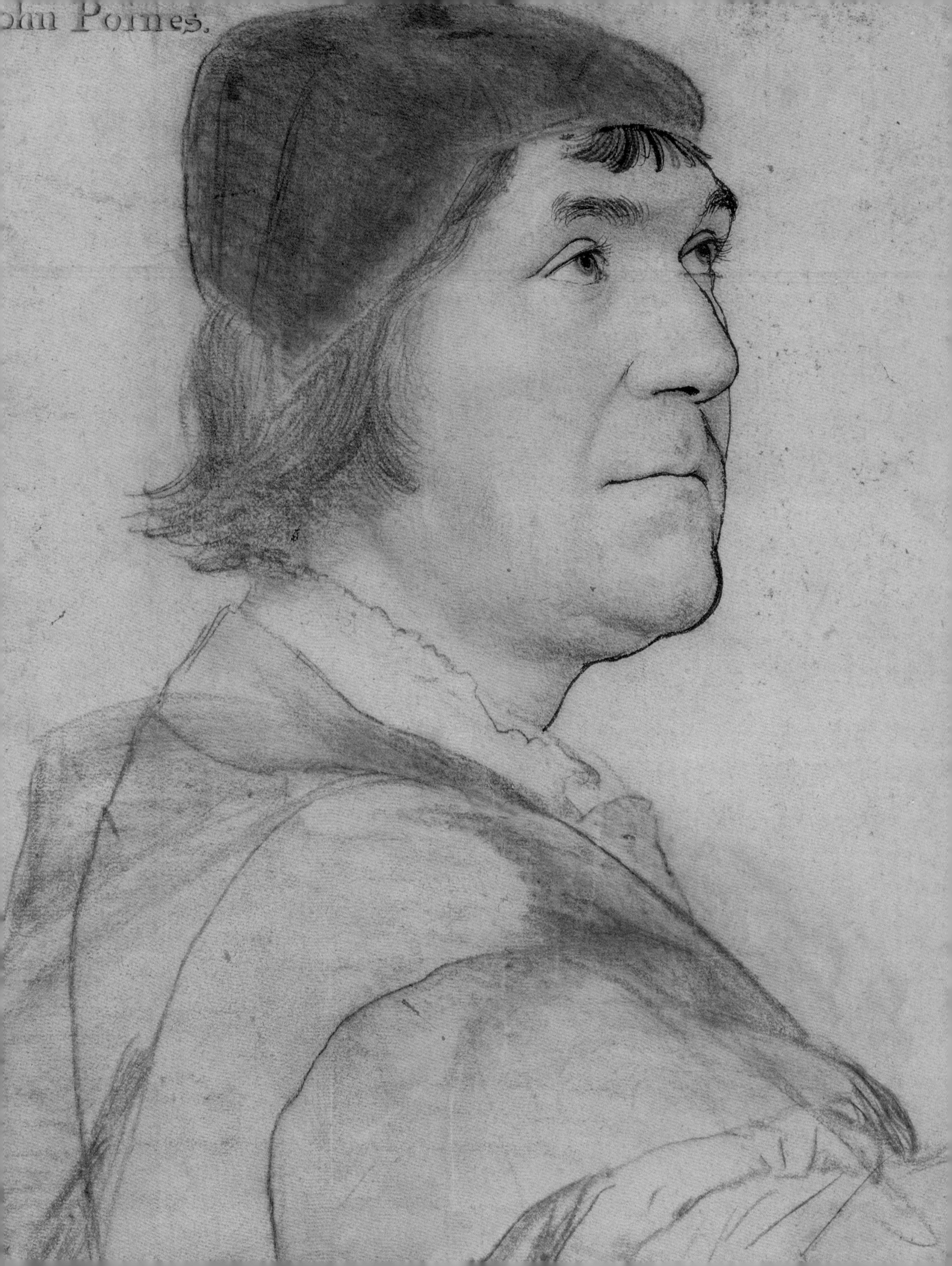
ohn Poines.

Hans Holbein: Portrait Artist at the Tudor Court

Hans Holbein's portraits are arrestingly beautiful. Between 1526 and his death in 1543 he drew and painted the elite of the Tudor court, setting onto paper, parchment and panel their confidence and finery, and it is easy to see why the men and women he depicted sought his work. His painted portraits, sometimes placed against a background enlivened with twisting vines, antique-style pillars or the shadow of the sitter, gleam with shining satin, gold thread and expensive jewellery, which frame the warmth of his subjects' faces. His miniatures, small enough to be held in the palm of the hand, are in such vivid colours that they appear as jewels themselves. His drawings, made as preparatory studies for these finished portraits, are a masterclass in manipulating materials to convey a likeness. Coloured chalks – smudged, dampened, sharpened or scribbled – inks and watercolour are all employed, sometimes in the tiniest of touches, to capture the glint of an eye, the softness of black velvet or the curve of a cheekbone. Looking closely, it is possible to imagine Holbein, too, peering in towards his sitter to see the detail of an iris, of an embroidered collar, of a tiny gold tag sewn onto a hat.[1] Sometimes we feel the artist's frustration: he struggled to depict the left eye of the wealthy and learned Duchess of Suffolk, scratching the circle of her iris repeatedly with his pen, and he was unhappy with the profile he had given the Page of the Chamber, William Reskimer, even as he turned from his drawing to panel, seemingly working on both simultaneously to reach a solution.

[OPPOSITE]
Hans Holbein, *John Poyntz*, *c.*1532 (see p. 60)

Born around 1497 in Augsburg, the son, nephew and brother of artists, Holbein's skill as a painter had been apparent from an early age (Fig. 1).

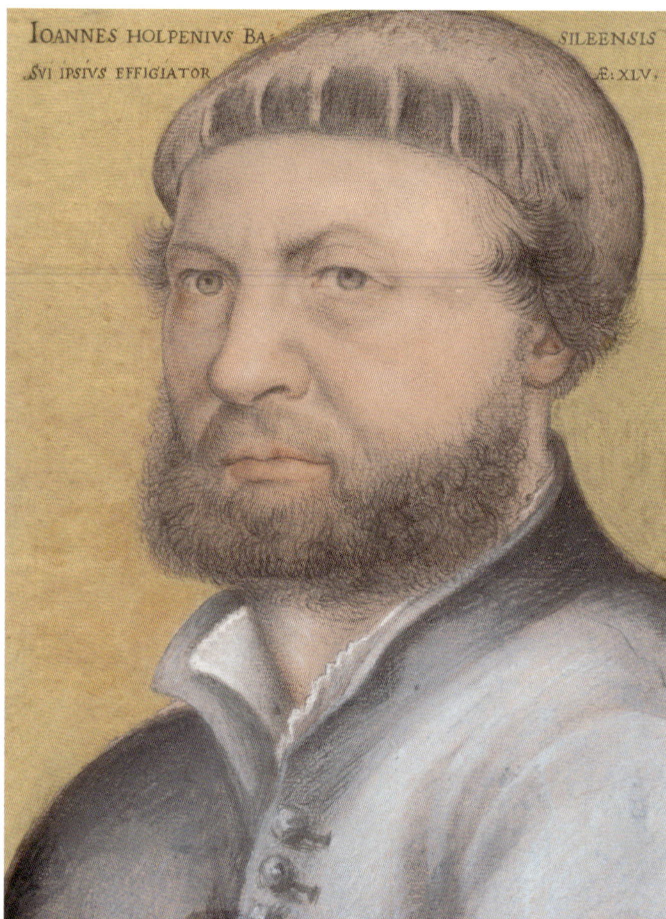

Fig. 1 **Hans Holbein, *Self-portrait*, *c.*1542–3, coloured chalks with pen and ink (and later gold background)**
Uffizi Gallery, Florence, 1890,1630

By the time he arrived in London to seek work in autumn 1526, he was already celebrated in the Swiss city of Basel, where he had lived since at least 1515, designing book illustrations and stained glass, painting religious panels, decorating façades with murals and making portraits of the city's ruling elite. He worked as a designer for Johannes Froben (*c.*1460–1527), a Basel printer who published the works of the Dutch scholar Desiderius Erasmus (1466–1536), who was also living in the city (Figs 2–3). By 1526, however, commissions in Basel were becoming harder to find, largely due to attacks on devotional images by those who promoted religious reform: 'the arts are not appreciated here', wrote Erasmus in August, while the artists of Basel complained to their city council that 'the painter's profession is in a bad way. Several painters have already abandoned their jobs'.[2] Among those to abandon a career in Basel in that year was Holbein.

The English court was not Holbein's first choice: in 1524 he had tried his fortune in France. Here, Francis I was gathering works by Italian artists at his

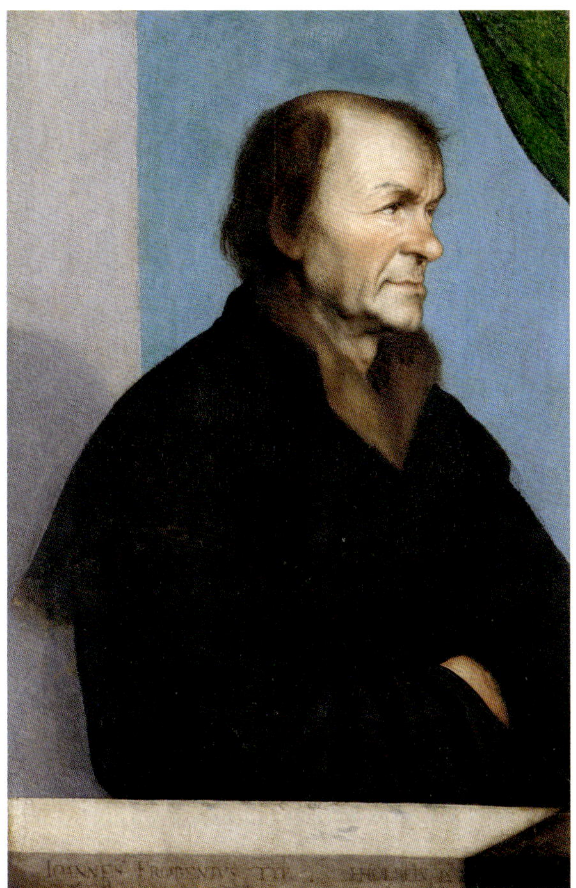

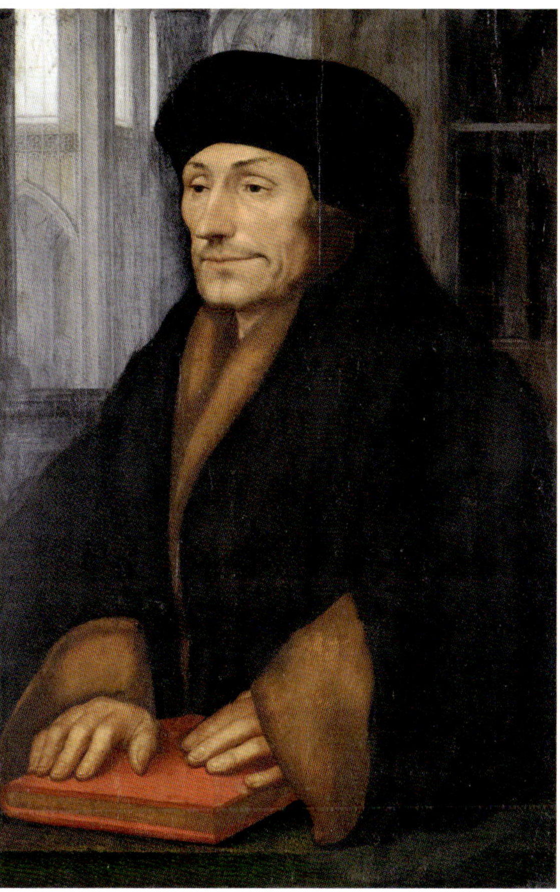

Fig. 2 **Hans Holbein, *Johannes Froben*, *c.*1522–3, oil on panel**
RCIN 403035

Fig. 3 **After Hans Holbein, *Desiderius Erasmus*, *c.*1520–40, oil on panel**
RCIN 403036

château of Amboise, among them Leonardo da Vinci (who had worked as 'first painter, architect and engineer' to Francis I from 1517 until his death in 1519), Fra Bartolomeo, Pietro Perugino and Andrea del Sarto.[3] It seems likely that Holbein hoped to be employed at the French court. He took with him a portrait of Erasmus on behalf of the sitter; the recipient of this gift is unrecorded, but it would act as valuable evidence of Holbein's skill and connections.[4] We know little about his itinerary in France, although two drawings of sculptures of the duc and duchesse de Berry show he visited Bourges, possibly on his way to or from Amboise (Fig. 4). Although he did not find a permanent position in France, Holbein's adoption of coloured chalks has been dated to this trip.[5] He had probably first encountered this technique in Augsburg where Hans Burgkmair and Leonhard Beck were using coloured chalks to make preparatory drawings for painted portraits in the early years of the sixteenth century (Fig. 5).[6] Indeed, the quality of the drawings of the duc and duchesse de Berry shows Holbein was already practised in this medium. But after his trip to France, coloured chalks became his preferred material for

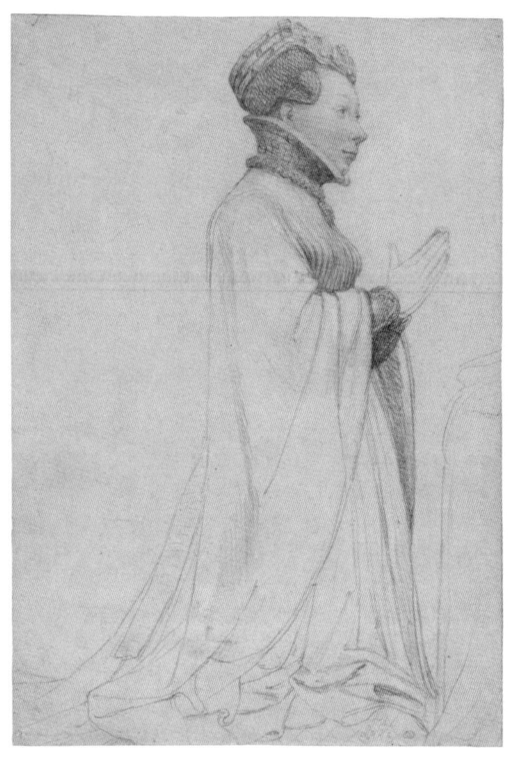

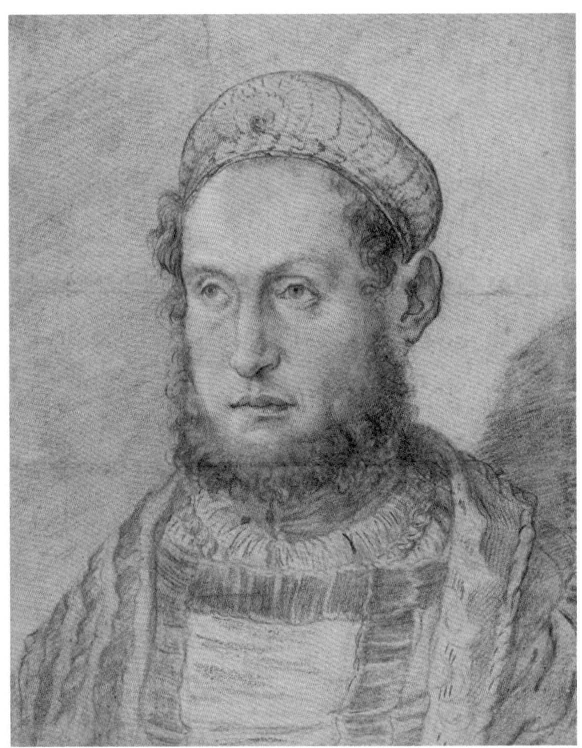

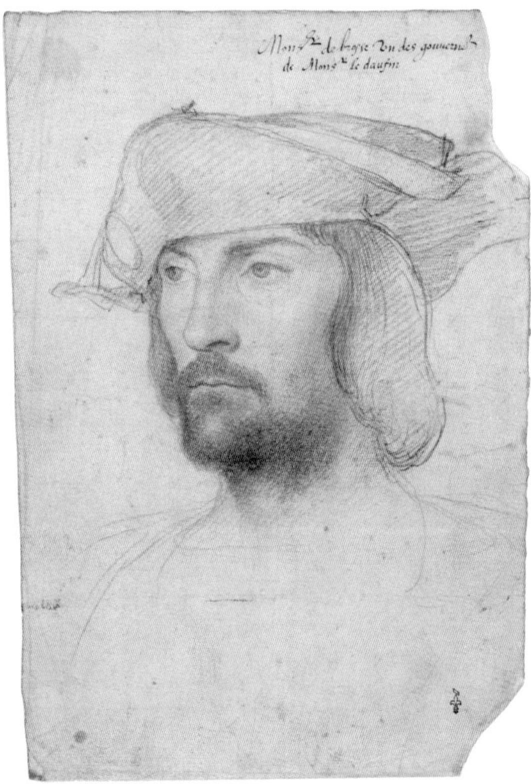
de Monsr le daufin

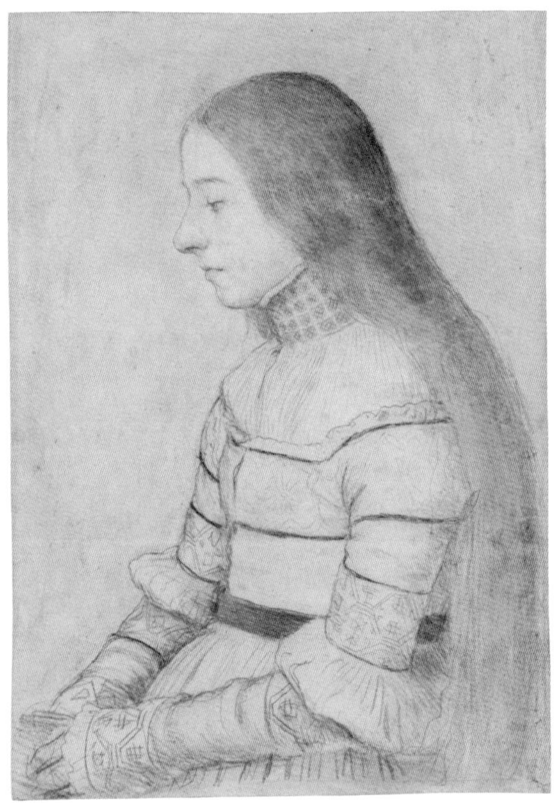

[OPPOSITE]:
Fig. 4 **Hans Holbein, *Jeanne de Boulogne, duchesse de Berry*, *c.*1524, black and coloured chalks**
Kunstmuseum, Basel, 1662.126

Fig. 5 **Hans Burgkmair (1473–1531), *Unknown man*, *c.*1505–7, black and coloured chalks**
Rijksmuseum, Amsterdam, RP-T-1948-140

Fig. 6 **Jean Clouet (1480–1541), *Jean de Barre, comte d'Etampes?*, *c.*1519, black and coloured chalks**
Musée Condé, Chantilly, MN163;B13

Fig. 7 **Hans Holbein, *Anna Meyer*, *c.*1525–6, black and coloured chalks**
Kunstmuseum, Basel, 1823.142

[RIGHT]
Fig. 8 **Hans Holbein, *Darmstadt Madonna*, 1525/6 and 1528, oil on panel**
Würth Collection, inv. 14910

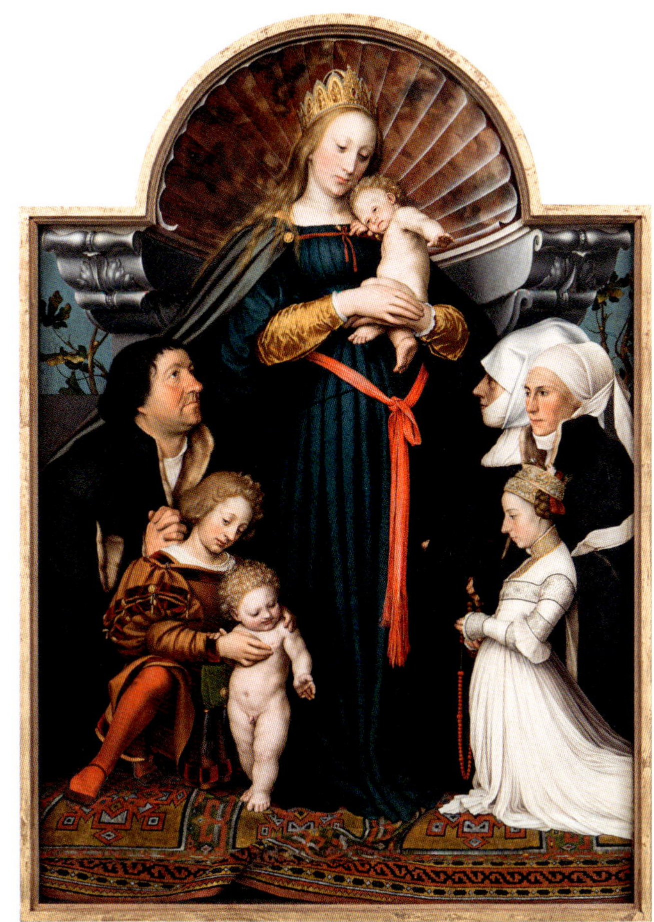

portrait drawings, suggesting the influence of work he saw at the French court where, alongside Italian artists, the Netherlandish painter and draughtsman Jean Clouet was making his name with chalk portraits of courtiers (Fig. 6).[7] Perhaps Holbein was impressed by the appeal of such drawings to Clouet's sitters and adopted the approach for commercial reasons. Returning to Basel, he drew the prominent Meyer family in chalks in preparation for a painted altarpiece (Figs 7–8).

In August 1526 Holbein set out from Basel for Antwerp, where he may have met the painter Quinten Massys, and then on to London, apparently carrying a letter of introduction from Erasmus to the lawyer, senior courtier and scholar Sir Thomas More.[8] Perhaps Erasmus gave Holbein the same advice he gave Nicholas Cannisius, who travelled to England the following year: 'you will meet many of the English nobles and men of learning. They will be infinitely kind to you, but be careful not to presume upon it: when they condescend, be you modest. Great men do not always mean what their faces promise, so treat them reverently, as if they were gods'.[9] If Holbein sought an introduction to these 'nobles and men of learning', Thomas More was the ideal man to provide it. Secretary to Henry VIII since 1518, and recently appointed to the influential position of Chancellor of the Duchy of Lancaster, More was part of a web of European intellectuals with Erasmus at its centre, which also included William Warham, Archbishop of Canterbury, John Fisher, Bishop of Rochester, and Sir Henry Guildford, a friend of the king. More was an accomplished author, and had already encountered Holbein's work, since Hans and his older brother Ambrosius had designed the woodcuts for an edition of More's daring social satire *Utopia*, published in Basel by Johannes Froben in 1518 (Fig. 9). Most importantly for Holbein, More was popular with Henry VIII and his queen Katherine of Aragon, with whom he dined regularly, and a close colleague of such important patrons as Thomas, Cardinal Wolsey.

More, who described the painter as 'a wonderful artist', provided Holbein with his first work in London.[10] He commissioned a group portrait of his family seated in an interior and a portrait of himself as a statesman, wearing magnificent velvets and furs and the Collar of Esses, which identified him as a senior court official. He must also have introduced Holbein to acquaintances, since by February 1527 the artist was working for Henry Guildford as part of a team designing decorations for a court entertainment at Greenwich. For this, Holbein contributed, among other paintings, a depiction of the siege of Thérouanne on the back of a triumphal arch.[11] The fall of the city of Thérouanne after the Battle of the Spurs in 1513

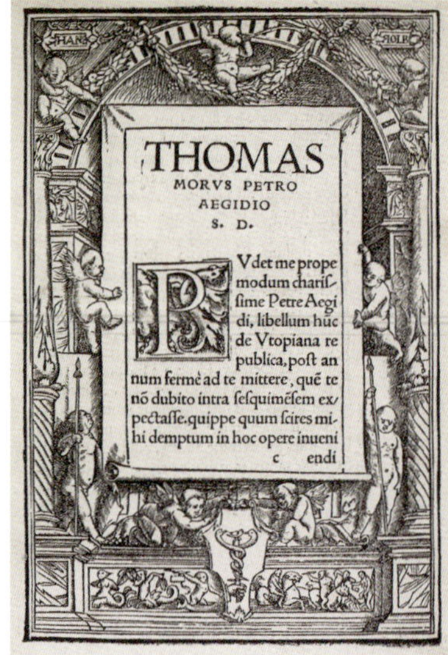

THOMAS
MORVS PETRO
AEGIDIO
S. D.

R Vdet me prope modum chariſſime Petre Aegidi, libellum hũc de Vtopiana republica, poſt annum fermè ad te mittere, quẽ te nõ dubito intra ſeſquimẽſem expectaſſe. quippe quum ſcires mihi demptum in hoc opere inueni endi

Fig. 9 **Sir Thomas More, *Utopia*, dedication page, 1518, printed book**
RCIN 1086970

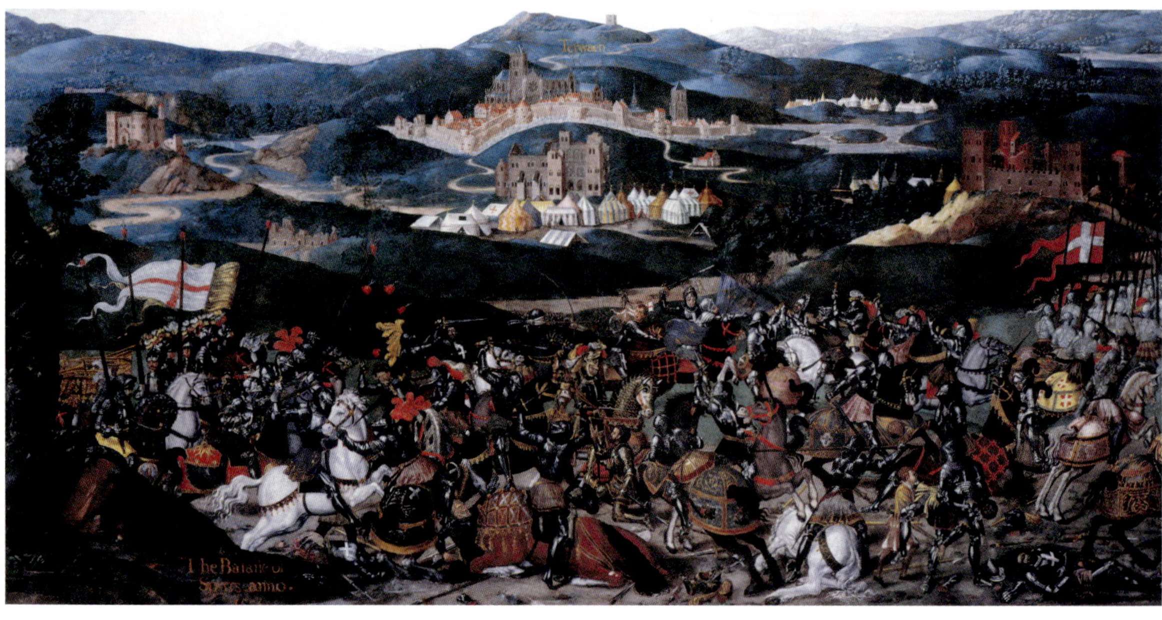

Fig. 10 **Flemish School, *The Battle of the Spurs*, *c.*1513–47, oil on canvas**
RCIN 406784

Fig. 11 **Hans Holbein,** ***A Lady with a Squirrel and a Starling (Anne Lovell?)*****, 1526–8, oil on panel**
National Gallery, London, NG6540

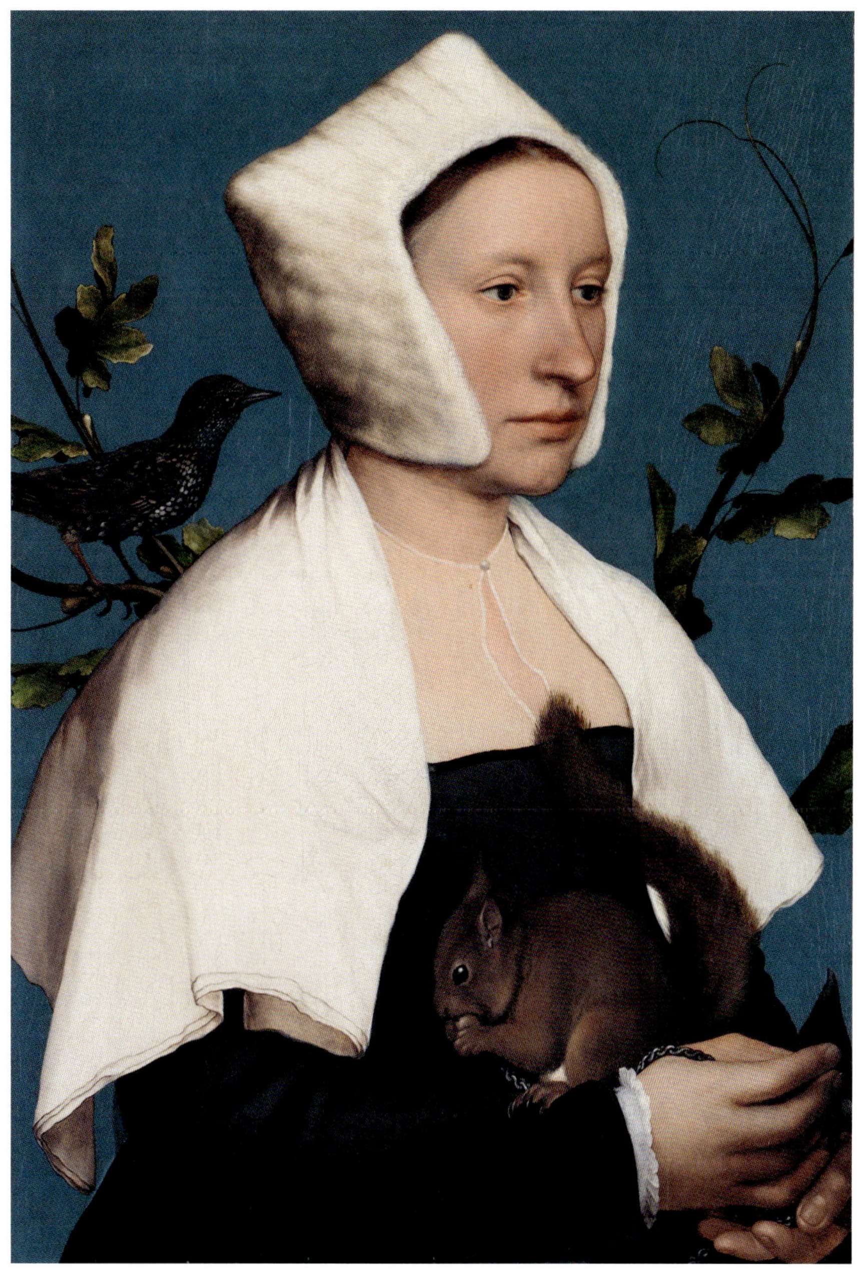

was a noted victory for Henry VIII against the French, and the king owned at least one other painting of the battle (Fig. 10). In the same year, William Warham commissioned Holbein to paint his portrait as a gift for Erasmus, who had sent his own likeness to the archbishop in 1524. More may also have provided an introduction to the German mathematician and designer of scientific instruments Nicolaus Kratzer, resident in England since about

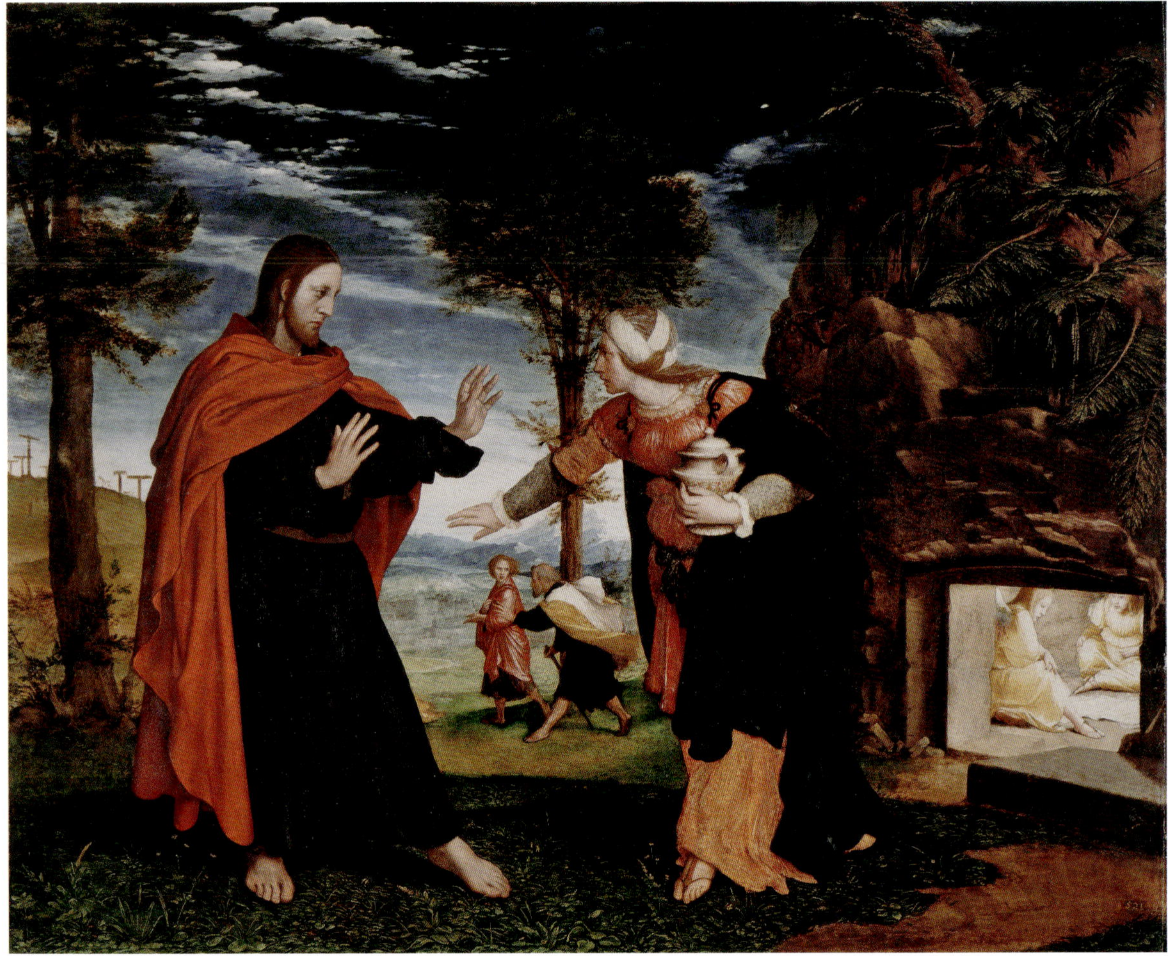

Fig. 12 **Hans Holbein, *Noli me Tangere*, 1526–8, oil on panel**
RCIN 400001

1516, who worked with the artist on the Greenwich decorations and whom Holbein painted in 1528.[12] Other commissions included a double portrait of the Norwich notary Sir Thomas Godsalve and his son John, and a portrait of a woman who may be Anne Lovell, of East Harling in Norfolk (Fig. 11). Non-portrait commissions at this period are less well recorded, but may have included a small and tense *Noli me Tangere*, showing Christ addressing Mary Magdalene after the Resurrection, which seems to have been painted in England between 1526 and 1528 (Fig. 12).[13]

Despite finding a willing group of patrons in England, in 1528 Holbein returned to Basel, where he had a wife and young children. He risked losing his Basel citizenship if he was absent for more than two years, but there may have been other reasons for his journey. In the summer of 1528 there was an epidemic of the deadly sweating sickness in England. Even if Holbein did not flee the illness, the escape of courtiers to their country estates may have led to

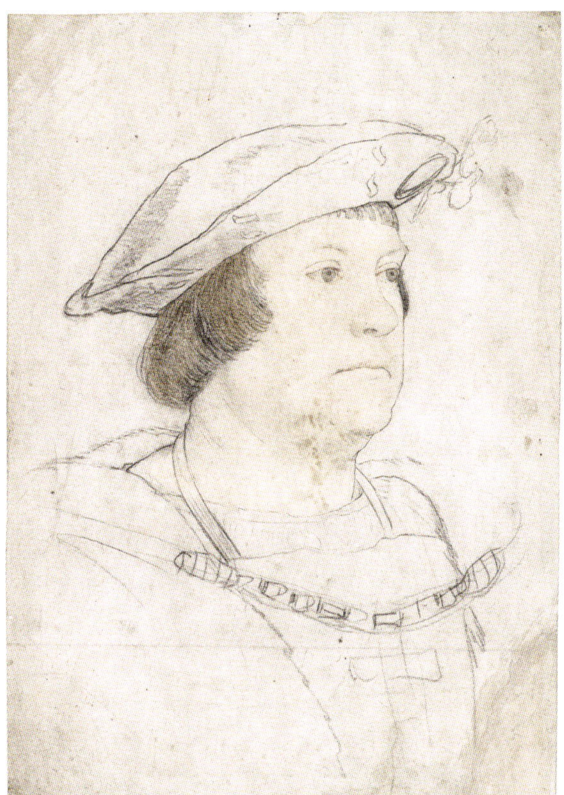

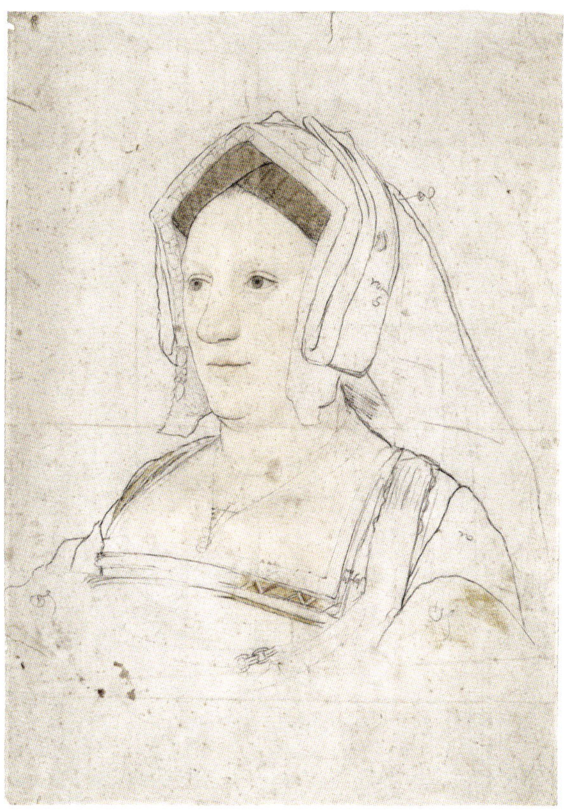

Fig. 13 **Hans Holbein, *Unknown man (Sir Edward Guildford?)*, *c.*1528, black and coloured chalks**
Kunstmuseum, Basel, 1662.122

Fig. 14 **Hans Holbein, *Unknown woman (Eleanor, Lady Guildford?)*, *c.*1528, black and coloured chalks**
Kunstmuseum, Basel, 1662.123

a downturn in commissions. Or did the death in April 1528 of Albrecht Dürer, the favoured artist of the Holy Roman Emperor, suggest a vacuum that Holbein hoped to fill? In 1533 he would apply praise originally written for Dürer to his own portrait of the German merchant Derich Born, hinting at a parity of the two artists. There is certainly a possibility that he intended to set down roots in Basel in 1528, since he purchased a house there.[14] At the same time, he did not abandon England entirely: on his return to Switzerland he must have been in the middle of a commission from the Guildford family, taking with him drawings of Mary Guildford and also of a couple who may be Henry's half-brother Edward and his wife Eleanor (Figs 13–14). These three drawings, all on the same paper that Holbein had used for his drawings of Henry Guildford and Thomas More, remain in Basel, among the works collected by the Amerbach family in the sixteenth century from Holbein's descendants or workshop.

Holbein is recorded working on a project in Basel in October 1531 but had returned to London by July 1532, when he painted a portrait of an unknown merchant.[15] Again, this return may have been a compromise rather than his original intention: Erasmus complained that he delayed for a month in Antwerp 'and would have stayed longer', perhaps hoping to gain

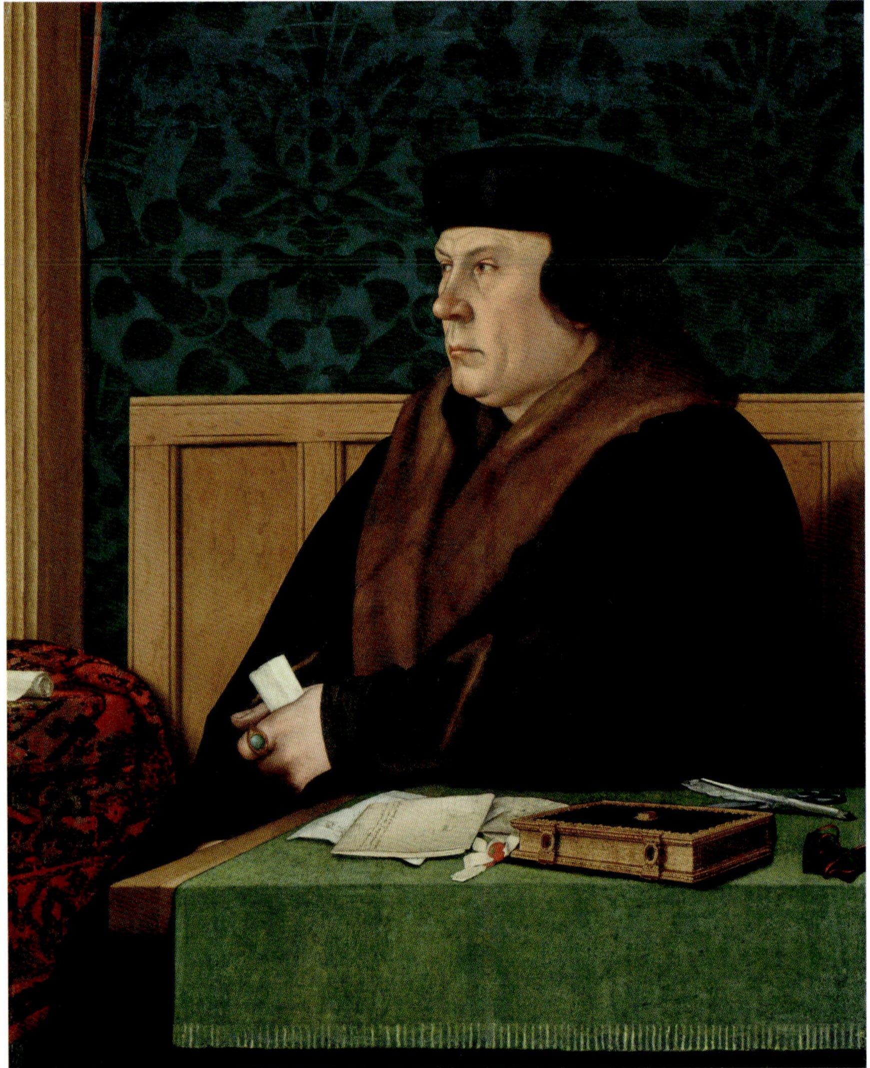

Fig. 15 **Hans Holbein, *Thomas Cromwell*, 1532–3, oil on panel**
Frick Collection, New York, 1915.1.76

sufficient commissions to remain in that city, where a newly founded bourse was attracting a wealthy merchant community.[16] It may indeed have been mercantile commissions that brought Holbein back to London, since some of his earliest portraits after his return, including that of July 1532, were made for members of the London Steelyard. This was an enclosed community of merchants from the Hanseatic League, a confederation of traders from northern and central Europe. The Steelyard was situated on the north bank of the Thames, and the Hanseatic merchants based there enjoyed special trading privileges.[17] Holbein made at least seven portraits of Hanseatic sitters soon after his return to London. Beyond portraiture, Holbein carried out large-scale commissions for the Steelyard merchants, designing the community's pageant

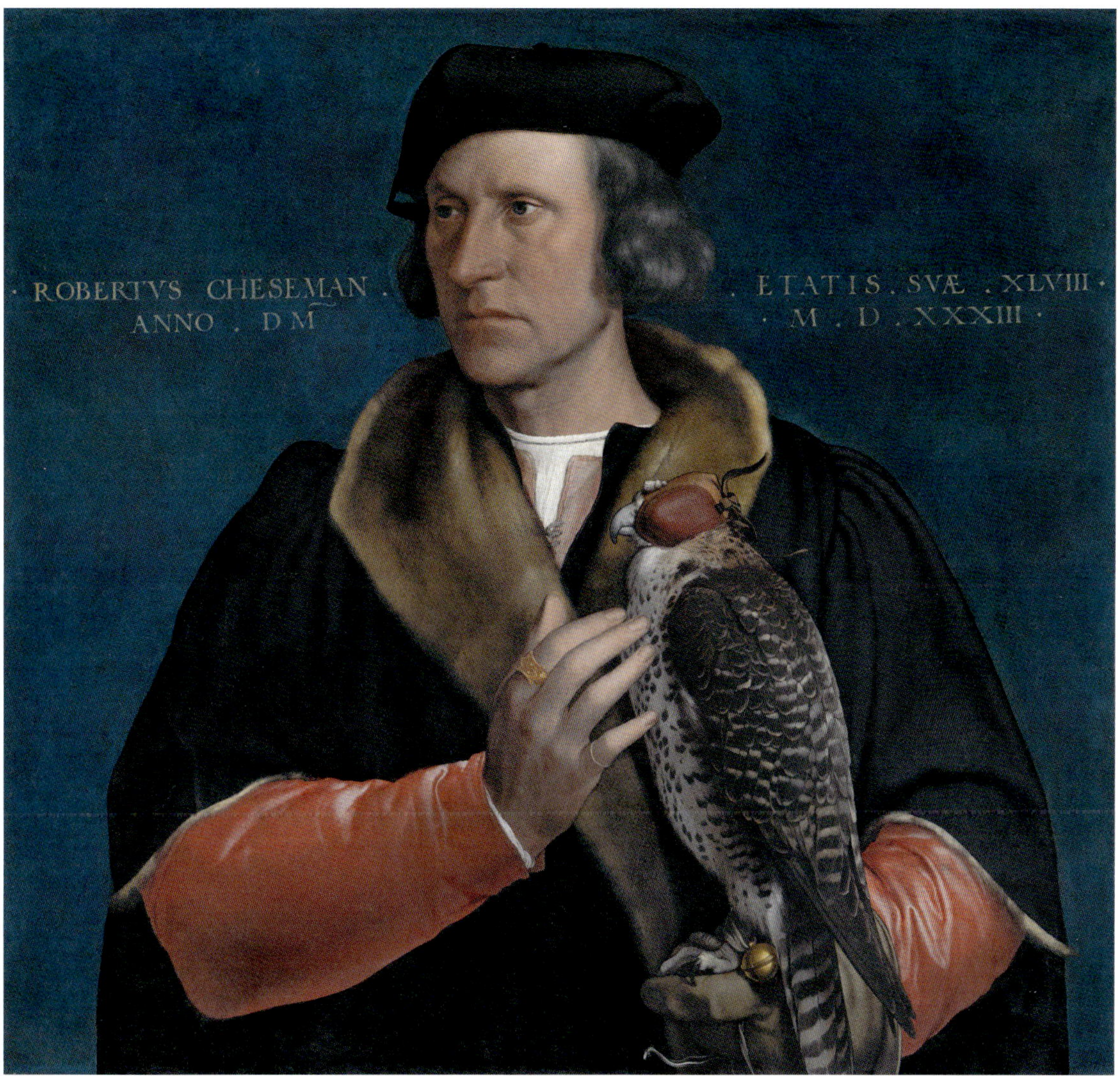

Fig. 16 **Hans Holbein, *Robert Cheseman*, 1533, oil on panel**
Mauritshuis, The Hague, 276

arch for Anne Boleyn's royal entry into London in May 1533 and paintings on canvas of the *Triumph of Riches* and the *Triumph of Poverty*, which were displayed in the dining hall of the Steelyard.[18]

For the Steelyard merchants, the commissioning of a Holbein portrait must have been a statement of prosperity and success, and an increasing group of English patrons, too, sought paintings from the artist. Thomas Cromwell commissioned a fine portrait to celebrate his appointment as Master of the Jewel House: the painting can be closely dated as he only held this post from April 1532 until 1534, and it must therefore be one of the first commissions that Holbein received on his return to London (Fig. 15).[19] In 1533 the wealthy Middlesex MP Robert Cheseman commissioned a painting of himself holding a falcon (Fig. 16), choosing to be shown as a man of leisure, unlike Cromwell's businesslike portrait. In the same year, Holbein received a prominent commission to paint two French visitors to London, the ambassador Jean de Dinteville and the bishop Georges de Selve (Fig. 17). He produced a panel rich in symbolic allusions to the two sitters, depicting them against the rich green curtain he had used to such effect in the portraits of Thomas More and Henry Guildford.

Few drawings survive for commissions of 1532–3, perhaps suggesting that sheets from these dates were lost or disposed of before Holbein's death. From the mid-1530s he appears to have retained his portrait drawings more systematically, since a large group showing English sitters survives in the Royal Collection. These include drawings from Holbein's first visit to England, and many drawings made after his return to London in 1532.[20] Very few of Holbein's drawings from the English period can be connected to autograph paintings or miniatures. As it seems likely that all were made with a finished work of art in mind, this may suggest that, combined with the loss of drawings from 1532–3, there are commissions from Holbein's first years after his return to London about which we have no information. Even on the surviving evidence, it is obvious that Holbein was extremely busy from the moment of his return, probably working simultaneously on a number of different projects.

The range of Holbein's sitters in the 1530s make clear that he was not allied to any court faction or religious ideology. He received commissions from religious conservatives and reformers, from adherents of Katherine of Aragon, and of Anne Boleyn. He painted dynastic groups for both Charles Brandon, Duke of Suffolk, and Thomas Howard, Duke of Norfolk, the rival dukes of East Anglia. Politicians such as Richard Southwell, ambassadors such as Thomas Wyatt and soldiers such as George Cobham all sought Holbein portraits, as did more minor court officials, including the Page of the Chamber, William Reskimer. The identities of a number of his sitters are unknown to us, and there are figures at court who it seems inconceivable did not commission a portrait. Did Holbein, for example, paint the brilliant and dissolute Francis Bryan, nicknamed the Vicar of Hell, who was a close associate of so many men and women portrayed by the artist? If so, such a portrait is not known today.

Many of Holbein's sitters, like Bryan, had travelled in mainland Europe and would have been familiar with the developments in art and architecture taking place across the continent. Among them, Thomas Wyatt spent much time in Italy and Spain and narrowly missed being caught in the 1527 Sack of Rome.[21] He may have seen such glories as the newly carved choir stalls and altarpiece of San Benito el Real in Valladolid and Raphael's *Transfiguration* in San Pietro in Montorio in Rome. The latter was commissioned by Cardinal Giulio de' Medici, by then Pope Clement VII, but previously Cardinal Protector of England and absentee Bishop of Worcester. Perhaps Wyatt even managed to visit the

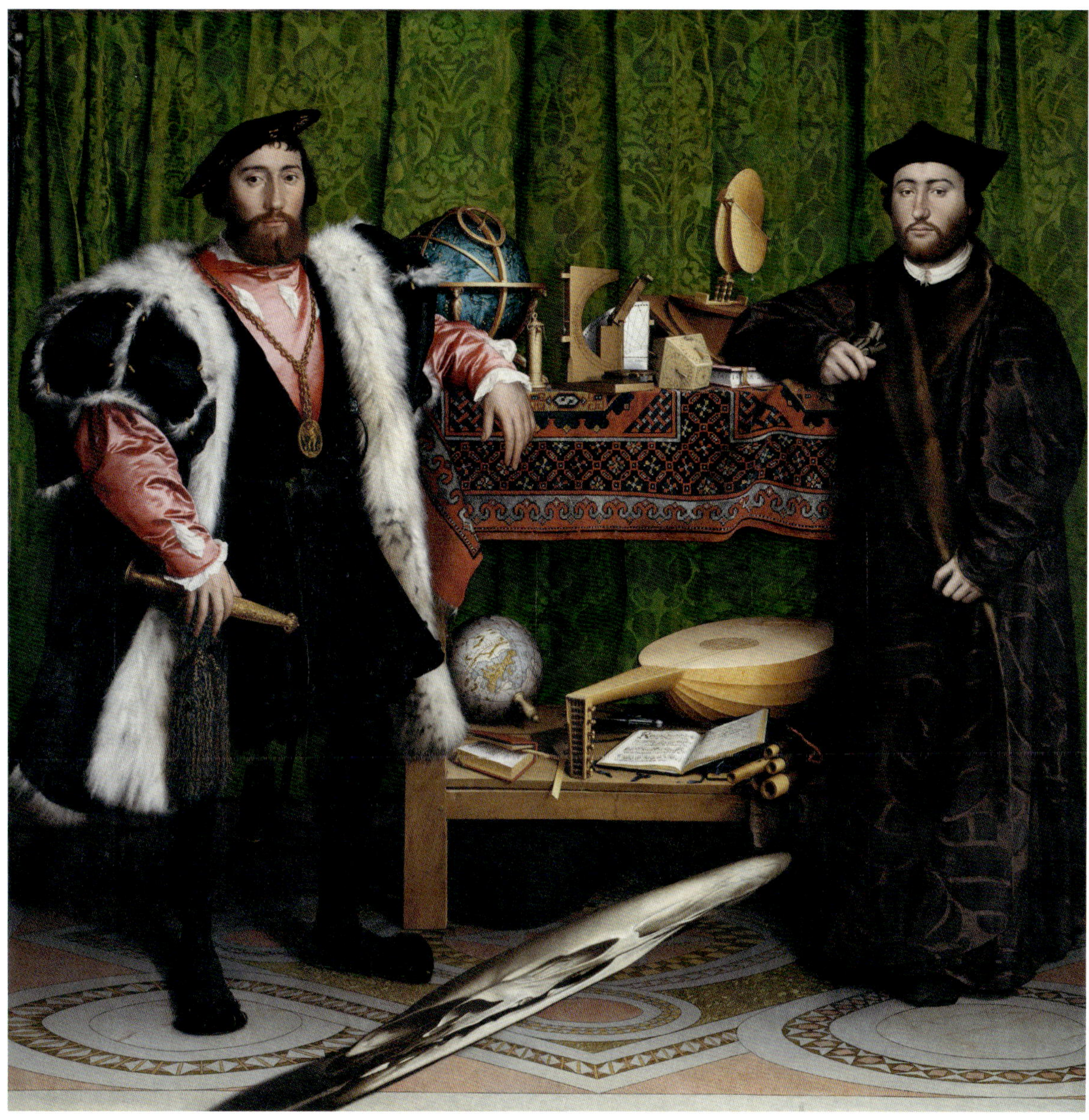

Fig. 17 **Hans Holbein, *The Ambassadors*, 1533, oil on panel**
National Gallery, London, NG1314

Sistine Chapel to gaze at its recently painted ceiling by Michelangelo. Others would have seen examples of foreign drawing, painting, printing and sculpture that had arrived in England, by trade or gift, or with the many craftsmen and women who crossed the Channel, like Holbein, in search of work.

Personal associations must have been important in gaining commissions, with Holbein's reputation being passed on by word of mouth. Tudor elite society was sociable and intertwined. The accounts of Sir Thomas Lestrange, one of Holbein's many sitters in Norfolk, reveal that the Lestrange house at

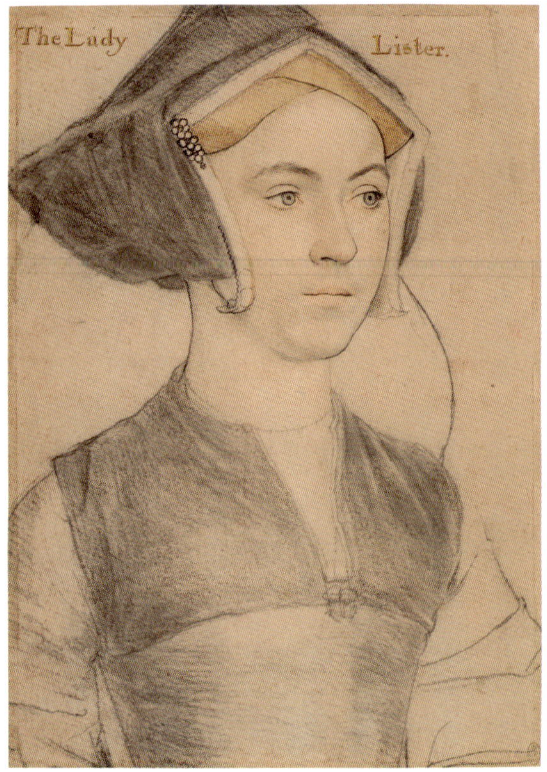

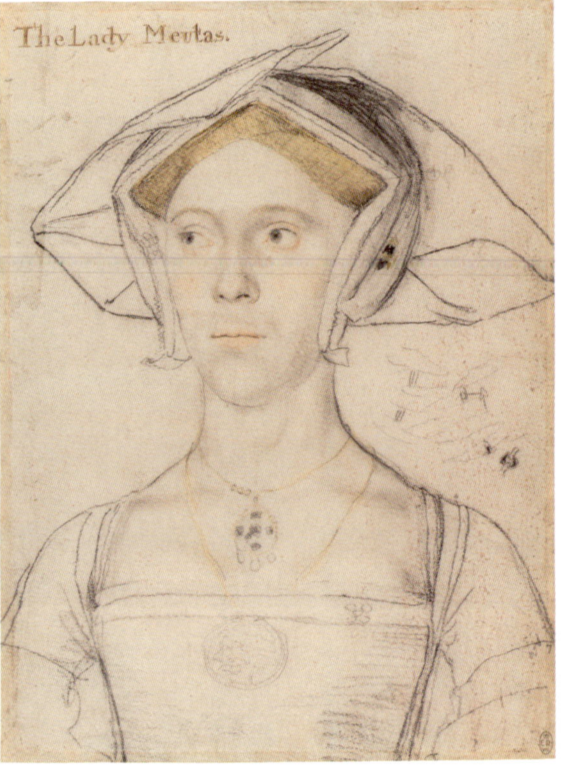

Fig. 18 **Hans Holbein, *Lady Lister*, *c.*1535–6, black and coloured chalks with ink on pink prepared paper**
RCIN 912219

Fig. 19 **Hans Holbein, *Joan, Lady Meutas*, *c.*1536–43, black and coloured chalks on pink prepared paper**
RCIN 912222

Hunstanton received a regular stream of visitors who came to stay, dine and talk, and that the Lestranges in turn paid visits to their county neighbours. In June 1527 the Lovell family were guests at Hunstanton Hall, staying for three days. Francis Lovell was Sheriff of Norfolk and would have worked closely with Sir Thomas in county affairs. At around the time of the visit his wife, Anne, who accompanied him to Hunstanton, was probably painted by Holbein in one of the artist's earliest commissions in England (see Fig. 11). Did this visit play a part in encouraging Sir Thomas to commission his own portrait from Holbein in 1536? Equally, it may have been the commissions from his brother- and sister-in-law, Baron and Lady Vaux, in around 1535 that spurred Lestrange to request a portrait. The Lestrange accounts show that Sir Thomas was probably aware of Holbein's work from at least 1527, and is likely to have discussed not only the Lovell painting but also the Vaux portraits before requesting his own. They hint at the importance of unrecorded conversations and meetings to Holbein's commissions. Similarly, commissions from the Poyntz and Gage families may have followed Holbein's early work for the Guildfords, since these families were closely related by marriage.[22]

Such networks may explain the large number of Holbein sitters who lived in East Anglia. This was one of the richest areas of the country, with a wealthy elite who played a role in government and who could afford luxuries such as a Holbein portrait.[23] But the consistency with which East Anglian patrons commissioned works from Holbein is nonetheless notable. The Norwich notary Sir Thomas Godsalve and the Lovells of East Harling were among his first patrons, and Sir William and Margaret, Lady Butts, also of Norwich, were among his last. They were joined by Richard Southwell of Woodrising, John Godsalve of Norwich, the Dukes of Norfolk (Kenninghall) and Suffolk (Westhorpe), Mary Shelton of Shelton and Thomas Lestrange of Hunstanton. Charles Wingfield of Kimbolton lived at the fringes of the region. Did Holbein's commissions in East Anglia originate with the close-knit community illustrated in the Lestrange accounts? Did he sometimes travel to his sitters rather than them coming to him, perhaps setting out on a tour of clients during one of the periods when outbreaks of contagious illness took hold in London or the court was absent on progress? Is it significant that he is the only artist working in England in the first half of the sixteenth century whose will records his ownership of a horse?

Regardless of where Holbein recorded his likenesses, it seems that his portraits usually began with a drawing taken at a sitting.[24] These acted as a record of his sitter's appearance, and were sometimes also used as patterns from which the key outlines were traced onto a panel for painting. In a few instances, such as the drawing of Lady Vaux, lines from the tracing are visible on the verso. Holbein's process in making a drawing can be seen in the two drawings of Henry Howard, Earl of Surrey, one of which was abandoned at an earlier stage than the other. This shows how Holbein built up his likenesses in careful layers of chalk, ink and wash. Sometimes he inscribed notes to record the colour or fabric of a sitter's dress. Holbein's portrait drawings are worked up to different degrees, perhaps a reflection of the time available for a sitting: in the case of Thomas Wyatt, Holbein concentrated on the face, indicating Wyatt's hat and clothes with only the briefest of outlines, while the drawing of the man thought to be Ralph Sadler carefully illustrates the sitter's dress as well as his countenance. The drawing of of Lady Lister is very comprehensively worked, while that of Joan, Lady Meutas, suggests hurry, with rough strokes to indicate the shading of her headdress and bodice, and a slight sketch of hands placed as an aide-mémoire to the right of the sitter's cheek (Figs 18–19). Was there an aspect of showmanship in the more finished portraits, which Holbein could flourish at the end of a session as testament to his

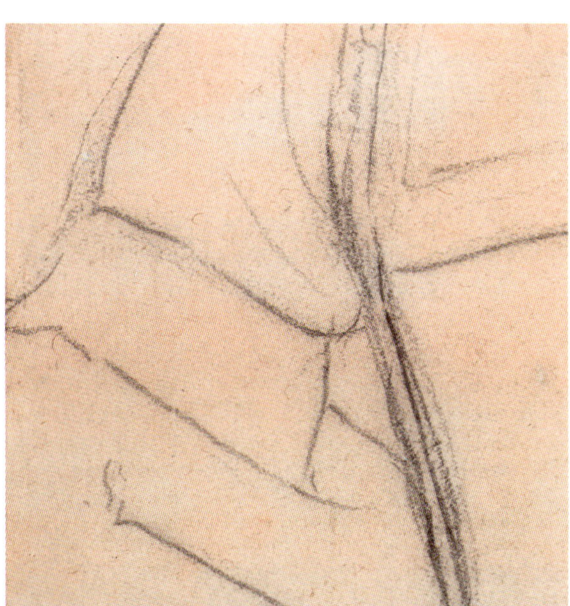

Fig. 20 **Hans Holbein, *Frances, Countess of Surrey* (detail of proper right arm), *c.*1535–6, black chalk on pink prepared paper**
RCIN 912214

artistry? If he had the time to work up a drawing, it could therefore be an investment in reputation, but the more hurried drawings served equally to record what he needed to create a final painting.

Holbein must have known how his finished portrait would look before he started the drawing, as he posed his sitters, some (such as John Poyntz and Thomas Wyatt) dramatically.[25] The individual drawings in the More family group all show their subject largely as they would appear in the final work, whether seated in profile, looking downwards or facing to the side. It has been suggested that only the most senior courtiers, for example, Guildford and Norfolk, were portrayed three-quarter length, and it is notable that only royal sitters such as Henry VIII and Christina of Denmark are depicted full length (see p. 25).[26] For individual portraits made in England it seems likely that Holbein provided a range of options at a range of prices: in an interior with objects, in a plainer interior, against a plain background of blue or green, against a plain background with a vine, or with a curtain, in a roundel large or small, or as a miniature.[27] Did sitters and artist build the composition from available options as a process of discussion? Perhaps Derich Born chose both the vine and a parapet so Holbein could add the inscription he had offered to the young sitter. Did the Lovells pay more for a portrait with a vine and animals than William Reskimer, who is accompanied by a vine alone? Despite the possibility of a stock approach, each of Holbein's paintings and drawings is entirely individual, each subtly different from the others in process. Sometimes he would take a pen or brush and trace outlines in ink, and at other times work sheets up in soft chalk alone. It is impossible to imagine his sitters as anything other than delighted with the result.

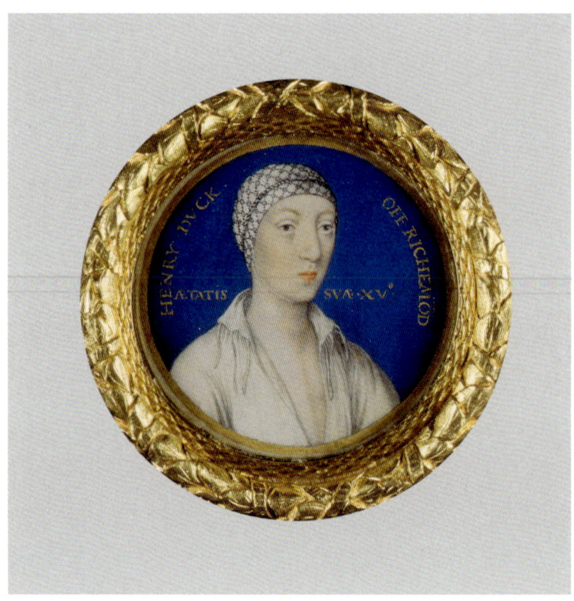

Fig. 21 **Lucas Horenbout (*c.*1490/5–1544),** ***Henry Fitzroy, Duke of Richmond and Somerset*****, *c.*1533–4, watercolour on vellum laid on playing card**
RCIN 420019

Although it is clear that Holbein had the finished work in mind when he embarked on his drawing, there was nonetheless a process of refinement from paper to panel.[28] This can be seen in the drawings, where Holbein has essayed an outline in faint strokes before firmly setting the final contour (Fig. 20; see also p. 88). This iterative process continued on the panel. Recent examination has shown how he worked again and again on the outline of Derich Born's face, seeking to find the right line. Holbein lengthened and thinned Henry Guildford's profile in the finished portrait to make him appear more elegant and imposing.[29] The clothing of some sitters, among them the man traditionally known as Simon George, was altered and developed from drawing to the final painting.[30] In the cases of Anne Lovell, who is accompanied by a

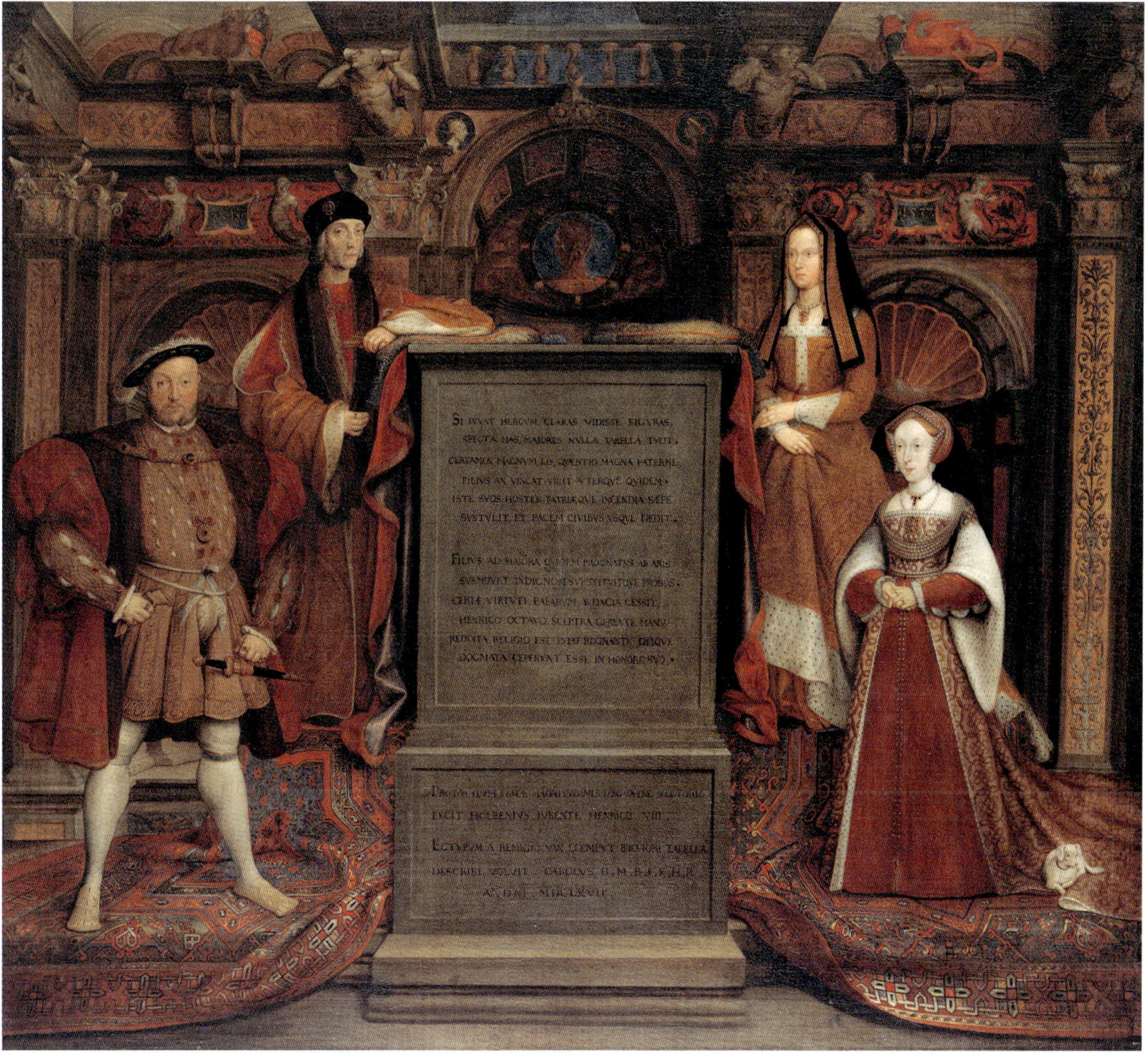

Fig. 22 **Remigius van Leemput (d. 1675) after Hans Holbein, *Henry VII, Elizabeth of York, Henry VIII and Jane Seymour*, the 'Whitehall mural', 1667, oil on canvas**
RCIN 405750

squirrel and a starling, and an unknown man with a hawk in The Hague, the animals were added towards the end of the painting process.[31] Could William Reskimer, too, have been intended to hold an animal or object? This might explain the strange twisting of his hands, which appear to cup and grip an invisible mass (see p. 108).

Holbein's drawings were sometimes used to make miniatures rather than panel paintings. He is reported to have learnt the technique of miniature from another Tudor royal painter, the Flemish artist Lucas Horenbout, who had arrived in England by 1525. Horenbout was an accomplished miniaturist, making portraits of, among others, Henry VIII and the king's illegitimate son, Henry Fitzroy (Fig. 21).[32] Holbein's earliest surviving miniatures date from the second half of the 1530s, suggesting he adopted the technique after his return to England in 1532. Both preparatory drawing and finished miniature by Holbein survive in the case of Elizabeth, Lady Audley, and it seems likely that other of the drawings were made with miniatures rather than panel paintings in mind. It is easier to imagine the intimate portrait of Anne Boleyn as a handheld miniature than a panel displayed on a wall. Might the finished portrait of Katherine, Duchess of Suffolk, also have been a miniature, to accompany those of her sons? If more of the drawings than we expect were to be reproduced at this small scale, this might explain the lack of surviving panel paintings, which has long perplexed writers on Holbein.

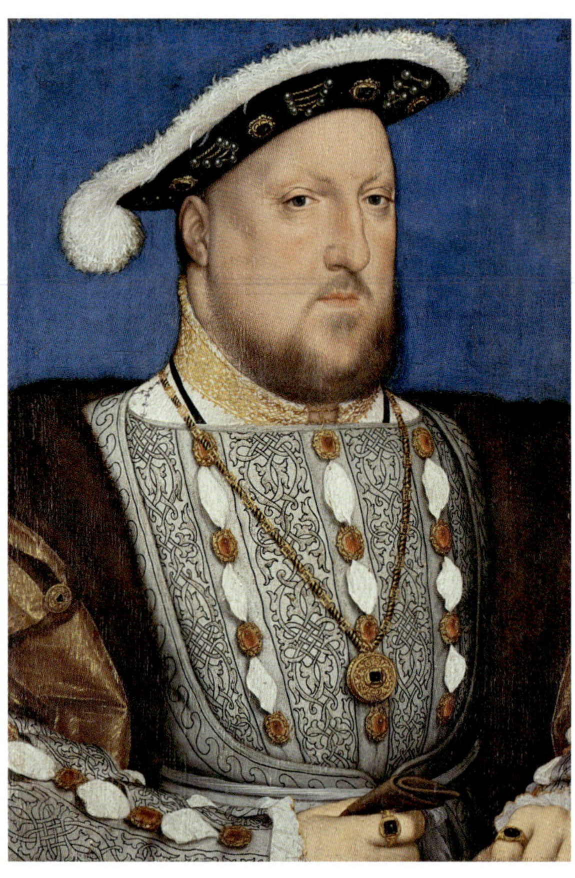

Fig. 23 **Hans Holbein, *Henry VIII*, c.1537, oil on panel**
Museo Nacional Thyssen-Bornemisza, Madrid, 191 (1934.39)

The choices made by artist and sitter in the development of the portrait must have been influenced by its intended destination and purpose. The archives are largely silent on the way in which Holbein's portraits were used: they do not appear in the wills of any of his known sitters.[33] But they were surely as much status symbols as the metalwork, tapestries and books that were itemised in wills such as that of Richard Southwell, who listed over the course of 16 pages the luxuries which, along with the income from his thousands of sheep, made his life so comfortable and signalled his success so clearly. Portraits were commissioned to mark special occasions like marriage, or as gifts for family or lovers.[34] Among the humanist circle who were Holbein's first patrons in England, portraits were commissioned as gifts and as mementos. When Erasmus sent his portrait by Holbein to Warham in 1524, it was so that the archbishop should 'have some piece of your Erasmus, in case God should call me hence'.[35] A different form of commemoration is demonstrated by portraits of female sitters, such as that of Anne Lovell, which coincide with the birth of heirs.[36] Where original panel portraits survive, they are often traced to the descendants of the sitter, suggesting that many were hung in their subjects' houses rather than presented as gifts. Does the proliferation of early copies reflect the wish of children and grandchildren to own portraits of their forebears? There are a surprising number of copies of the portrait of Nicholas Poyntz, but perhaps this is less surprising when his many children are taken into account.[37]

In the case of portraits of royal sitters, there is much more information on use and display. Holbein was appointed King's Painter at some point before

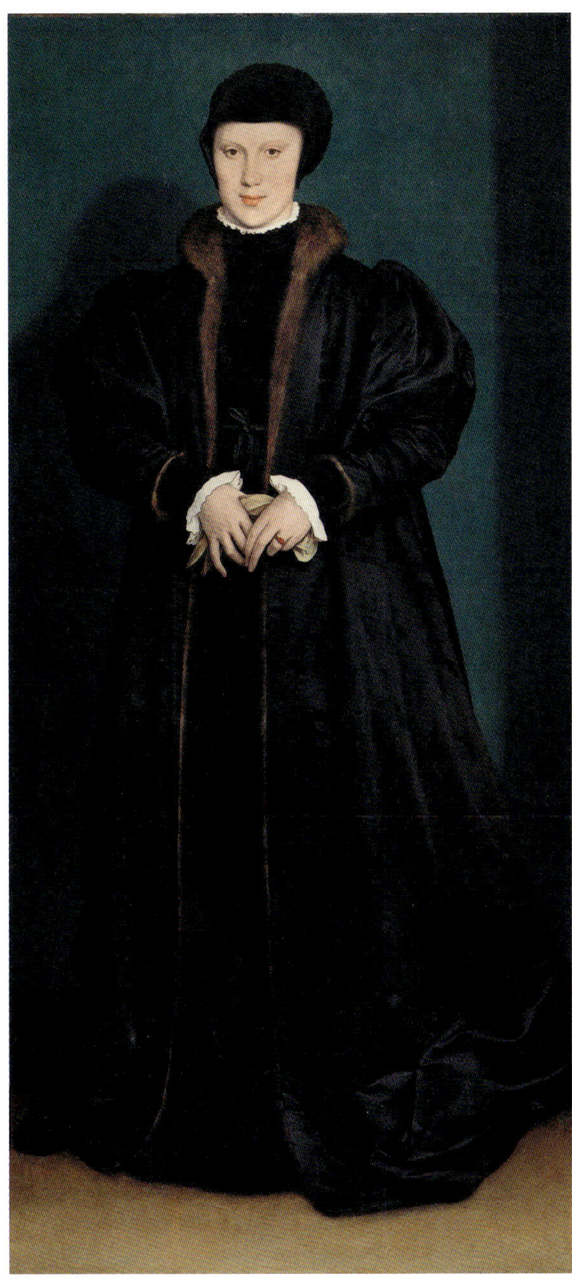

September 1536, when he is first described in this post by Nicholas Bourbon.[38] He had been undertaking royal commissions soon after his return to London.[39] As King's Painter, Holbein received a salary of £30 a year, slightly less than his contemporary Lucas Horenbout, who had also been awarded the title.[40]

Holbein's earliest royal portrait was probably the drawing of Anne Boleyn in a simple cap and furred gown. If this portrait was, as seems likely, intended as a miniature, to be looked at in private, then Holbein's portraits of Henry VIII and his third wife, Jane Seymour, had a much wider audience. Jane was the mother of Henry's first legitimate male heir, Edward. She was among those featured in a dynastic mural, lost to fire in 1698, which Holbein created on the wall of the Privy Chamber at Whitehall Palace where Henry greeted important guests (Fig. 22).[41] Here, the king and queen, and the king's father and mother, were painted at life size standing around a tablet with an inscription celebrating the Tudor succession. Holbein also made individual portraits of the king and queen from the same likenesses (Fig. 23).[42] His portrait of Henry became the most widely recognised image of the king in the second half of the sixteenth century, when it was frequently reproduced.[43] Beyond these formal portraits, a limning of Solomon and the Queen of Sheba has long been regarded as a flattering allegory of Henry as the wise biblical king, perhaps painted as a gift for the monarch.

Jane Seymour died in 1537, and in 1538 and 1539 Holbein made several journeys to northern Europe to take likenesses of potential wives for Henry VIII. Among his sitters was the recently widowed Christina of Denmark, Duchess of Milan, who was living in Brussels. Following a three-hour sitting in March 1538, Holbein produced (probably after his return to England) a full-length portrait for the king (Fig. 24). Henry also owned a half-length portrait of the duchess, which differs in a number of details from Holbein's original full-length version and is likely to have been created by an artist associated with Holbein from drawn studies or a lost half-length painting made as a result of the sitting (Fig. 25).

Fig. 24 **Hans Holbein, *Christina of Denmark*, 1538, oil on panel**
National Gallery, London, NG2475

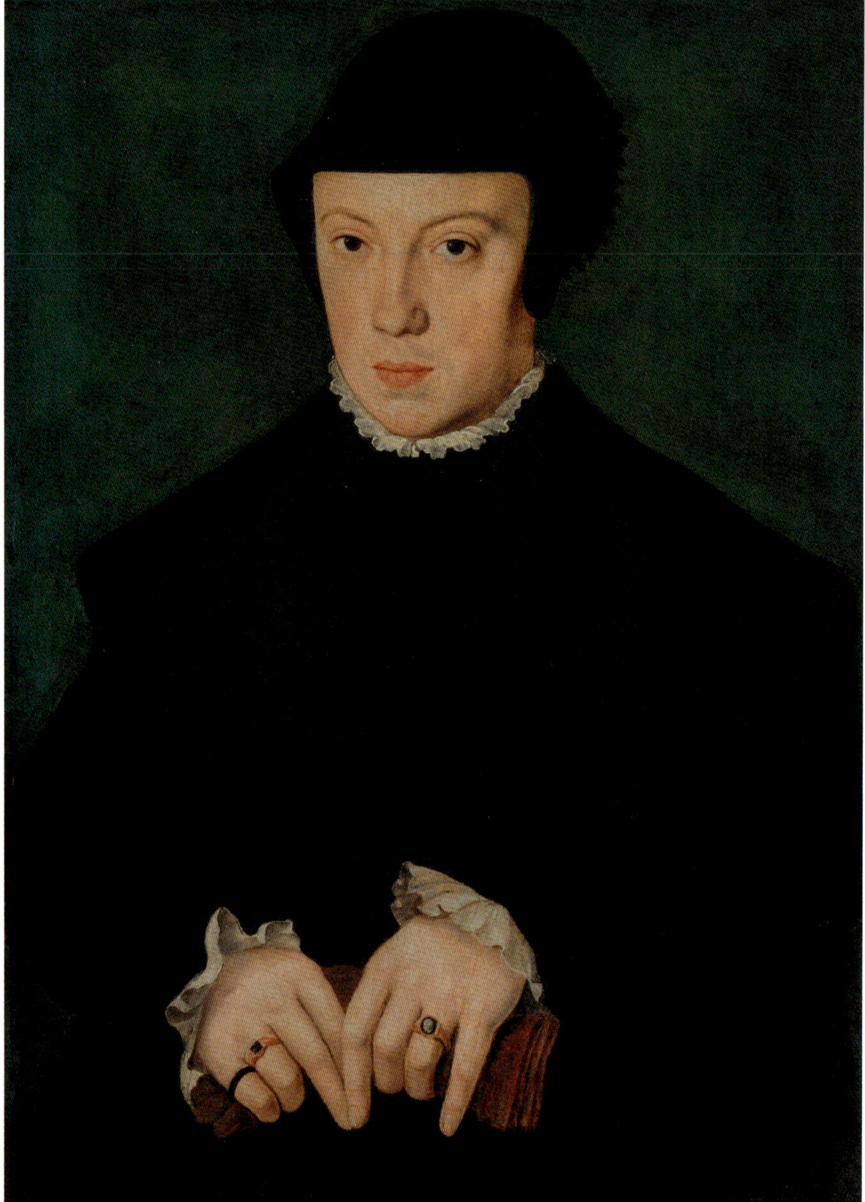

Fig. 25 **After Hans Holbein, *Christina of Denmark*, *c.*1538, oil on panel**
RCIN 403449

Another prominent royal project of 1538 was a portrait of the young Prince Edward, almost certainly 'the pictour of the p[ri]nce grace' presented by the artist to the king as a New Year's gift on 1 January 1539 (see Fig. 50).[44] In autumn 1538, while working on this painting, Holbein briefly visited Basel, where he arrived in the manner of a returning hero, wearing fine clothes and spending liberally. The reformer and pastor Rudolf Gwalther reported in a letter to his mentor, the theologian Heinrich Bullinger, that Holbein had 'praised the happy condition of

England' during his visit.[45] Whether this was bravado or an honest assessment is unclear, but Holbein was now committed to his career at the Tudor court and told his audience his stay in Basel would be short.

The year 1539 saw Holbein travelling to the Duchy of Cleves in north-west Germany to take the likeness of other potential wives for Henry. The king had already been supplied with portraits of Anne of Cleves and her sister Amalia, which had been passed in May 1539 to the ambassadors Nicholas Wotton and Richard Berde. Nervously, Wotton and Berde warned that '[a]s muche as we hadde not seene the ij ladyes, we shulde [not be] able to advertise his Majestye whether theyr imaiges wer [l]yke to theyr persones'.[46] Concern about the accuracy of the portraits led to Wotton and a colleague, Dr Peter, receiving instructions to 'freendly desier' to see the women 'in suche place as they might fyll their eyes wt the sight and contemplation of them seing it laye in oon of their lottes to be there Quene'.[47] Disquiet continued and Holbein was dispatched to Cleves to paint portraits that were, presumably, considered trustworthy by the English court. He produced a three-quarter-length painting and a miniature of Anne (Fig. 26). He may, too, have produced a miniature of Henry's next queen, Katherine Howard, although the traditional identification of the sitter as Katherine is tentative and her identity remains uncertain.

In 1541 Holbein was recorded as resident in the parish of St Andrew Undershaft, on Aldgate Street in the City of London.[48] His neighbours in the parish included Thomas Eden, Clerk of the Star Chamber, and Sir William Pickering, a diplomat and close friend of Thomas Wyatt and Henry Howard, Earl of Surrey. Holbein was one of a number of 'strangers' or foreigners in the parish.[49] He retained his links with the immigrant community throughout his time in London, designing, for example, metalwork to be made by the Flemish goldsmith Hans of Antwerp. Such association may have been a matter of choice, linguistic convenience or pragmatism, but there is also a sense that segregation was conditioned by the customs of London: John Godsalve issued licences for those running tennis courts restricted to foreign players, suggesting that immigrants were unable to use the domestic facilities.[50] It may have been such restrictions that encouraged Holbein, along with many others, to become a denizen (that is, to adopt English nationality) in 1541.[51]

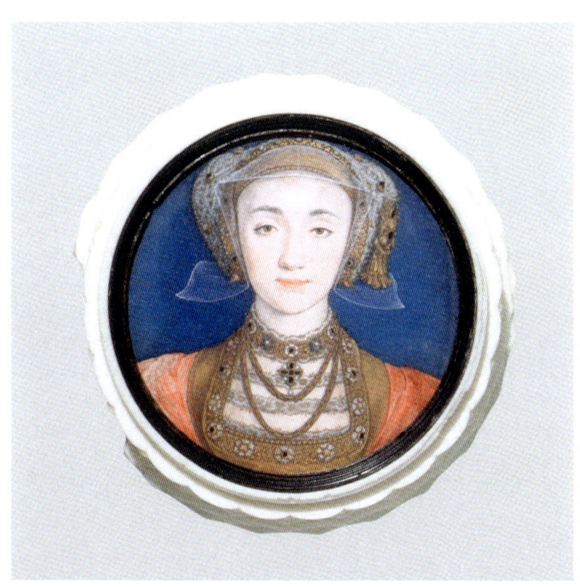

Fig. 26 **Hans Holbein, *Anne of Cleves*, 1539, watercolour on vellum laid on playing card**
Victoria and Albert Museum, London, P.153:1,2-1910

Holbein's commissions for English patrons extended beyond portraiture. He continued to design woodcuts for books, including the title page of the 1535 Coverdale Bible, the first full English translation of the Bible (Fig. 27).[52] A painted allegory of the Old and New Testaments probably dates from the mid-1530s although nothing is known about the circumstances of its production (Fig. 28).[53] Alongside prints, Holbein designed metalwork and jewellery. Although none of the pieces themselves remain, among the surviving drawings are designs for a standing cup for Jane Seymour, and for pendants with intertwined 'H' and 'A' (perhaps for Henry and Anne Boleyn) and 'H' and 'I' (possibly for Henry and Jane Seymour).[54] One of his last commissions must have been the design, with Nicolaus Kratzer, for an elaborate salt cellar with an integral clock (Fig. 29), which Anthony Denny presented to Henry VIII as a New Year's gift in January 1544.[55] By this time Holbein was dead.

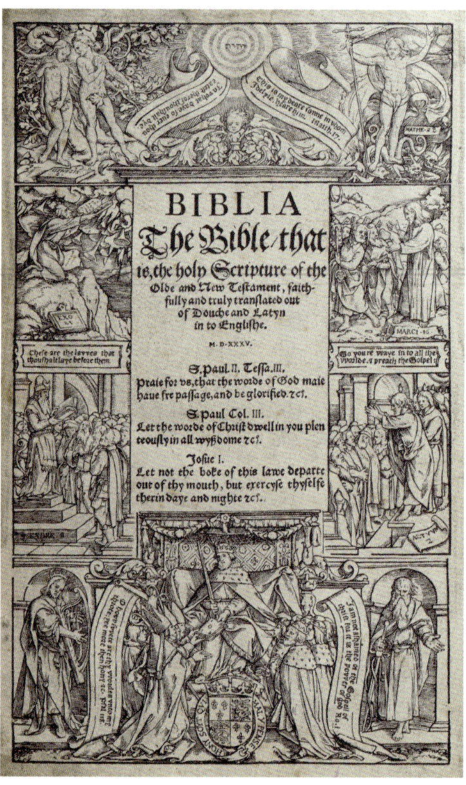

BIBLIA
The Bible/that
is, the holy Scripture of the
Olde and New Testament, faith-
fully and truly translated out
of Douche and Latyn
in to Englishe.

M.D.XXXV.

S.paul.II. Tessa.III.
Praie for vs, that the worde of God maie
haue fre passage, and be glorified. &c.

S.paul Col. III.
Let the worde of Christ dwell in you plen
teously in all wysdome &c.

Josue I.
Let not the boke of this lawe departe
out of thy mouth, but exercyse thyselfe
therin daye and nighte &c.

Fig. 27 **Hans Holbein, *Coverdale Bible*, title page, 1535, woodcut**
RCIN 1051852

Holbein made his short will on 7 October 1543 and he had died by 29 November, when Hans of Antwerp, one of his executors, took out letters of administration.[56] Holbein asked that 'all my goodes ... and also my horse' be sold to pay his debts and to provide for the care of two young children in London 'wich be at nurse'. His executors were four foreigners resident in London: Hans of Antwerp; Anthony Snecher, an armourer; Ulrich Obringer, a merchant; and Harry Meynert, a painter. Although no mention of Holbein's studio contents appears in the will, three books containing drawings probably made their way almost immediately into royal hands: a book of designs for jewellery (now in the British Museum), a book of designs for standing cups and weapons (Fig 30; previously in the collection of Thomas Howard, Earl of Arundel, but subsequently lost) and a book of drawings for portraits (now in the Royal Collection).[57] Whether these books were compiled by the artist or by his executors is unclear. It is notable that none of Holbein's portrait drawings (with the exception of that of Anne Boleyn) have work on the verso, which may indicate that they were stored in an album at an early date. There must have been an element of selection, too: the majority of the portrait drawings are highly finished. There are likely to have been other studies of, for example, sitters' hands, of which few have been preserved. The drawing of Mary, Dowager Duchess of Richmond's costume may confirm that Holbein developed a number of studies of a sitter.

What was the purpose of retaining these drawings? Did Holbein anticipate that sitters may want subsequent copies of their paintings or was he forming an archive of material? In the case of sitters such as Jane Seymour, whose portrait was circulated widely, it is clear from its condition that the drawing has been kept and reused, but for other, less elevated sitters the demand for additional

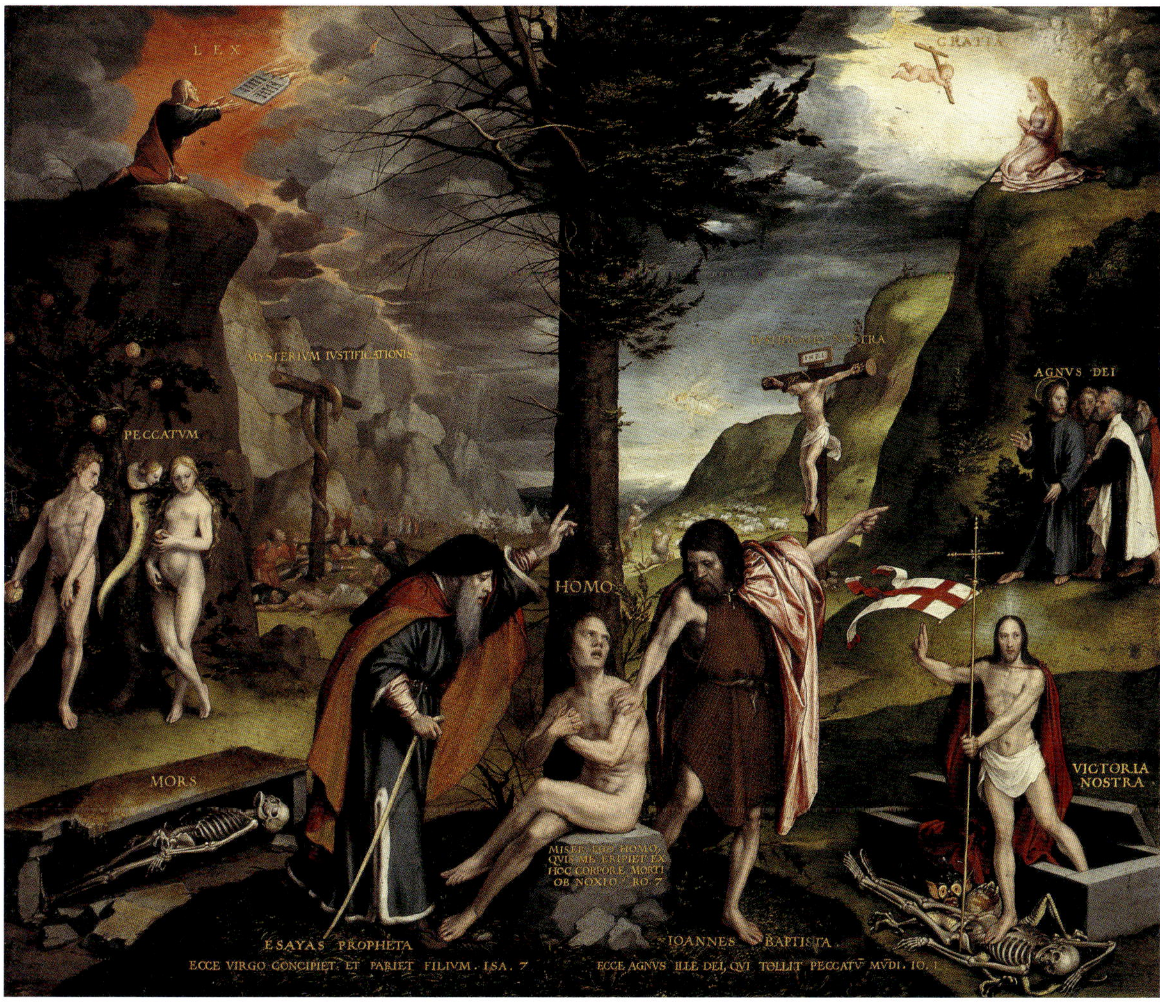

Fig. 28 **Hans Holbein, *An Allegory of the Old and New Testaments*, mid-1530s, oil on panel**
National Galleries of Scotland, Edinburgh, WA1863.424

portraits must have been uncertain. Perhaps Holbein retained his sheets as this was the period in which drawings became collectors' items, preserved by those who sought examples of an artist's work.[58] Whether it was Holbein or one of his executors who assembled the group of portrait drawings now in the Royal Collection, any process of selection will have affected our view of the artist since we see only the most polished drawings today. Holbein was a brilliant portraitist, but the sense of him effortlessly throwing off an elegant drawing of the man or woman in front of him may not reflect a reality in which he made numerous studies to arrive at a final picture. The surviving drawings represent only part of the process of creation.

Nor is the group of portrait drawings we see today the group that entered royal ownership after Holbein's death. The portrait drawings passed through a number of hands in the sixteenth century and drawings left and joined the

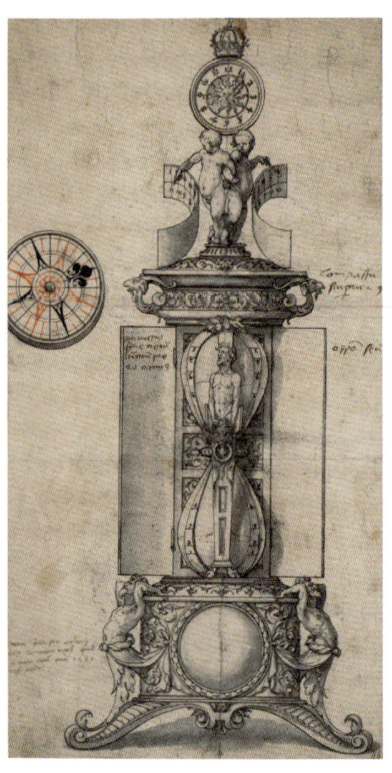

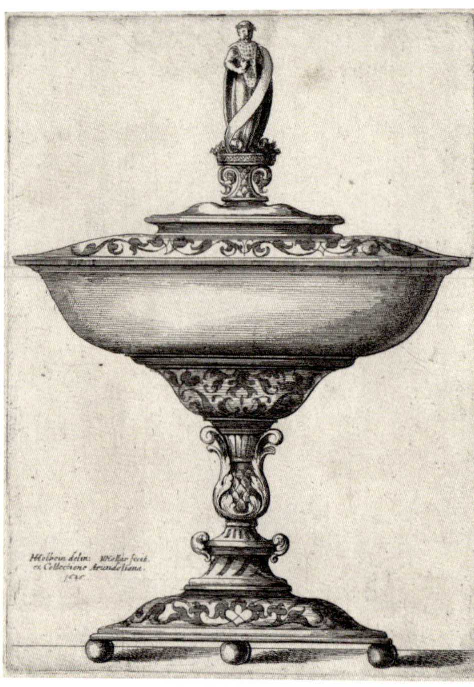

[LEFT]
Fig. 29 **Hans Holbein, *Design for a clock salt for Anthony Denny*, 1543, pen and ink with wash**
British Museum, London, 1850,0713.14

Fig. 30 **Wenceslaus Hollar (1607–77) after Hans Holbein, *Wide cup on ball feet*, 1646, etching**
RCIN 805003

[OPPOSITE]
Fig. 31 **Follower of Hans Holbein, *Edward VI, c.*1550, black and coloured chalks on pink prepared paper**
RCIN 912202

group during that time.[59] The book (known since the late sixteenth century as the 'Great Book') is first recorded at Whitehall Palace in 1547, in an inventory taken at the accession of Edward VI. It was surely, therefore, previously owned by Edward's father, Henry VIII. The book seems to have passed from Edward VI to Henry FitzAlan, 12th Earl of Arundel. After the earl's death it was acquired by his son-in-law, the bibliophile and collector John, Lord Lumley. In an inventory of Lumley's collection taken in 1590, the volume was described as 'A great booke of Pictures doone by Haunce Holbyn of certeyne Lordes, Ladyes, gentlemen and gentlewomen in King Henry the 8: his tyme, their names subscribed by Sr John Cheke Secretary to King Edward the 6 wch booke ws King Edward the 6'.[60] Lumley bequeathed the book to Henry, Prince of Wales, and it was passed with his possessions to his younger brother, who became Charles I in 1625. Charles passed 'the book of Holbin's [*sic*] drawings; wherein manie heads, which were done with Cryons' to William Herbert, 3rd Earl of Pembroke, in exchange for a painting by Raphael. Pembroke passed the book 'soe soone as hee receaved it' to Thomas Howard, 14th Earl of Arundel, whose enthusiasm for Holbein saw him form the greatest collection of the artist's work assembled outside Basel.

After Arundel's death in 1646, the location of the book was unknown until 1675, when it was described as 'happily fallen into' the collection of Charles II, a notable collector of drawings. In 1690 Constantijn Huygens recounted seeing 'four or five books with drawings, including some by Holbein and Leonardo

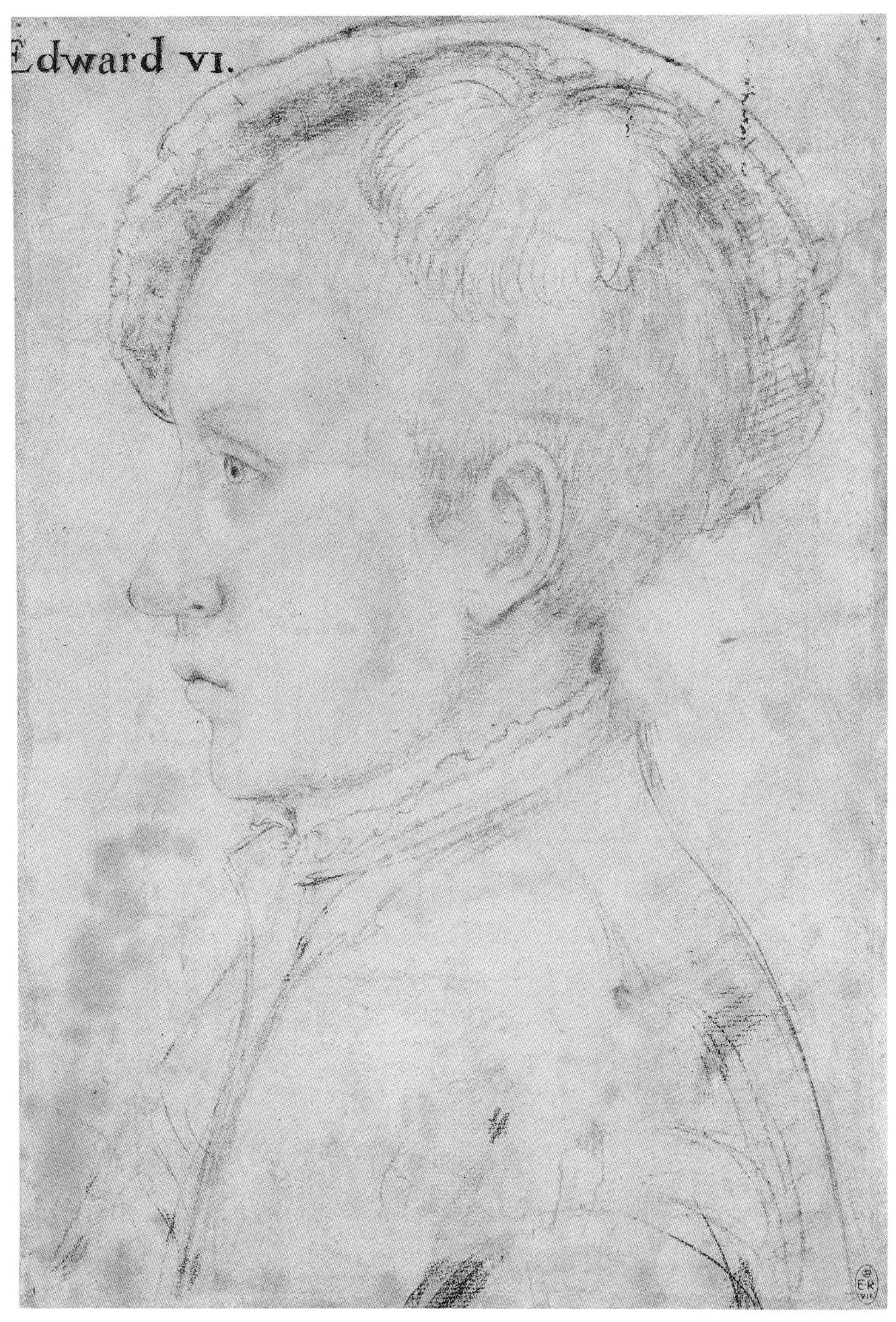
Edward VI.

da Vinci' in 'the rooms below the King's study' at Whitehall.[61] By this time, it was noted that many of the drawings had been 'spoyled by the injury of time and the ignorance of such as had it in custody'.[62] The loss of pigment seen to a varying degree on the sheets must have been partly due to their function as artist's patterns, and partly due to handling by later owners as they turned the pages of the Great Book.

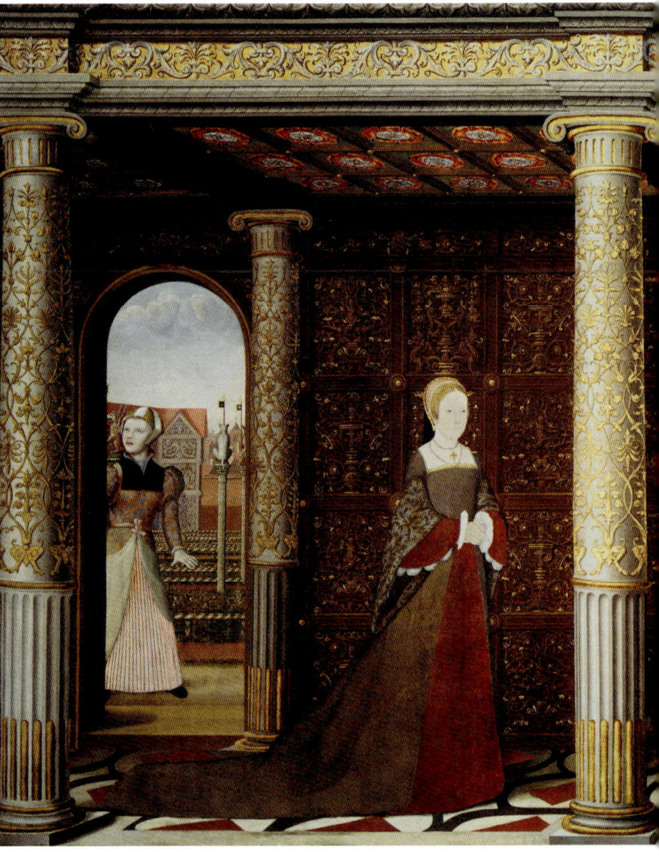

Fig. 32 **British School, *The Family of Henry VIII*, *c.*1545, oil on canvas**
RCIN 405796

On 7 August 1735, Viscount Percival, 1st Earl of Egmont, visited Queen Caroline's lodge at Richmond where he saw 'the famous collection of Holbein's heads of eminent persons in King Henry 8th reign. They are 63 in number, upon half-sheets of paper, and seem the sketches made for his portraits in oil. The Queen found them neglected in a book, shut up in a common table drawer'.[63] The drawings that Percival saw at Richmond are probably the 63 in the collection bearing an inscription in a neat hand identifying the sitter (see p. 60). These inscriptions appear to have been added at the instigation of Queen Caroline, and to be copies of the names Sir John Cheke inscribed in the book when it was in the ownership of Edward VI. By 1743, when George Vertue listed the drawings, then hanging in the Queen's Closet at Kensington Palace, he counted 89 he thought to be by Holbein. Those drawings not displayed at Richmond probably remained in the original book until they were removed for display at Kensington, at which time their accompanying inscriptions were copied onto them in a cursive hand (see p. 114).

A number of the drawings listed by Vertue are not by Holbein and drawings have clearly joined the group in the 200 years since Holbein's death.[64] Interestingly, many of these are comparable in technique to the autograph drawings and appear to be by artists working closely with Holbein. Among these is the portrait of John Fisher made, probably in the second half of the sixteenth century, by an artist familiar with Holbein's technique. A group of good copies of Holbein's drawings, dating from around the same time, was once in the collection of Lady Elizabeth Germain (1680–1769), who inherited some collections from Thomas Howard, Earl of Arundel.[65] These may have been made when the book was in the possession of Henry FitzAlan, Earl of Arundel, or John, Lord Lumley. A handful of drawings that seem to date from the reign of Edward VI may be evidence that Holbein's studies were available to the next generation of court artists, among them William Scrots, as is a large painting

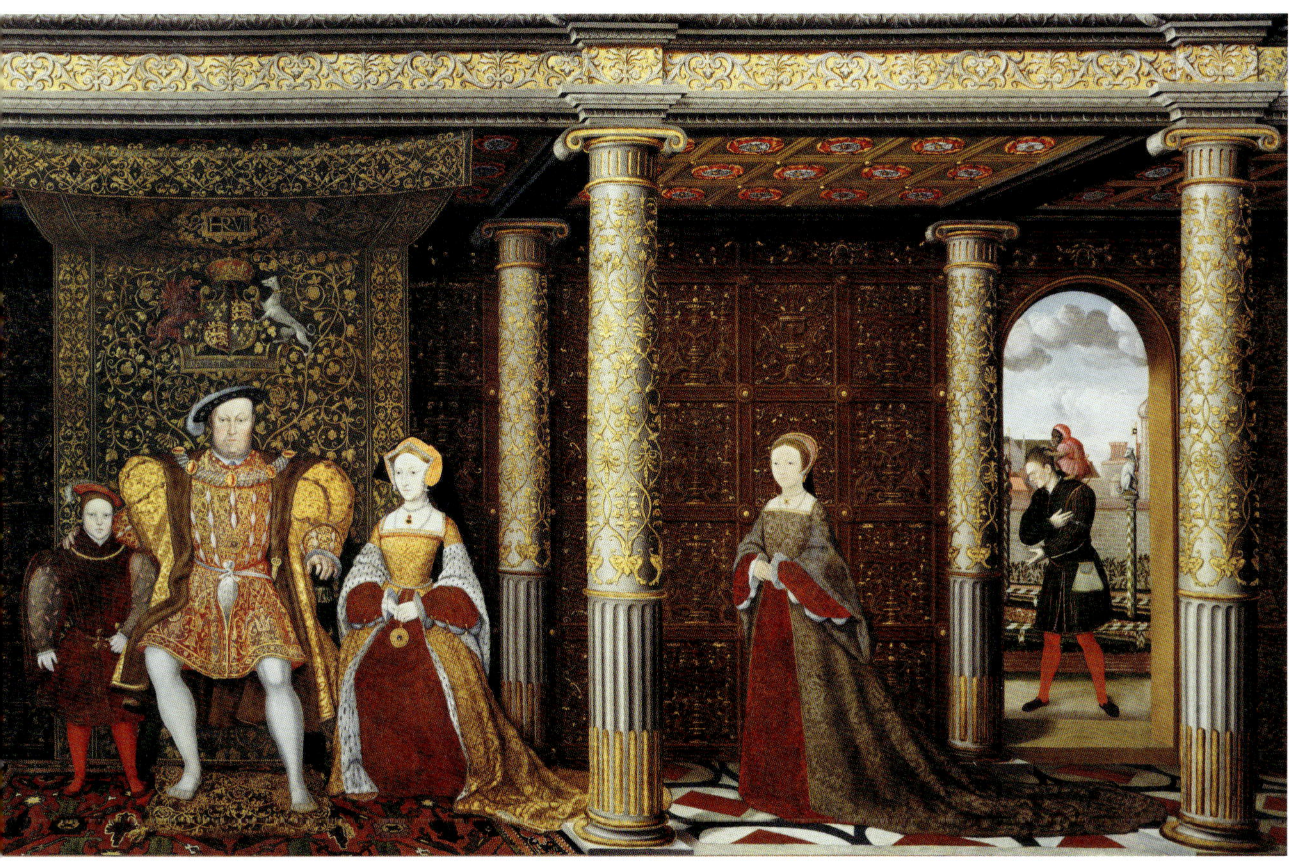

of Henry VIII and his family by an unknown artist, which draws closely on Holbein's models (Figs 31–32).[66]

In 1575 the Italian artist Federico Zuccaro made a visit to London, where he encountered the works of Holbein. As well as making copies of Holbein's Steelyard *Triumphs*, Zuccaro visited Baynard's Castle, the residence of Henry Herbert, 2nd Earl of Pembroke, where he saw Holbein's portrait of Christina of Denmark.[67] Did he also see the book of portrait drawings, then in the possession of Henry FitzAlan, Earl of Arundel, who was based at Arundel House a little further up the north bank of the river? Holbein's paintings in England, Zuccaro later told the engraver Hendrick Goltzius, 'were better than those of Raphael of Urbino'.[68] Holbein's star has never waned. His portraits, particularly, have been valued from the moment of their creation, sought after by sitters and collectors, and enjoyed by those who for centuries have marvelled at the skill of this 'wonderful artist', who so brilliantly depicted the men and women of Henry VIII's court.

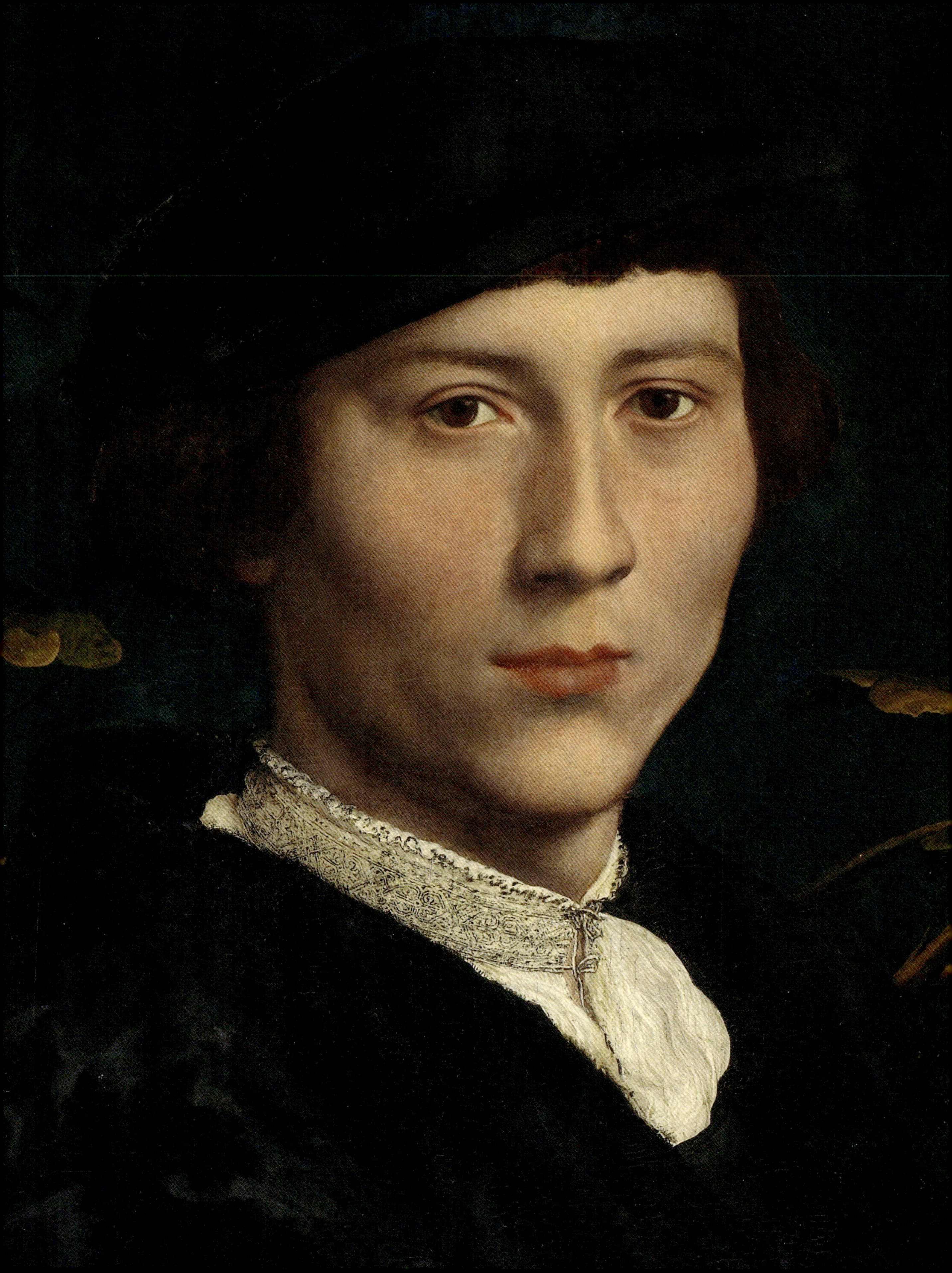

CATALOGUE

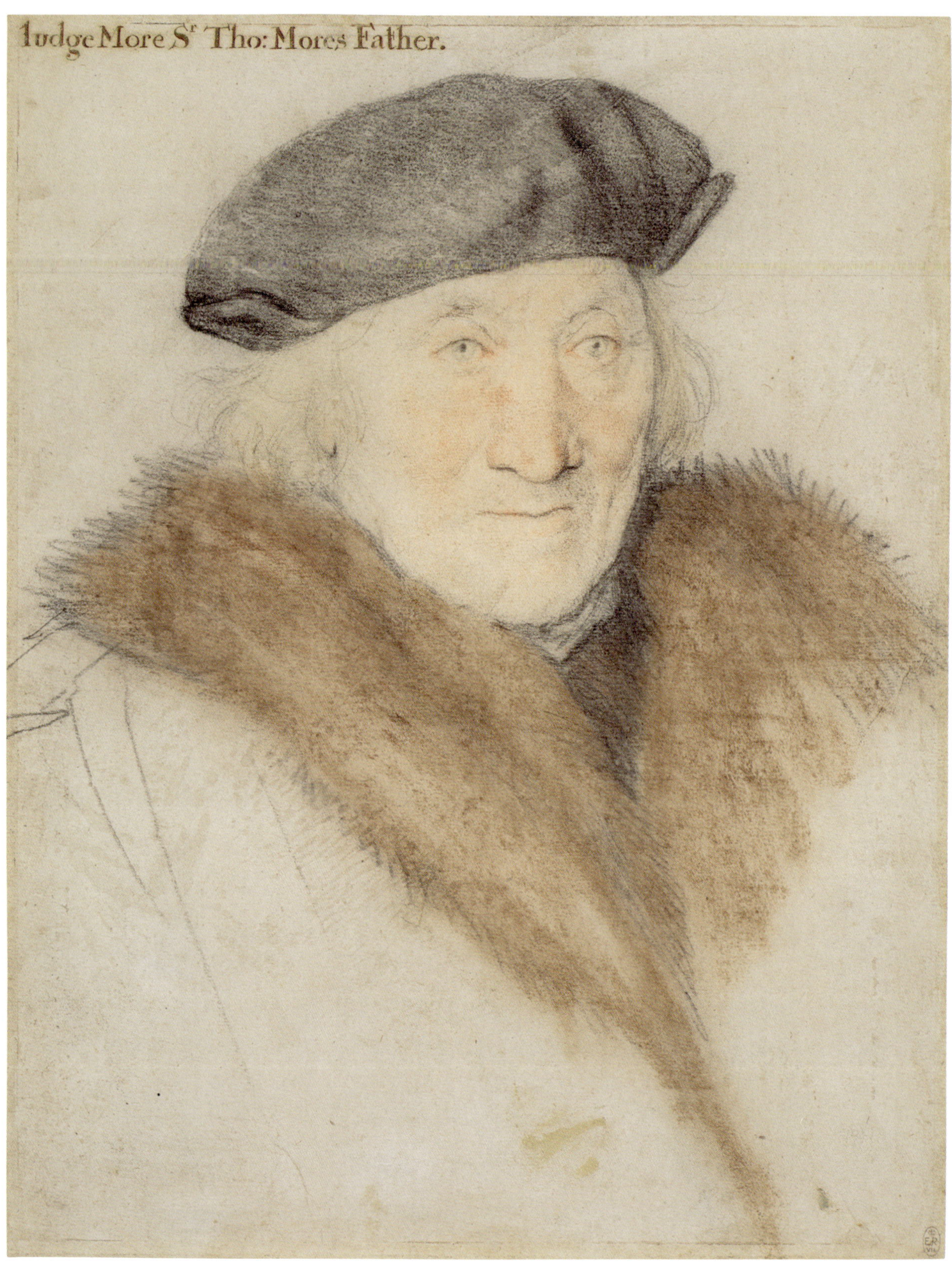
Iudge More Sr Tho: Mores Father.

Sir John More (*c*.1451–1530)

1526–7
Black and coloured chalks
35.1 × 27.3 cm
RCIN 912224

[BELOW]
Fig. 33 **Hans Holbein, *Sketch for the More Family Group*, *c*.1527, pen and ink**
Kunstmuseum, Basel, 1662.31

When Holbein arrived in London in the autumn of 1526, he seems to have carried a letter of introduction from the Dutch scholar Desiderius Erasmus, then resident in Basel, to Sir Thomas More. A prominent lawyer, royal administrator and author, More had recently been appointed Chancellor of the Duchy of Lancaster. On 18 December 1526 More acknowledged Holbein's arrival, writing to Erasmus: 'Your painter friend, my dear Erasmus, is a wonderful artist. I fear he will not find English soil as rich and fertile as he had hoped. But I shall do my best to make sure it is not completely barren.'[1]

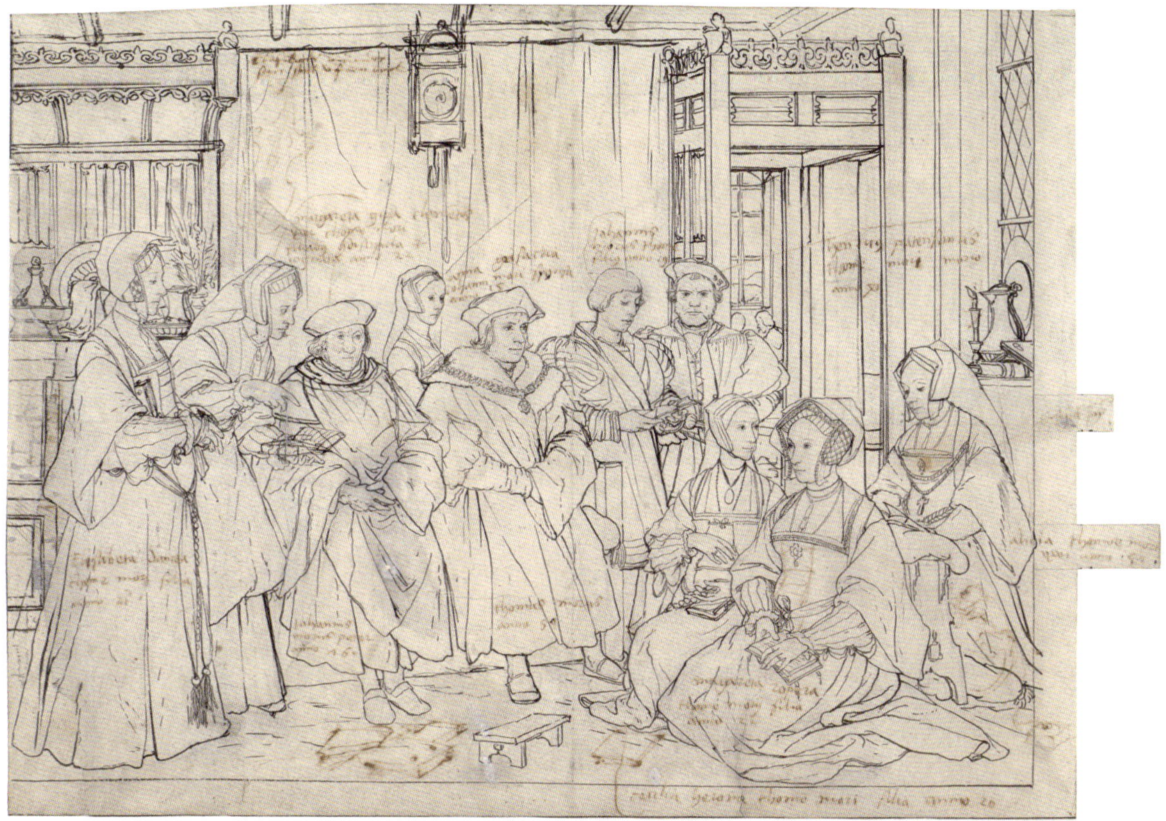

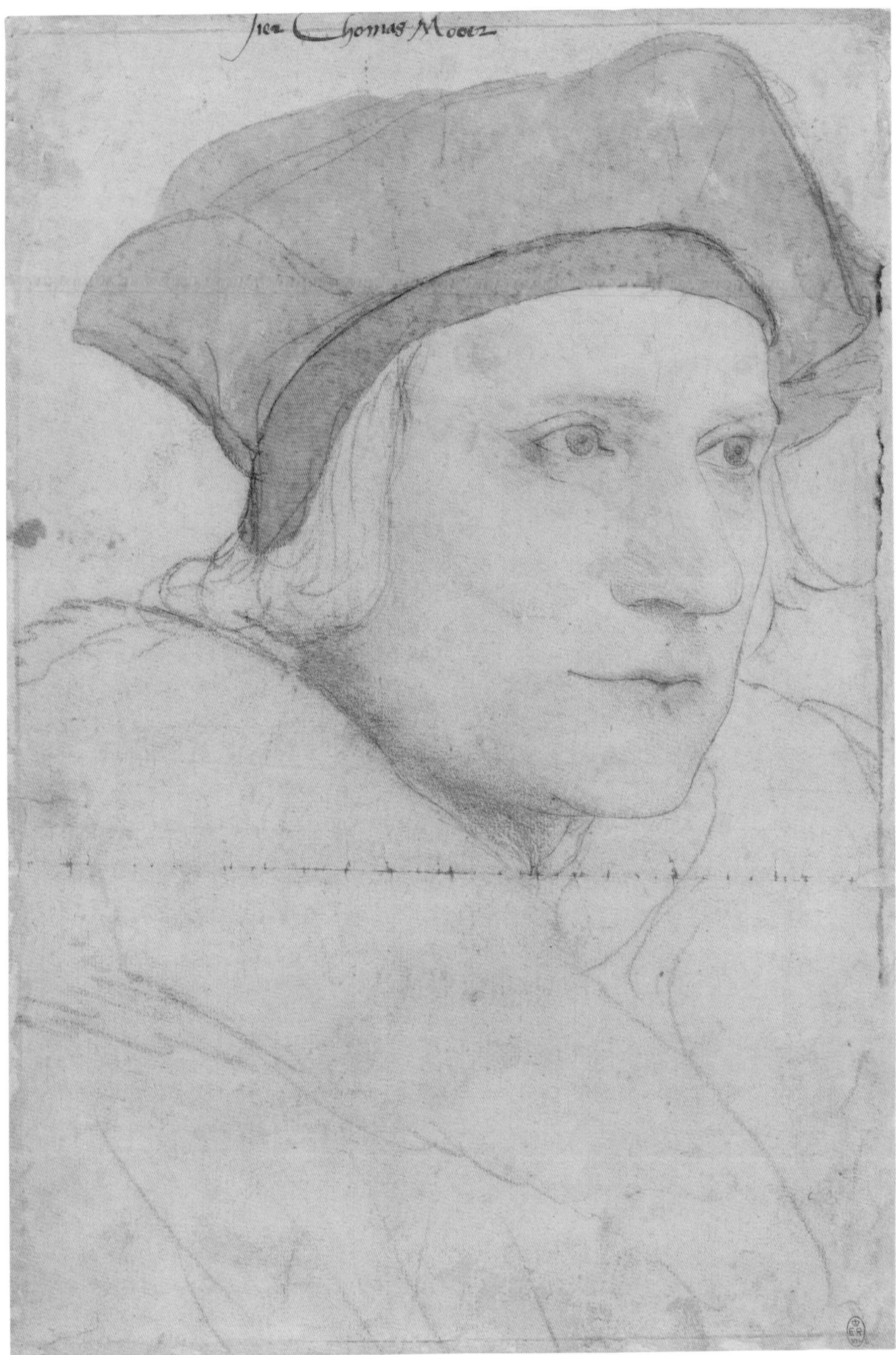
Sier Thomas Moore

Among Holbein's earliest commissions in England were two paintings for More: a single portrait (see Fig. 35) and a group portrait of the More family, shown seated in an interior.[2] The latter was probably intended for display in More's house. Although Holbein's finished painting of the family group was destroyed by fire in the eighteenth century, most of Holbein's studies of the individual sitters survive, as well as a sketch plan for the overall composition which Holbein gave to Erasmus when he returned to Basel in 1528 (Fig. 33). An early copy by Rowland Lockey at Nostell Priory in West Yorkshire may record the appearance of the final painting (Fig. 34).

There are ten figures depicted in the group composition. Drawings survive of More himself; his father, Sir John More; his son, also John; his married daughters Elizabeth Dauncey and Cicely Heron; and two adopted daughters, Margaret Giggs and Anne Cresacre. Anne would shortly marry John More the Younger. Drawings of More's wife Alice, his eldest daughter Margaret and a

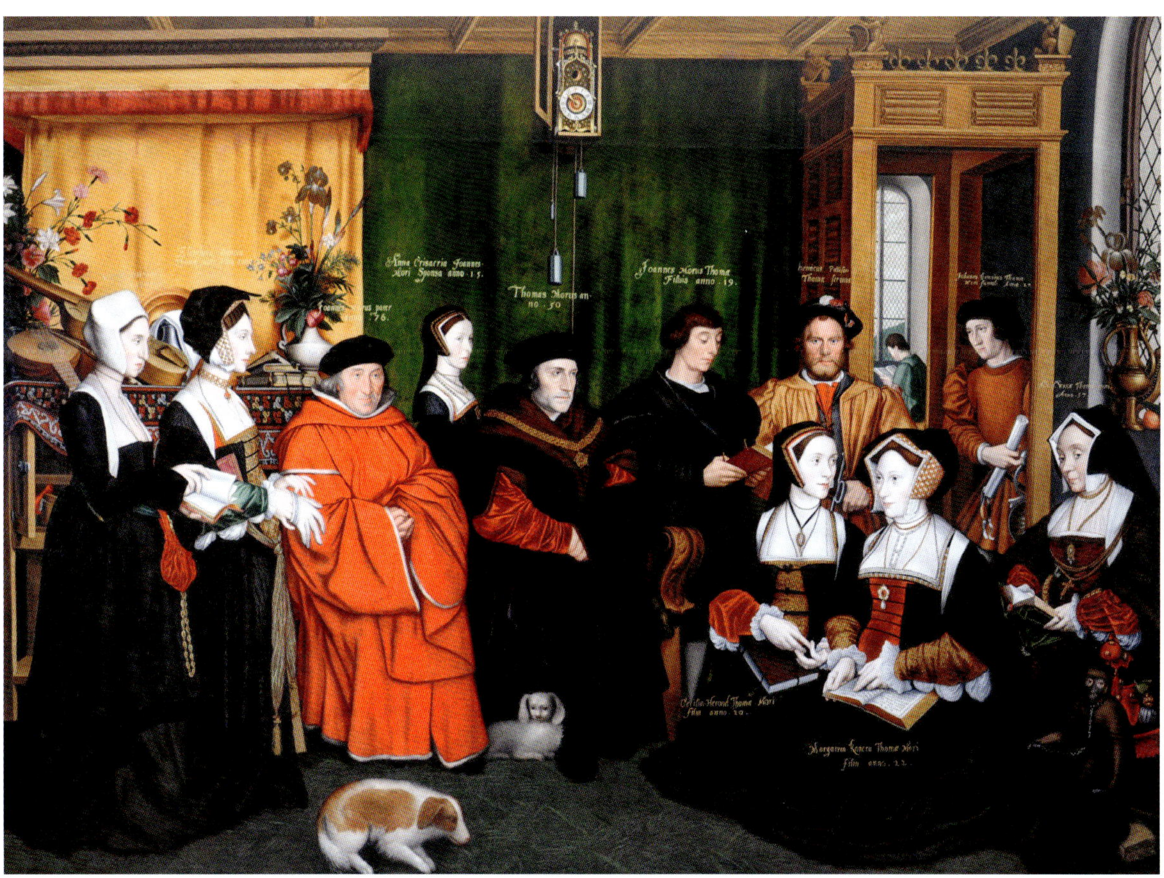

[ABOVE]
Fig. 34 **Rowland Lockey (*c.*1565–1616) after Hans Holbein, *The Family of Sir Thomas More*, 1592, oil on canvas**
National Trust, Nostell Priory, Yorkshire, 960059

Sir Thomas More (1478–1535)
1526–7
Black and coloured chalks with brown wash
37.6 × 25.5 cm
RCIN 912225

family servant, Henry Patenson, are not known to survive. Both Margaret Giggs and Elizabeth Dauncey are misnamed in the eighteenth-century inscriptions on the drawings.

Each of the drawings is in coloured chalks, and shows the sitter carefully posed as he or she will appear in the finished work. The back of the chair on which Anne Cresacre sits while she is drawn is lightly sketched, but she was shown as if standing in the final painting. The sketch surviving in Basel (which was annotated with the sitters' identities for Erasmus by Nicolaus Kratzer) is a working drawing that shows Holbein making alterations to the composition.[3] These include the addition of a viol hanging on the wall behind the head of Sir John More, a monkey nestling in Alice More's skirts and books scattered around the floor, while a candle on the windowsill to the far right is to be deleted. In the final painting, the position of Margaret Giggs has been altered: while in the drawing she leans over Judge More's shoulder to point out a passage in a book, in the painting, she stood to the far left behind Elizabeth Dauncey, still gesturing to the volume, but wearing a fur cap rather than an English hood. This change was made by Holbein before he drew Giggs, who is shown standing upright in the fur cap in the Royal Collection drawing.

The drawing of Sir Thomas More (p. 38) appears different from the rest, and its attribution to Holbein has been doubted, but it is on the same paper as the others from this group.[4] It is less finished and at a larger scale, but has clearly been used for transfer to another sheet or to the painting surface, since blind lines traced with a stylus can be seen, particularly to the right of More's proper left cheek. It may represent a different stage in Holbein's working process, since the other drawings in the group show few, if any, signs of transfer.[5] An early inscription at top centre indicates that this sheet has a separate early history from the majority of the drawings: perhaps when the Great Book was compiled, the more highly worked drawing of More was selected for inclusion. As a portrait of Thomas More, who was executed for his opposition to Henry VIII's religious reforms in 1535, this sheet would nonetheless have held some appeal, and was apparently preserved and added to the group by one of the Holbein collectors who subsequently owned the drawings.

[OPPOSITE]
Elizabeth Dauncey (b. 1506)
1526–7
Black and coloured chalks
36.7 × 26.0 cm
RCIN 912228

[PAGE 42]
John More (1509–47)
1526–7
Black and coloured chalks
38.1 × 28.1 cm
RCIN 912226

[PAGE 43]
Margaret Giggs (1508–70)
1526–7
Black and coloured chalks
38.5 × 27.3 cm
RCIN 912229

[PAGE 44]
Cicely Heron (b. 1507)
1526–7
Black and coloured chalks
37.8 × 28.1 cm
RCIN 912269

[PAGE 45]
Anne Cresacre (*c.*1511–77)
1526–7
Black and coloured chalks
37.2 × 26.6 cm
RCIN 912270

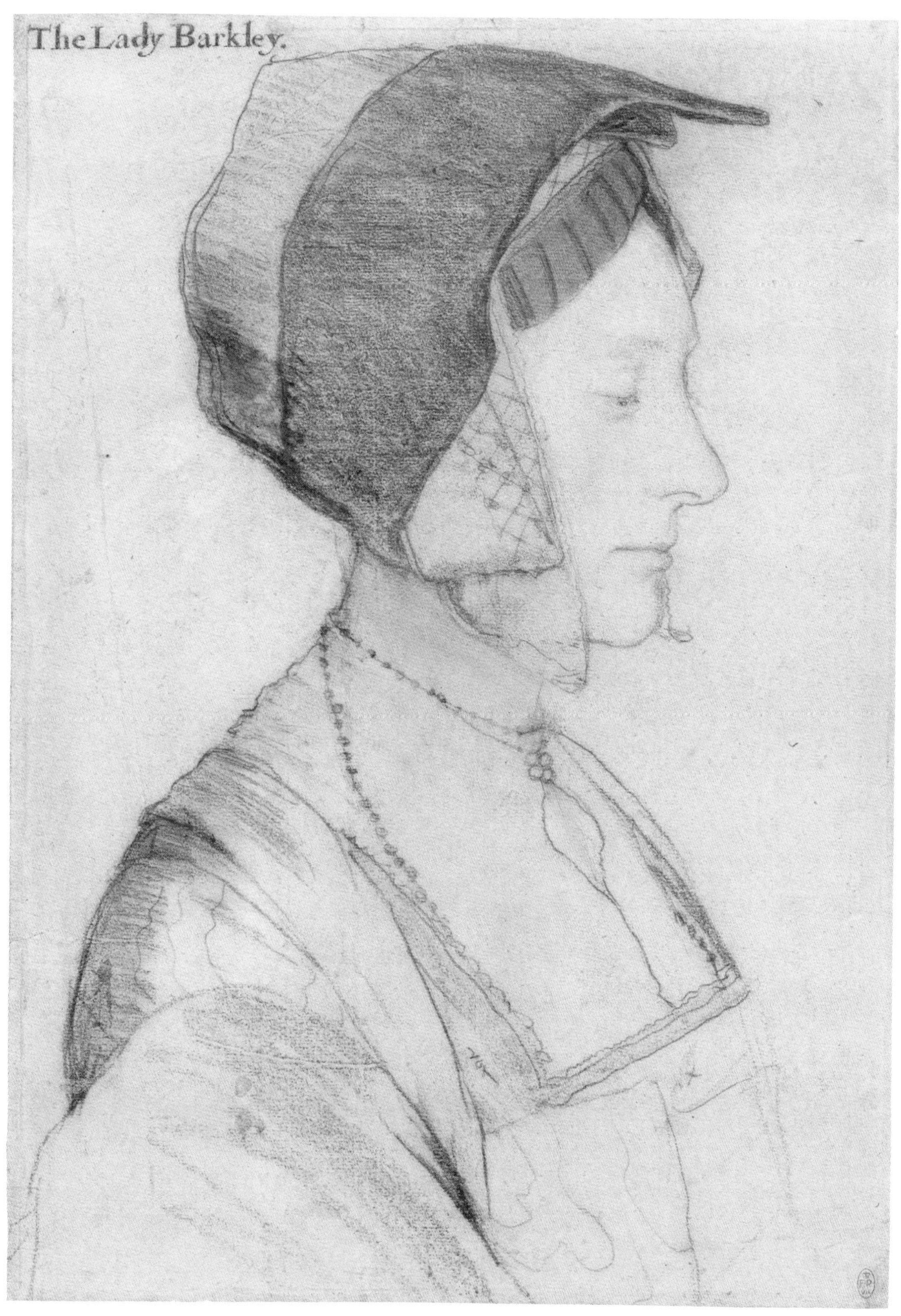
The Lady Barkley.

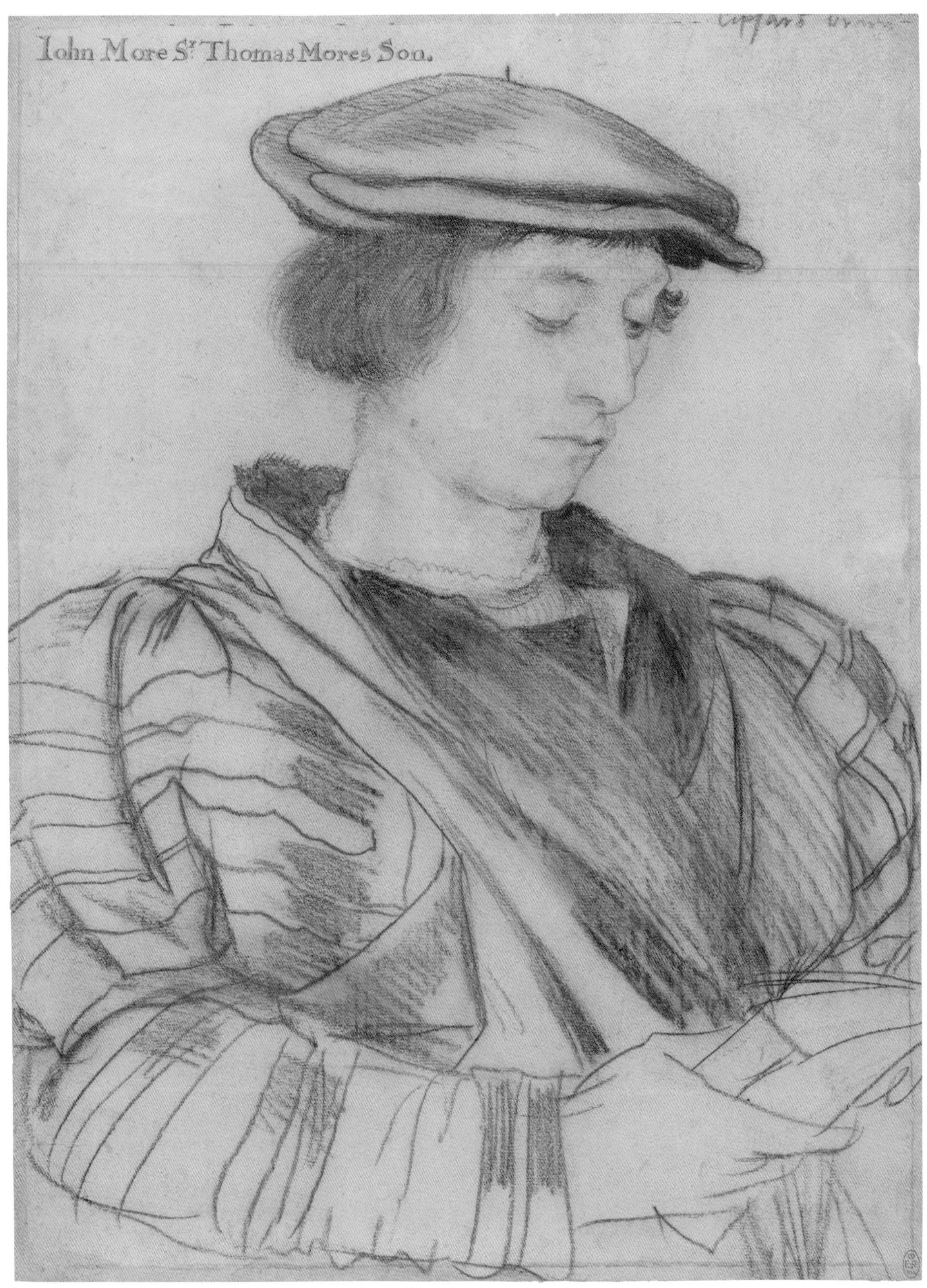
Iohn More Sr Thomas Mores Son.

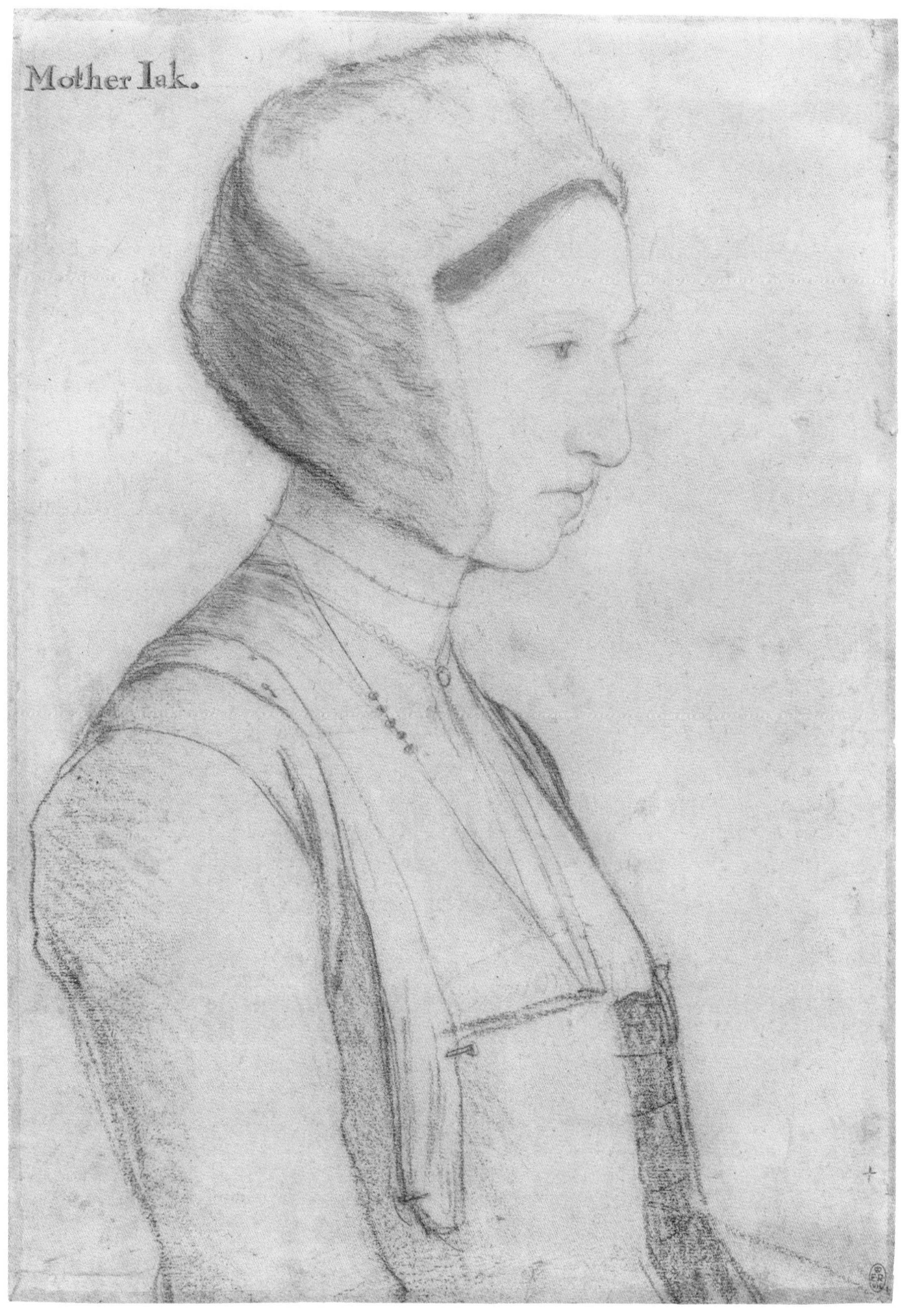
Mother Iak.

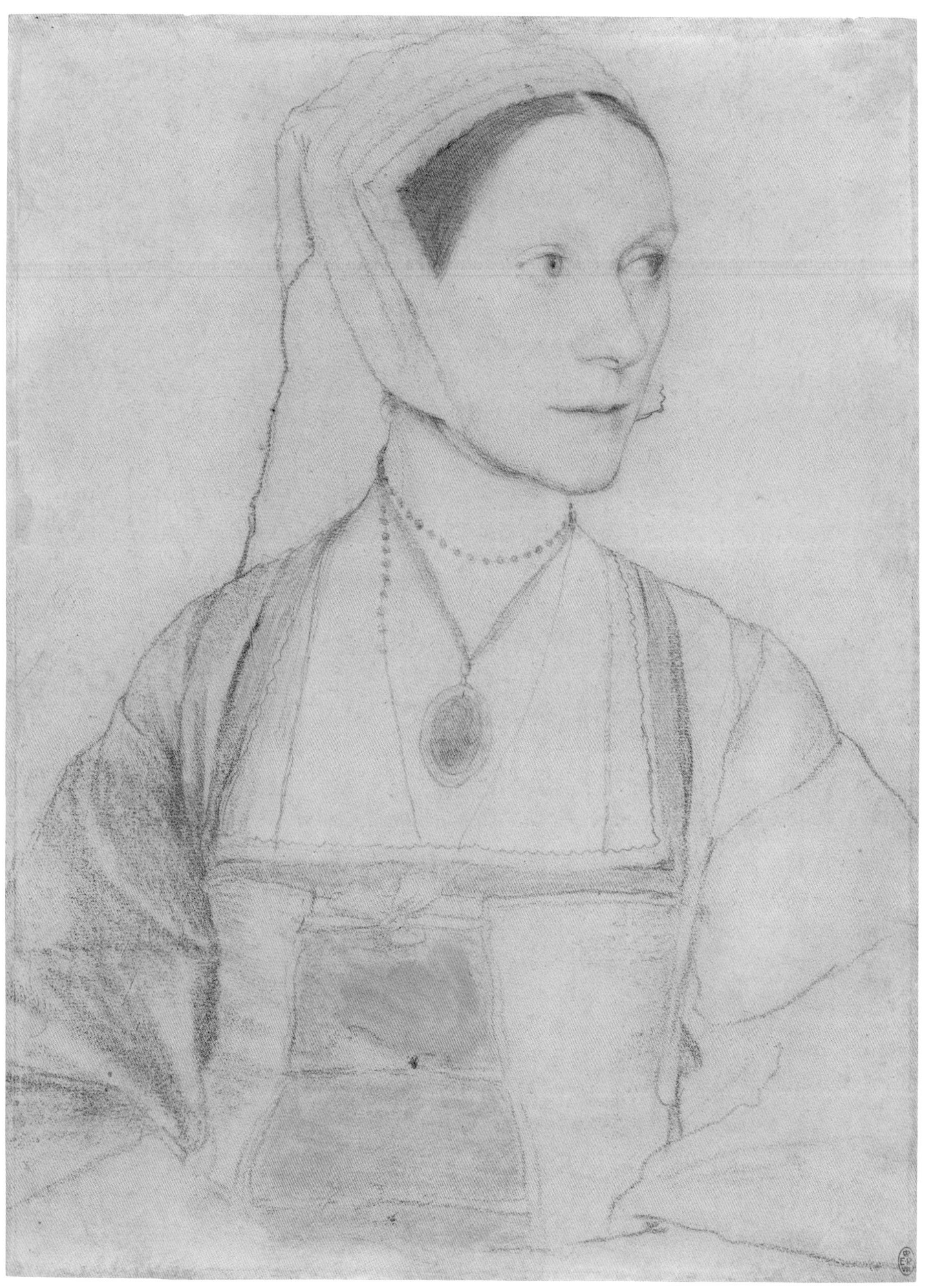

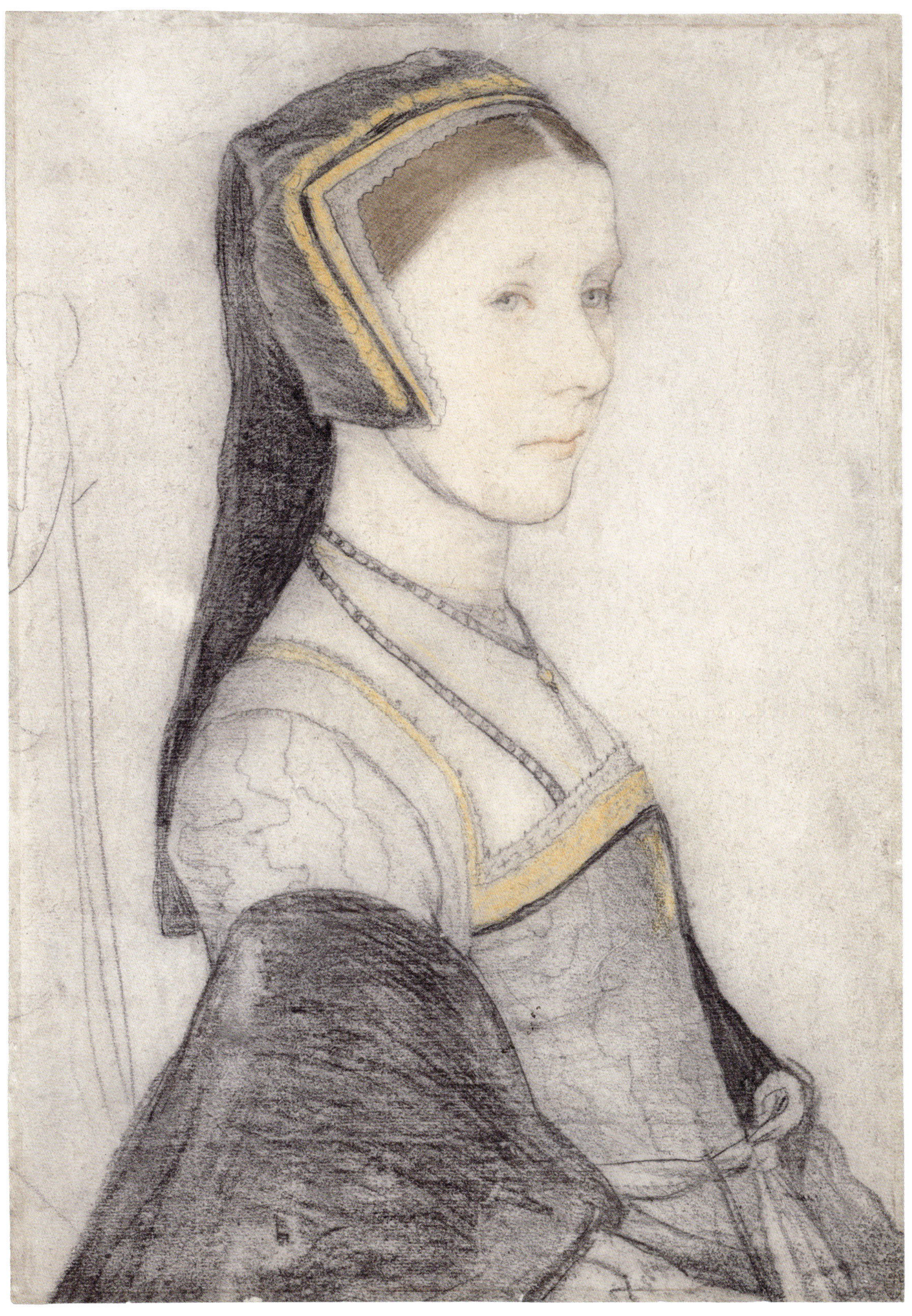

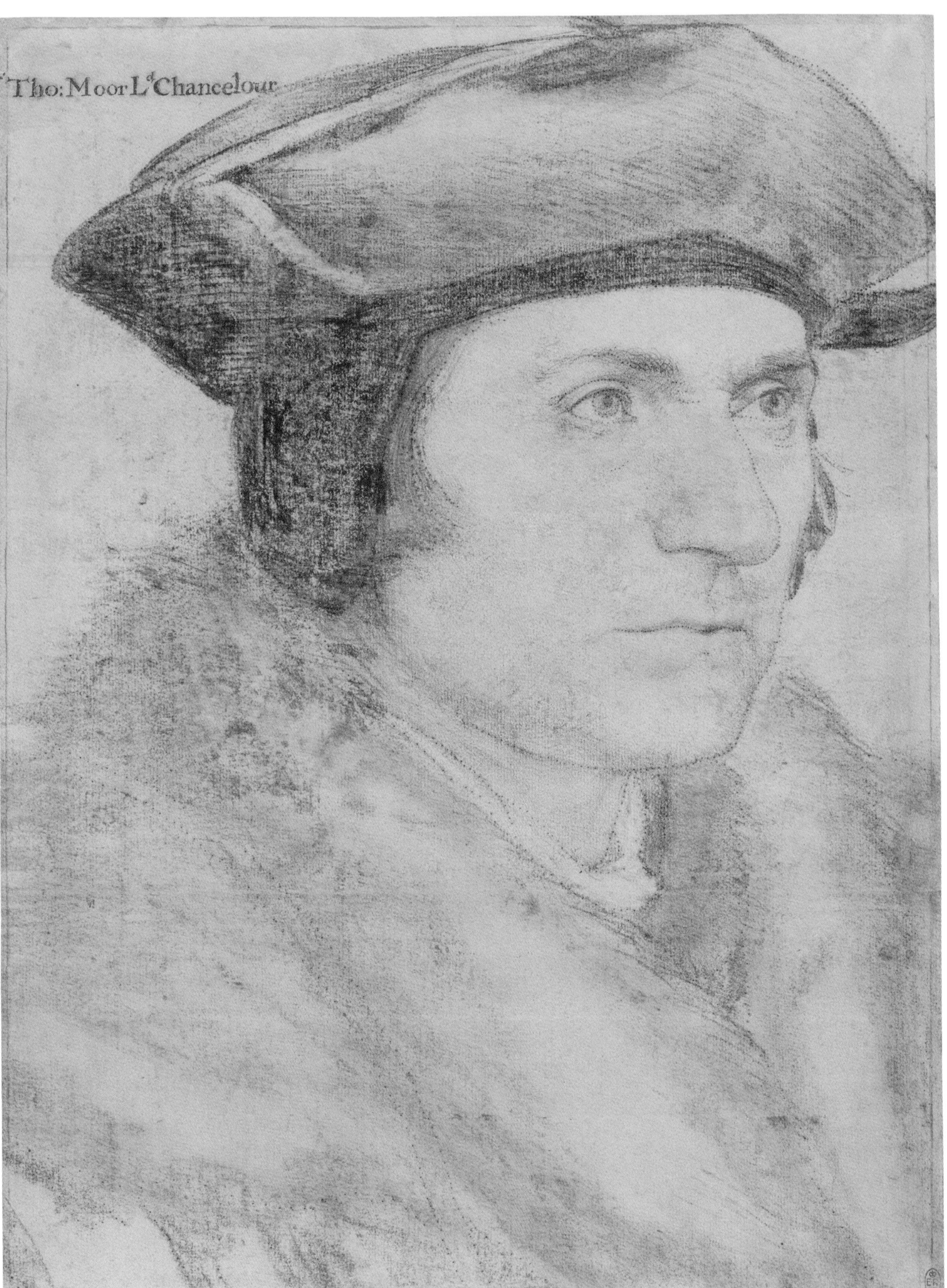
Tho: Moor Ld Chancelour

Sir Thomas More (1478–1535)

1527
Black and coloured chalks, the outlines pricked for transfer
39.7 × 29.9 cm
RCIN 912268

This is a study for a portrait of Sir Thomas More dated 1527, showing the sitter half-length, against a green curtain and wearing his Collar of Esses (Fig. 35).[6] The papers Holbein used at this period bear two different watermarks: the drawings for the More family group (see pp. 38–45) are on paper with one type, while this drawing, that of Sir Henry Guildford (p. 52) and the two unknown sitters now in Basel (see Figs 13–14), are on paper with another. On this basis, this seems likely to be the second commission given by More to Holbein shortly after the artist arrived in London in 1526.

The drawing demonstrates Holbein's masterful use of coloured chalks. He appears to have erased areas of the brown chalk to give a sheen to More's fur collar. Small strokes of black chalk around the chin suggest stubble, which is seen in the final painting, as is the redness around More's eyes. The outlines of the drawing have been pricked with a pin to transfer them to another surface, probably another sheet of paper, which Holbein could work on further.[7] Holbein also used pricking to transfer the cartoon of the Whitehall mural (see Fig. 22), but this is the only one of his surviving portrait drawings that is pricked and it is unclear why he used the technique here. Infrared examination of the finished portrait shows how Holbein altered the composition on the panel after he had transferred the initial design, continuing to refine the portrait as he worked, as he did with many of his portraits.[8]

While Holbein's portrait of William Warham (p. 49) was intended as a gift, the purpose of More's portrait is not known. Although it has been demonstrated that it had left England by the end of the sixteenth century, whether this was during More's lifetime or in the aftermath of his death cannot be determined.[9]

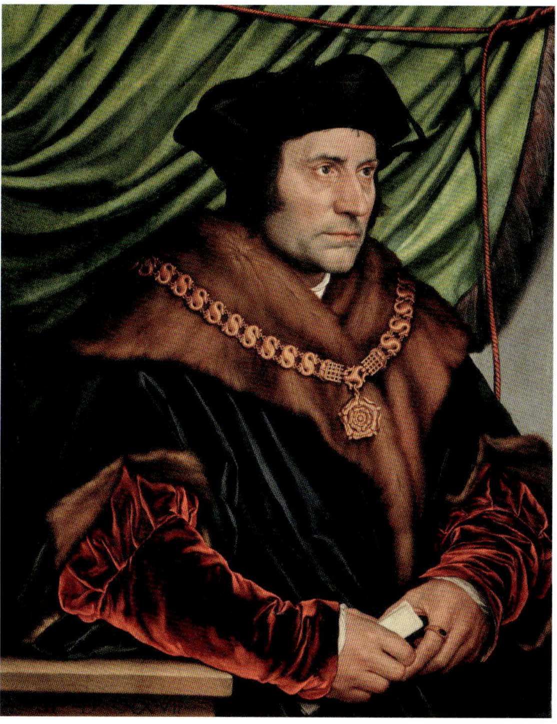

Fig. 35 **Hans Holbein, *Sir Thomas More*, 1527, oil on panel**
Frick Collection, New York, 1912.1.77

William Warham, Archbishop of Canterbury (1450?–1532)

1527

Black and coloured chalks

40.7 × 30.9 cm

RCIN 912272

William Warham was in his mid-seventies when Holbein took his portrait. After a distinguished ambassadorial career, he had been appointed Bishop of London in 1501, and Archbishop of Canterbury in 1503 (Fig. 36).[10] From 1504 to 1515 he simultaneously held the post of Lord Chancellor. As archbishop, he crowned Henry VIII on 24 June 1509. In 1527 he was, by virtue of his position, one of the leading voices in the debate over Henry VIII's wish to divorce Katherine of Aragon in favour of Anne Boleyn. Warham found himself pulled between loyalty to monarch and Church: the Spanish ambassador reported in May 1527 that the archbishop was trying to avoid attending court.[11] Having initially aided the king in the matter, in early 1532 (encouraged by John Fisher), Warham publicly opposed Henry's moves to take control of the Church in England, placing himself in direct conflict with the Crown. He died, of natural causes, in August 1532 and was buried in a chapel he had erected next to the site of the martyrdom of St Thomas Becket, to whom he had long been devoted, and whose own opposition to royal authority had recently been uppermost in his mind.

Like the drawings of Sir Thomas More (p. 46) and Sir Henry Guildford (p. 52), this is drawn entirely in chalk. Holbein has used a combination of brown and yellow chalks for the fur to suggest the fall of light. White chalk brightens the eyes.[12] A stylus has been used to trace over many of the outlines, probably for transfer to panel.[13]

It is thought that Holbein painted two versions of Warham's portrait.[14] One (now lost) was to be sent to Erasmus as a token of friendship in return for a painting of Erasmus sent by the philosopher to Warham; the other was for Warham's London residence, Lambeth Palace. Warham is seen before a green damask curtain, with a cross and mitre, the symbols of his archiepiscopal status, behind him. His pose echoes that of Erasmus in the portrait he had received as a gift in 1524.[15]

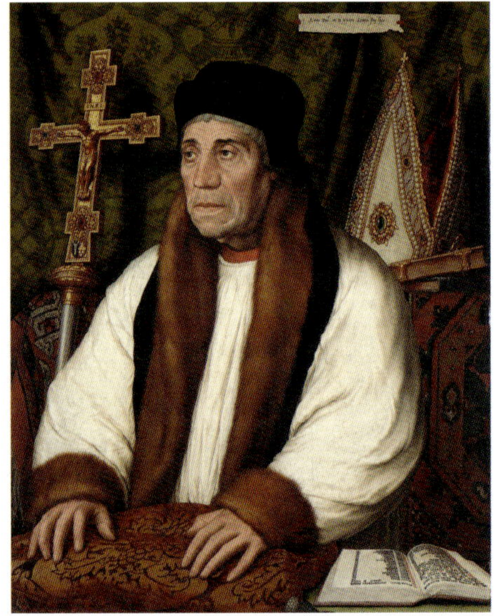

Fig. 36 **Hans Holbein, *William Warham, Archbishop of Canterbury*, 1527, oil on panel**

Musée du Louvre, Paris, 1344; MR 752

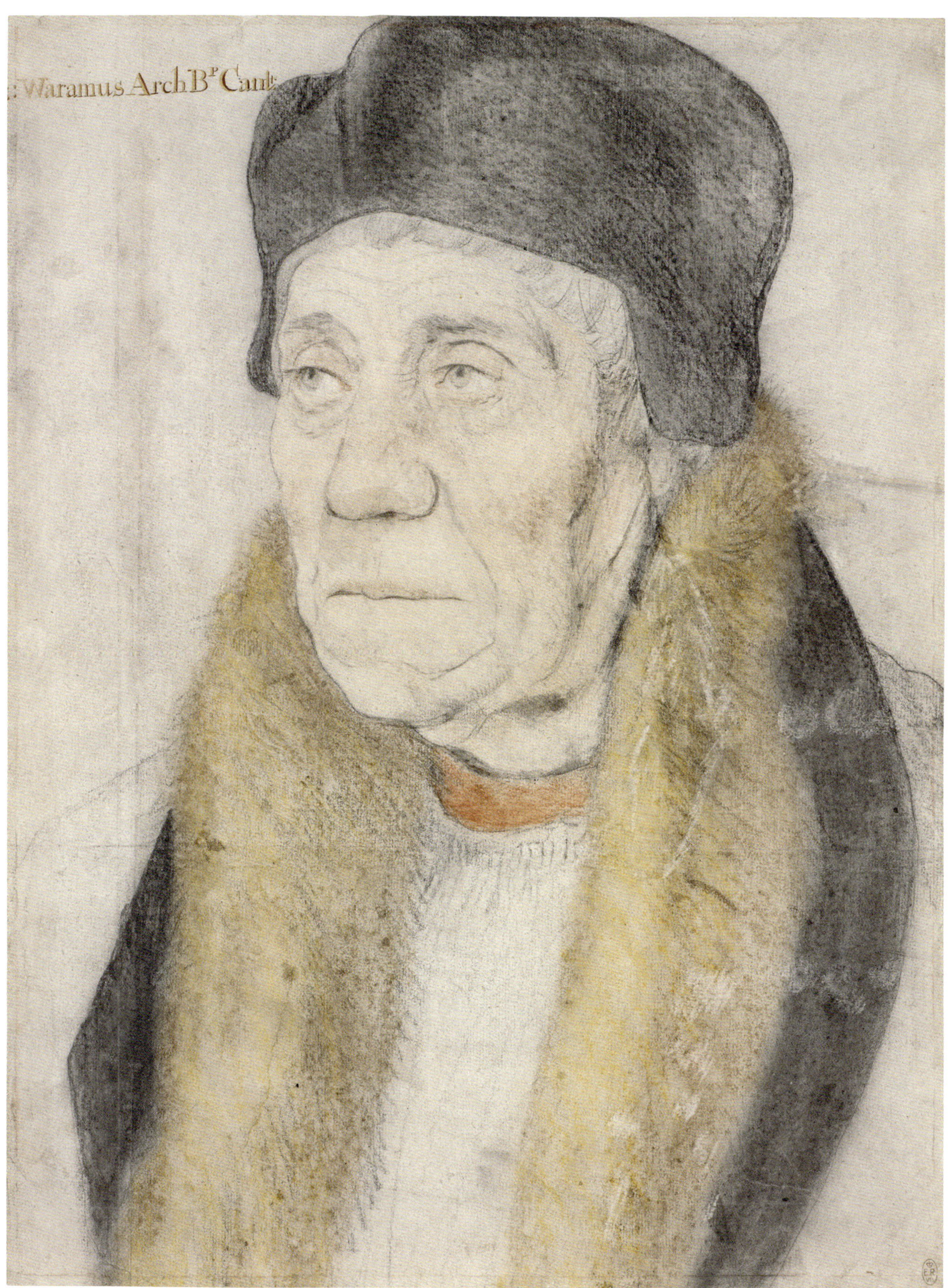
: Waramus Arch Bp Cant:

John Fisher, Bishop of Rochester (*c*.1469–1535)
Unidentified artist
1550–1600?
Black and coloured chalks with wash and ink on pink prepared paper
38.2 × 23.2 cm
RCIN 912205

John Fisher was appointed Bishop of Rochester in 1504. A learned and spiritual man, he gained a reputation as an ascetic. This impression has been compounded by portraits such as the present drawing, which show him gaunt and preoccupied, and by an inventory of his goods taken after his arrest, which records a sparsely furnished house.[16] The inventory, however, was taken after items of value had been confiscated and does not record the quantities of plate that passed into royal hands. Fisher was by no means entirely self-denying. He was a patron of Pietro Torrigiano, the Italian sculptor who was employed to work on the tomb of Lady Margaret Beaufort, Henry VII's mother, the construction of which Fisher oversaw. Torrigiano may also have made a terracotta bust of the bishop, and Fisher commissioned a tomb for his chantry chapel at St John's College in Cambridge based on Torrigiano's work.[17] Opposed to religious reform, Fisher was a vocal supporter of Katherine of Aragon in her struggle to prevent her divorce from Henry VIII and spoke against the king's move to take control of the Church. By the time Holbein returned to England in 1532, the bishop was in disgrace: he was arrested and imprisoned in March 1533 before being executed in 1535.

Although long attributed to Holbein, this drawing is probably by another artist, who echoes Holbein's use of pink prepared paper. The pink priming has been roughly applied in comparison to that on the Holbein sheets.[18] The facial features are more clumsily drawn than on any of Holbein's drawings and the modelling is largely in watercolour or wash rather than chalk. The drawing was started on a full sheet, which was then folded in half and worked up only on the top section of the paper, for what purpose is uncertain. An inscription in Italian, apparently referring to Fisher's execution, has proved hard to decipher, but suggests the drawing has a different early history from others in the group.[19] It may have been in Italian ownership, although it has also been proposed that the inscription may be connected with Thomas Howard, 14th Earl of Arundel.[20]

The drawing probably dates from the later sixteenth century when Fisher began to be revered as a Catholic martyr and large numbers of painted and printed portraits were produced to meet a growing demand for his image. Carlo Borromeo, Archbishop of Milan (1538–84), for example, included a portrait of Fisher in a gallery of models of episcopal conduct.[21] A date in the later sixteenth century would also explain a pattern for Fisher's face in the National Portrait Gallery, London, which is thought to have been used in a late sixteenth-century painter's workshop and which is based on the present drawing.[22] As a posthumous work, the portrait provides an idealised image of Fisher rather than his true likeness.

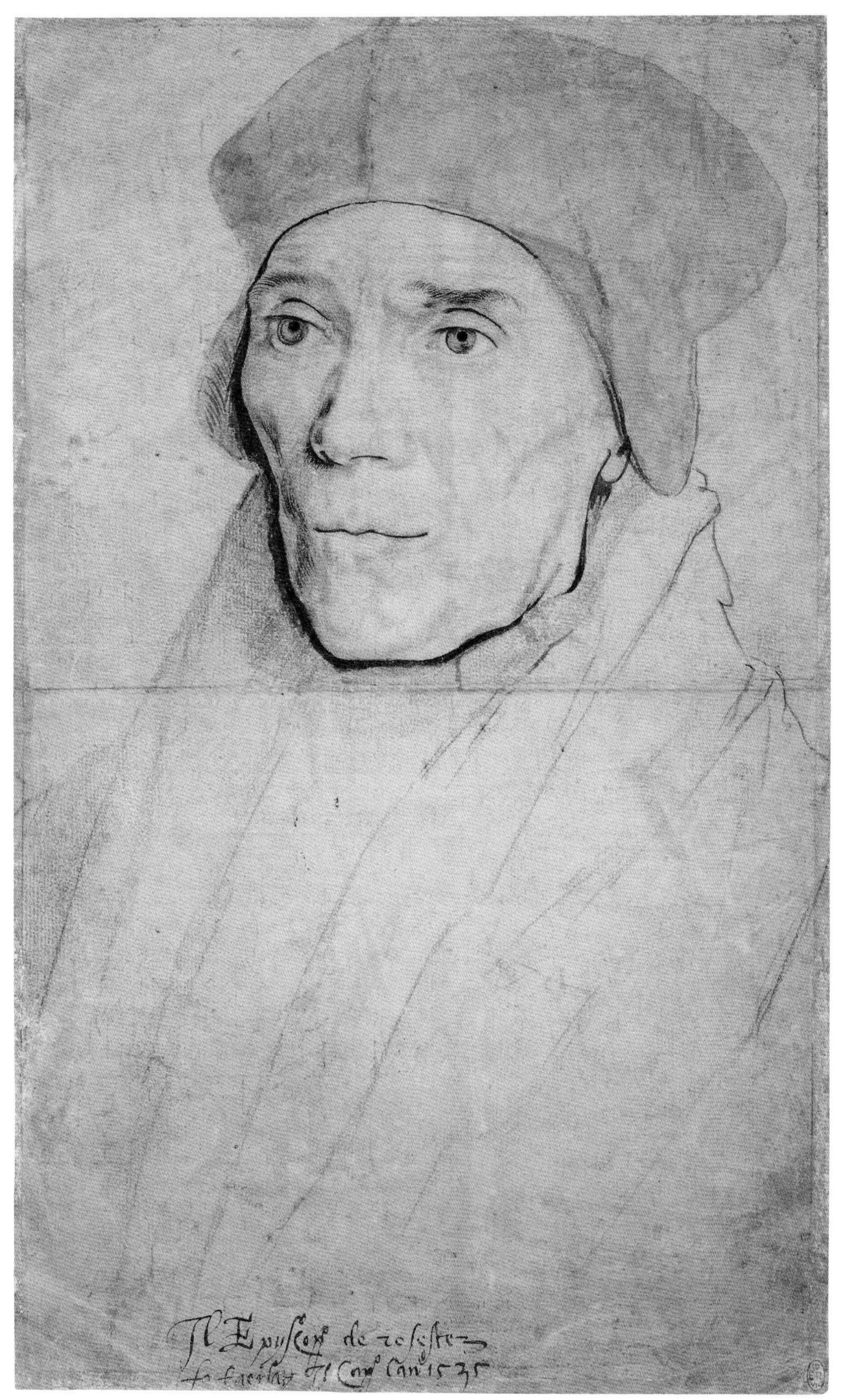

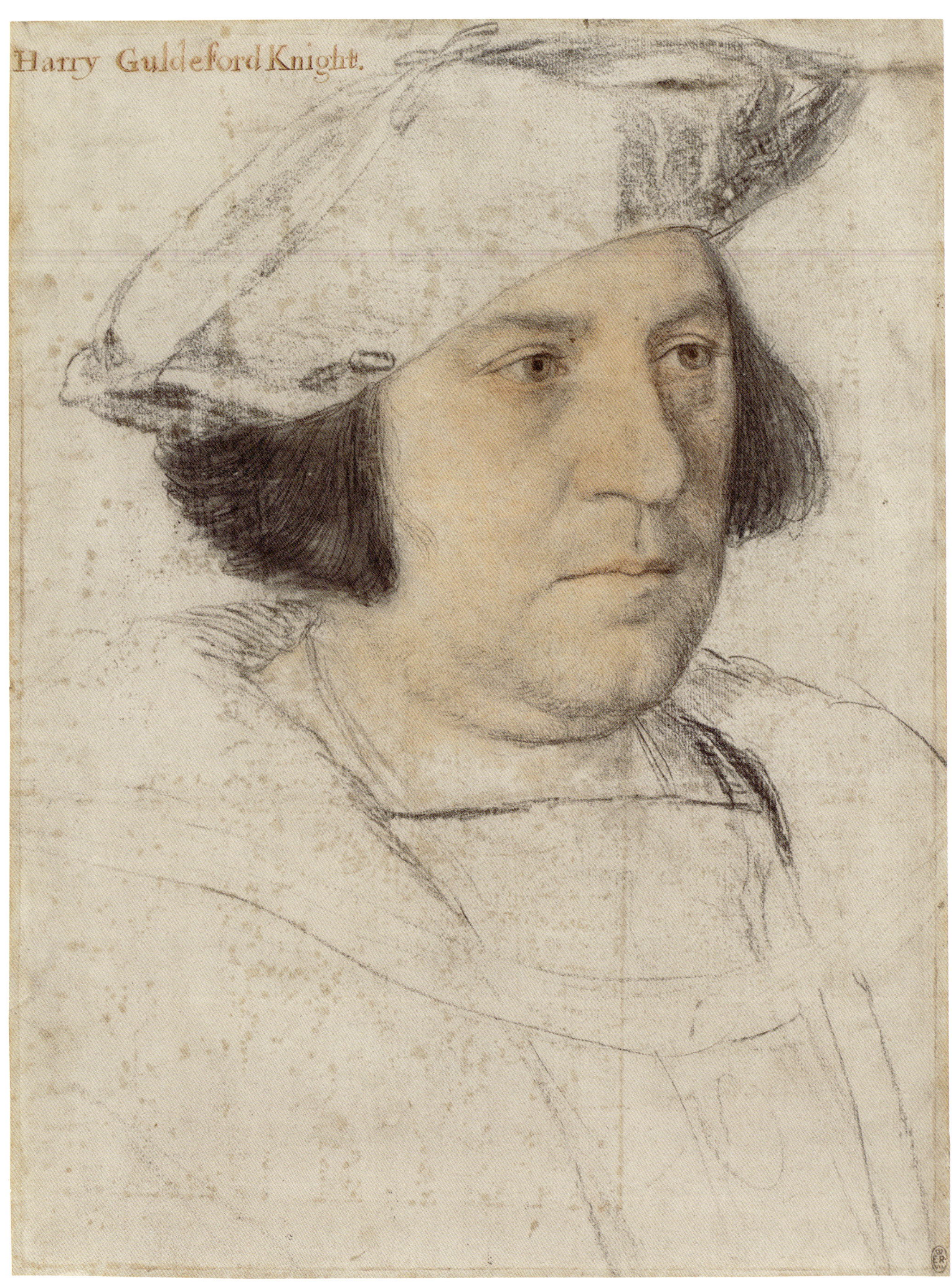
Harry Guldeford Knight.

Sir Henry Guildford (1489–1532)

1527
Black and coloured chalks with touches of brown ink
38.3 × 29.4 cm
RCIN 912266

Both Holbein's drawing and finished painting of Sir Henry Guildford are in the Royal Collection. Guildford's likeness is one of a pair with that of his wife Mary, now in St. Louis, Missouri. Holbein's drawing of Mary Guildford is in Basel, probably having been taken there by the artist in 1528 (Fig. 37). The couple, who had married in 1525, commissioned their portraits from Holbein in 1527, while the artist was working on painted decorations at Greenwich, under the supervision of Henry Guildford and Henry Wyatt. Shown against a brilliant blue background, the pair turn towards one another, he holding his staff of office, she a devotional book (p. 54 and Fig. 38). Behind Mary Guildford, a pilaster supports a curtain rail, which runs across both panels and from which hangs a bright green curtain. Beyond this is a twisting vine, which Holbein used in a number of his paintings, among them the portrait of William Reskimer (p. 109). The purpose of the vines in Holbein's paintings has never been satisfactorily explained and they may simply be intended to evoke the outdoors in the same manner as the trees and mountains that Holbein depicted behind the Basel lawyer Bonifacius Amerbach in 1519.[23]

Guildford is drawn almost entirely in coloured chalks, which have been smudged, hatched and dampened to create modelling and texture. A few lines of ink mark the bottom of his cap. The artist has struggled a little with the sitter's proper left eye,

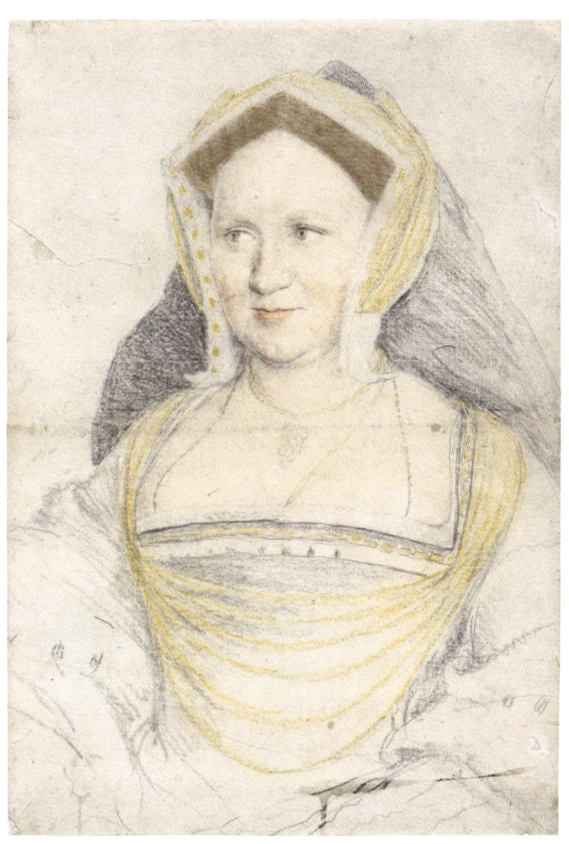

Fig. 37 **Hans Holbein, *Mary, Lady Guildford,* 1527, black and coloured chalks**
Kunstmuseum, Basel, 1662.35

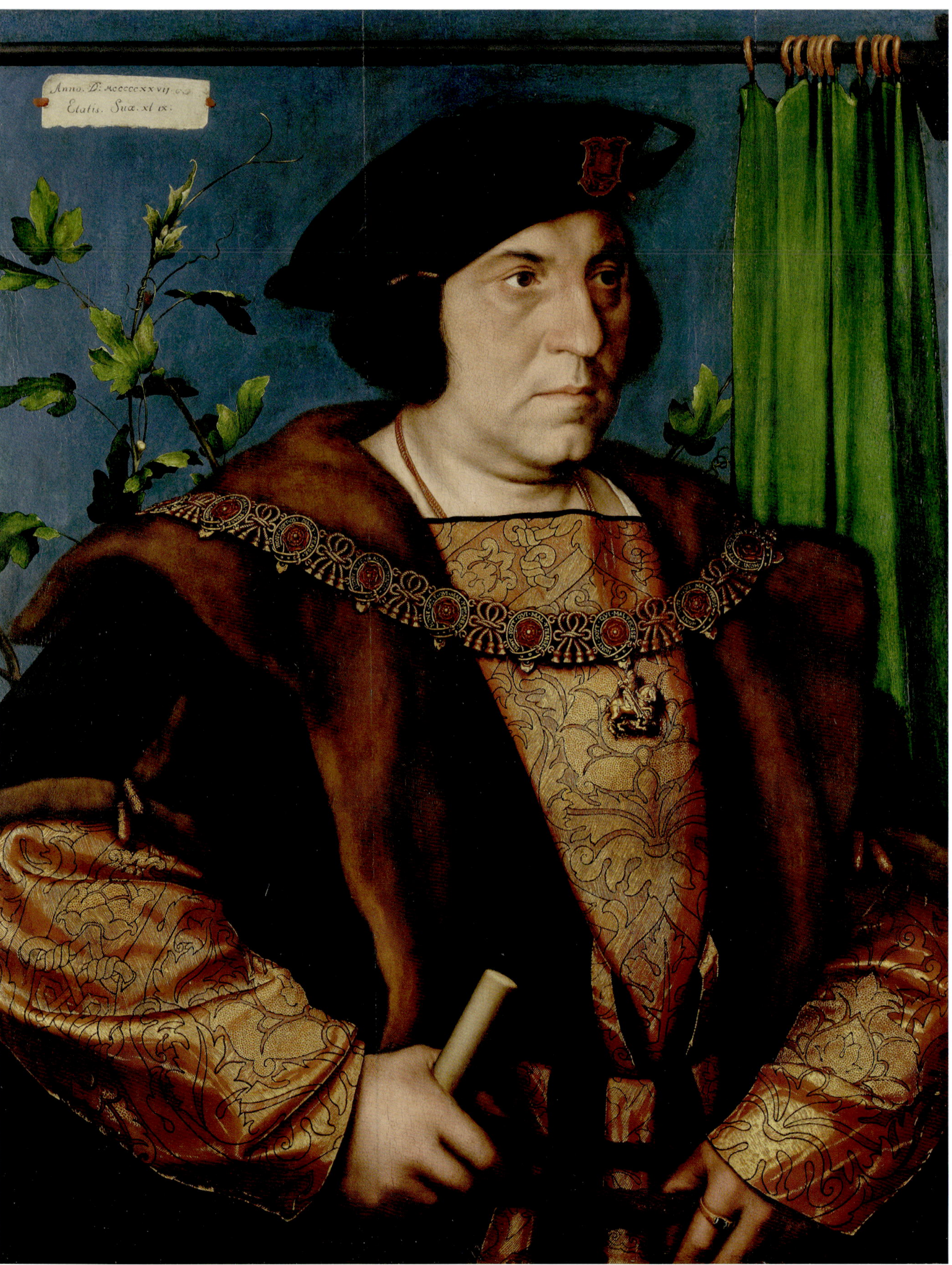
Anno. D: MCCCCCXXVII
Etatis. Suæ. xl ix:

which is strangely flat and misaligned, a challenge he resolved in the finished painting. Holbein made significant changes to both compositions as he worked, lengthening and slimming Sir Henry's face and altering Lady Mary's pose, so her body is angled towards her husband and she looks back to face the viewer. It has been shown that Holbein moved the outline of Henry Guildford around the panel to effect the changes to the design.[24]

From 1522, Henry Guildford, a contemporary and close friend of Henry VIII, held the senior position of Comptroller of the Household, the baton of which he holds in Holbein's portrait. He probably carried the royal standard at the Battle of the Spurs in 1513, and may be one of the stylised figures seen to the left of the painting of that engagement made for Henry VIII (see Fig. 10). In 1526 he was made a Knight of the Garter, the collar of which Holbein shows him wearing. Guildford was a correspondent of Erasmus, forming part of the group of learned men who gave Holbein his first commissions in England. Although he inherited little wealth, his accumulation of offices brought him a large income, which he lost as easily as he won. He died in 1532 in debt to creditors, including the royal goldsmith, Robert Amadas, to whom he owed £356 8s.[25] Among his executors were John Poyntz (p. 60) and Thomas Wyatt (p. 62).

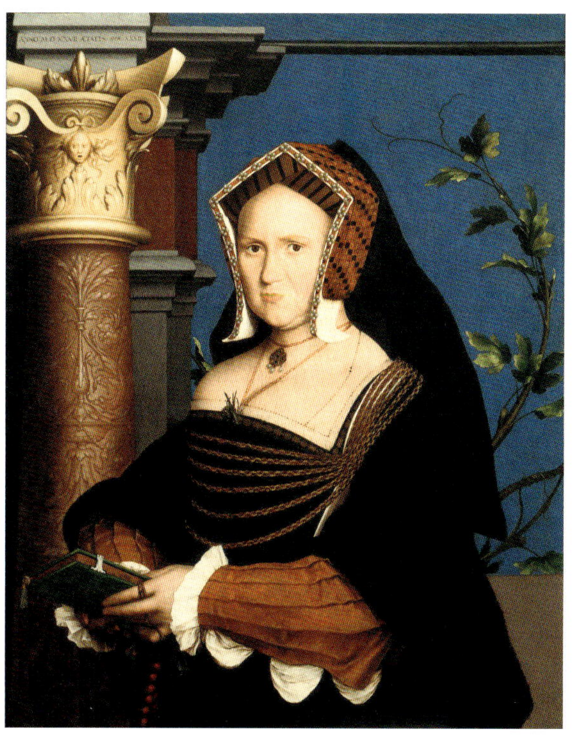

Fig. 38 **Hans Holbein, *Mary, Lady Guildford*, 1527, oil on panel**
Saint Louis Art Museum, Missouri, 1:1943

Sir Henry Guildford
1527
Oil on oak panel
82.7 × 66.4 cm
RCIN 400046

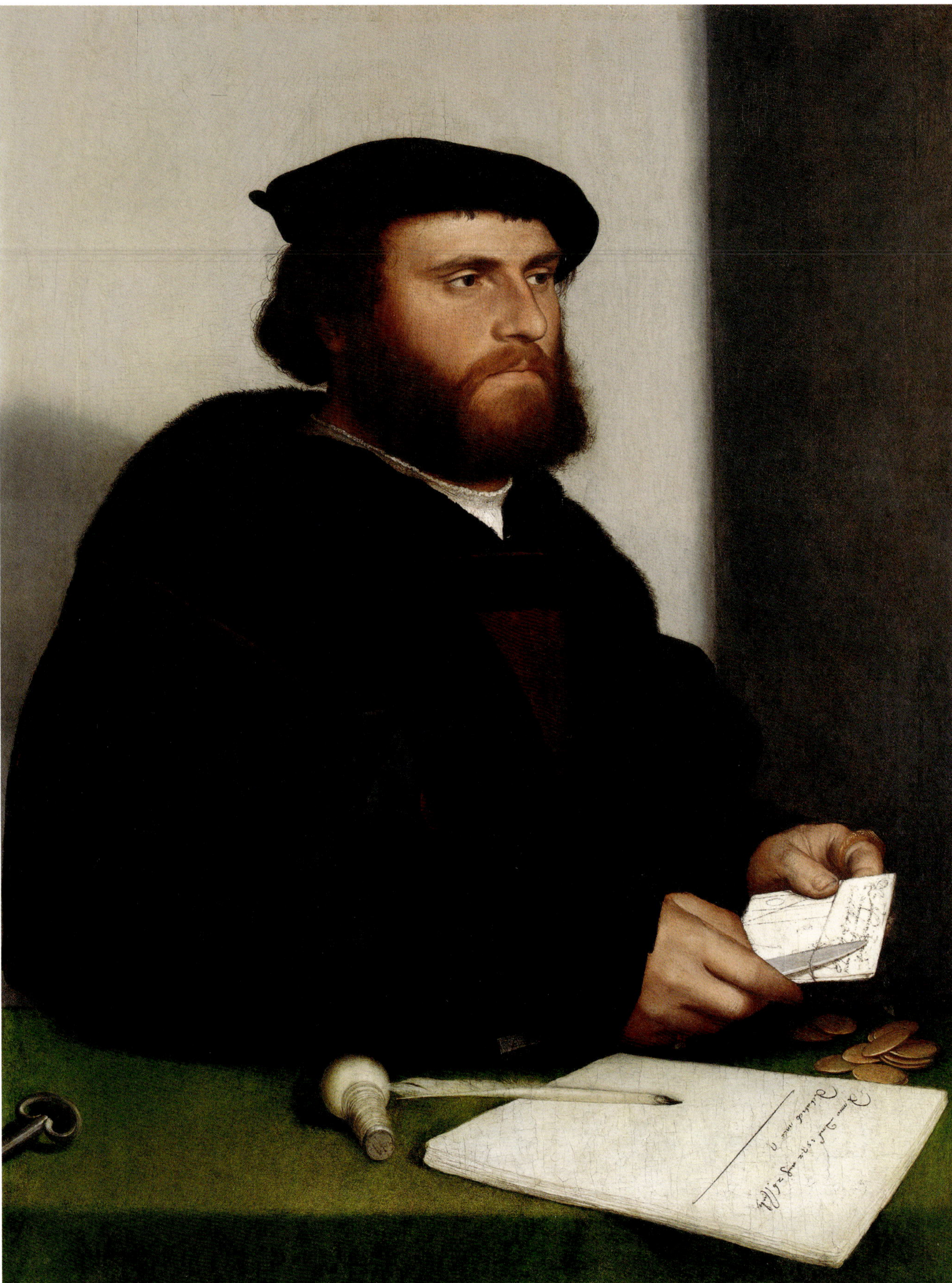

A Merchant of the Steelyard

1532
Oil on panel augmented with canvas
63.0 × 48.4 cm
RCIN 404443

This is among the first portraits painted by Holbein on his return to London, and is dated by an inscription on the paper lying on the table to July 1532. It is one of Holbein's portraits of merchants associated with the Steelyard, an enclosed trading compound on the site of today's Blackfriars station. A number of the Steelyard merchants commissioned portraits from Holbein after his return to London in 1532; seven of these can be identified with certainty today.[26] Although sometimes regarded as a set, these vary greatly in their approach, from figures placed against a plain background to those sat in elaborate interiors, and it seems likely that each portrait was an individual commission.[27]

The address on the letter the merchant holds in his hand appears to give his identity in a form Holbein would use on several of his Steelyard portraits.[28] This inscription, however, is badly rubbed, and it has proved impossible to interpret satisfactorily. It is generally agreed to include the word 'Stahlhof' (Steelyard) and to indicate that the sitter originated in Antwerp. Strangely, Holbein seems to have hidden the sitter's name behind the blade of the knife he is using to cut the thread around the letter. This has led to various suggestions about the sitter's identity and the painting has traditionally, and with little justification, been regarded as a portrait of the goldsmith Hans of Antwerp (*c.*1497–after 1550), who collaborated with Holbein on a number of projects. A small roundel in the Victoria and Albert Museum, London, sometimes attributed to Holbein, may show the same sitter.[29]

Although the sitter's identity is not known, the money and seal with a merchant's mark on the table in front of him confirm his mercantile status. A key to the far left was revealed in 2011, when the portrait was conserved, and may indicate that the merchant traded in particularly valuable goods, such as cloths of gold or jewels, which required secure storage.[30] Keys, as well as a seal and quill pen, occur in Holbein's contemporary portrait of Georg Gisze, also a Steelyard merchant, while that of Dirk Tybis, another member of the Steelyard painted in 1533, includes a quill, seal (with a stick of wax) and coins in the trough of an inkwell.[31] The sitter's fur collar has been added at a late stage of painting.[32]

The merchant's mark on the seal was revealed during recent conservation of the panel.[33] It bears a resemblance to the mark used by the merchant John Westbury, a London mercer, who died in June 1534 and whose mark appears in a group of letters relating to a consignment of goods lost in transport in 1533.[34] But since the sitter seems to have been a Steelyard merchant, John Westbury may be as unsatisfactory a candidate as Hans of Antwerp and the identity of the man in the picture remains a mystery.

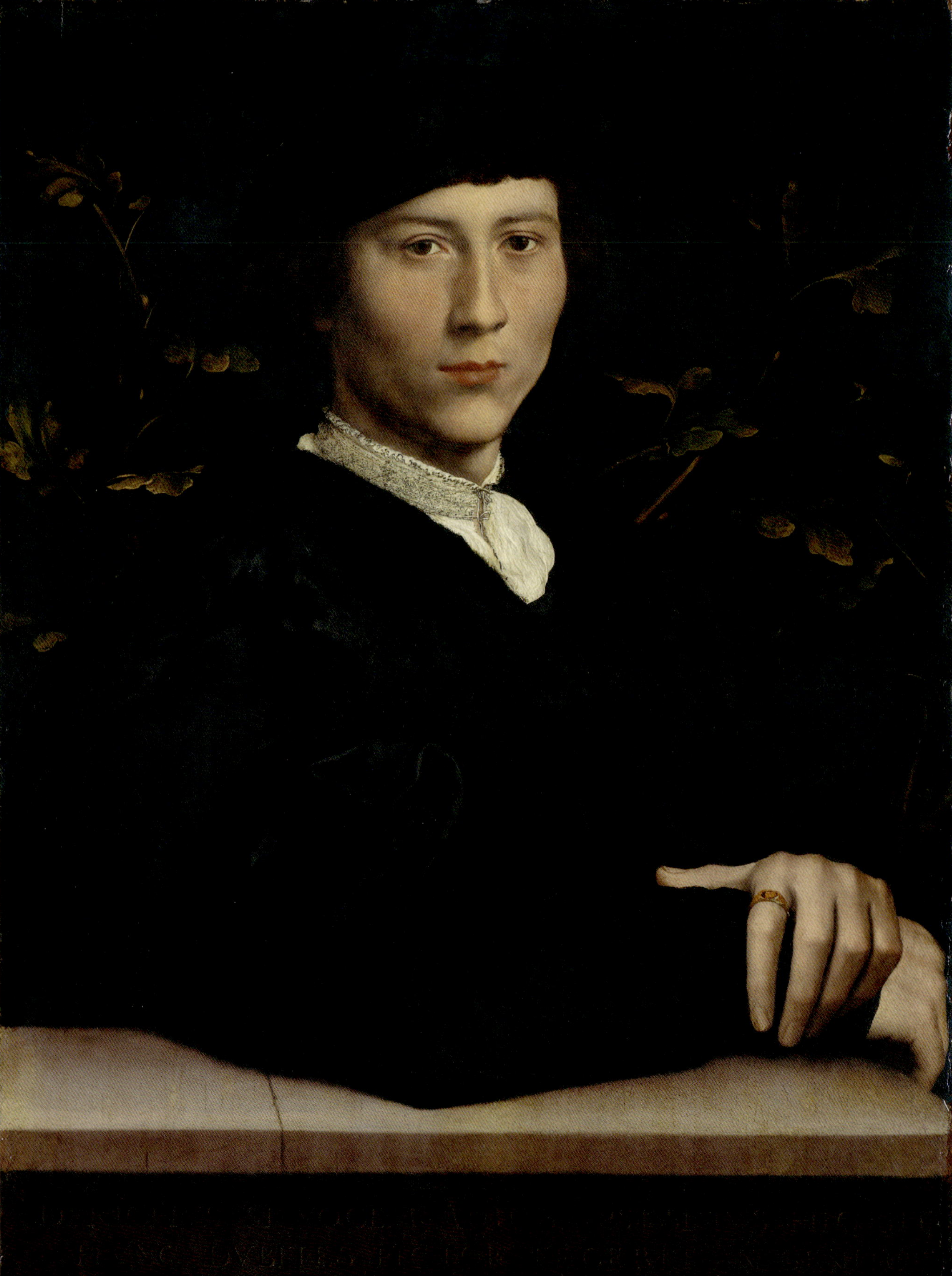

Derich Born (1509/10–after 1549)
1533
Oil on panel
60.3 × 44.9 cm
RCIN 405681

The German merchant Derich Born commissioned a portrait from Holbein in 1533, when he was 23 years old.[35] Born was one of the merchants based in the Steelyard and seems to have speculated in a variety of products: in 1536 he supplied Erasmus Kyrkenar, the king's armourer, with harnesses for use in the suppression of the rising known as the Pilgrimage of Grace. In 1541 a dispute with Charles Brandon, Duke of Suffolk, saw him and his brother expelled from the Steelyard. In 1549 he was recorded trading a consignment of towels in Antwerp and making a complaint about his expulsion.

Holbein painted this portrait on two boards of Baltic oak, joined down the middle of the sitter's face.[36] Recent conservation has demonstrated how Holbein's masterful depiction of Born was developed.[37] Over a grey ground, which gives the portrait its cool tonality, the artist built up face and body in smoothly applied layers set against a background of azurite. The contours of Born's face, hair, hat and shoulder were altered over the course of the painting; among other changes, the sculpted cheek and jawline of the sitter became more pronounced. Perhaps the most impressive aspect of the painting is Holbein's depiction of the textures of the black fabrics worn by Born, which vary from a shiny satin to a soft, short-haired fur, each of which reflects the light in a different way. Born is the only one of the Steelyard sitters to be shown against Holbein's characteristic vine, also seen in the portraits of Sir Henry Guildford (p. 54) and William Reskimer (p. 109).

With effortless poise, Born rests his arm on a parapet in front of him. On this is inscribed the sitter's name and age, and a tribute to Holbein's artistic brilliance: *DERICHVS SI VOCEM ADDAS IPSISSIMVS HIC SIT, / HVNC DVBITES PICTOR FECERIT AN GENITOR / DER BORN ETATIS SVÆ 23 ANNO 1533* ('If you added a voice, this would be Derich his very self. You would be in doubt whether the painter or his father made him. Der Born aged 23, the year 1533').[38] This inscription was surely Holbein's initiative rather than the sitter's. It quotes, almost verbatim, a tribute to a portrait by Albrecht Dürer of Kaspar Ursinus Velius, which had been published by Johannes Froben in Basel in 1522, with a title page designed by Holbein reused from an earlier publication.[39] Holbein may have been positioning himself as Dürer's successor, or he could simply have liked the sentiment: a common topos on Renaissance portraits, and one that was appropriate to this compelling image in which the sitter appears with arresting naturalism.[40]

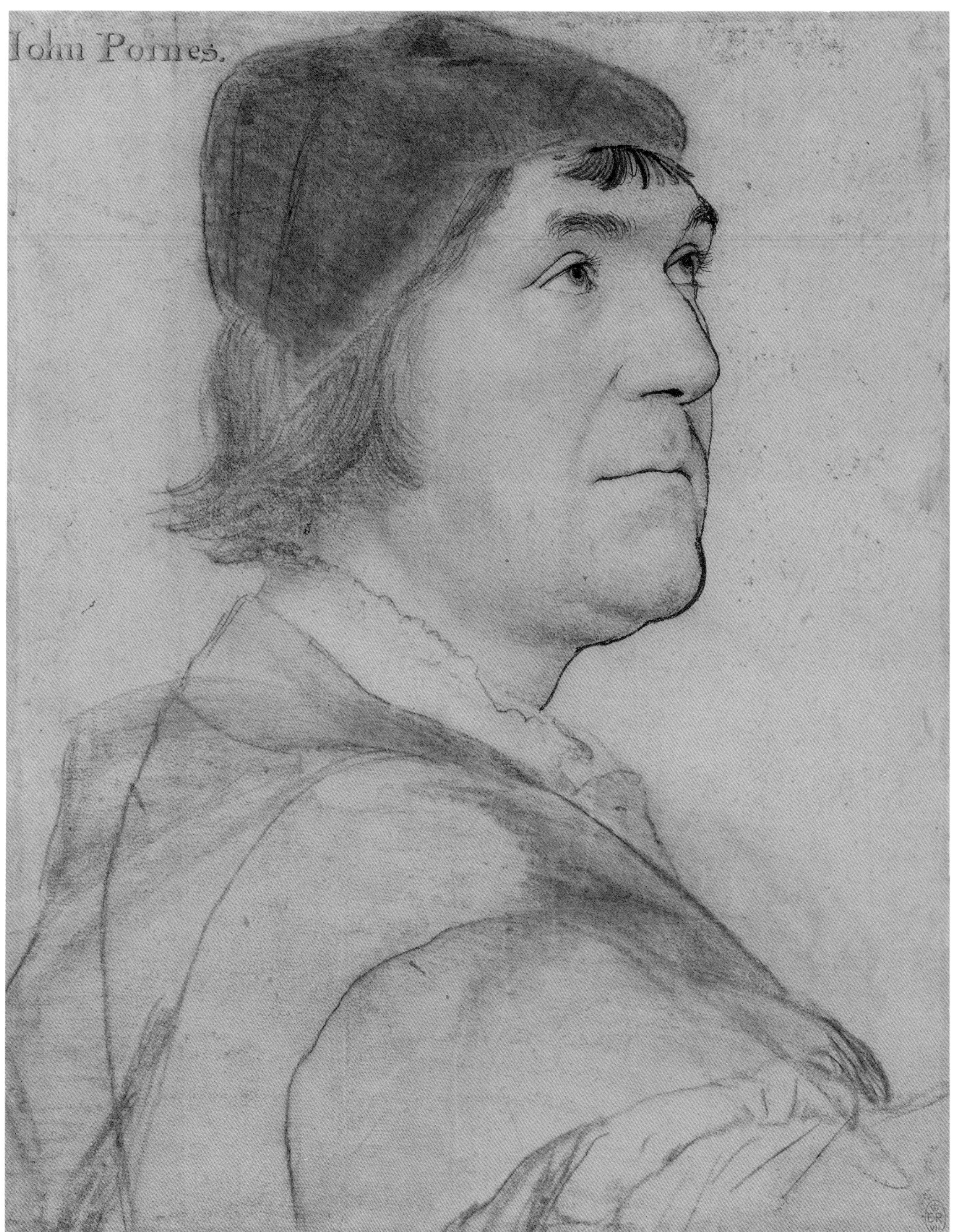
Iohn Poines.

John Poyntz (*c*.1485–1544)
c.1532
Black and coloured chalks with black ink on pink prepared paper
29.5 × 23.3 cm
RCIN 912233

John Poyntz held minor positions at court and attended Katherine of Aragon at the meeting at the Field of the Cloth of Gold in 1520.[41] He was the dedicatee of a French translation of Plutarch's treatise on friendship written at the French court in 1519, although the circumstances of this dedication are unknown.[42] In 1533 Poyntz spoke against the Act in Restraint of Appeals, which sought to obstruct the Pope's traditional authority in England. He was a friend of Thomas Wyatt (p. 62), whose poem 'To mine own John Poyntz' describes Wyatt's life in exile from court. Poyntz died in November 1544, possibly while part of the English military expedition in France. Poyntz was related to Sir Henry Guildford (whose mother Joan married as her second husband Poyntz's brother Anthony) and witnessed Guildford's will in 1532. This portrait may be one of a group of works for Guildford (p. 54) and his circle on which Holbein was working from 1527 until soon after his return to London in 1532.

Poyntz is shown from over his right shoulder, with his head turned sharply towards the right and his eyes focused on a point high above his head. The drawing is executed relatively hastily, with rough shading in the sitter's cap and a brief indication of an alternative profile for the clothing at his back. It is easy to imagine that Poyntz could not hold this pose for any length of time and that Holbein took the details he needed in chalk at speed before refining the facial features and dress either during the same sitting or later, when Poyntz was not present. The reason for this unusual pose is not clear, although it has been proposed that a finished portrait may have shown Poyntz looking up towards a religious figure in the same way that Holbein depicted Jakob Meyer zum Hasen in the Darmstadt Madonna of 1526 (see Fig. 8).[43] No painting by Holbein after this drawing survives, although a copy suggests Holbein discarded the cloak thrown over Poyntz's shoulder and painted him as if leaning on a parapet, somewhat like Derich Born (p. 58).[44]

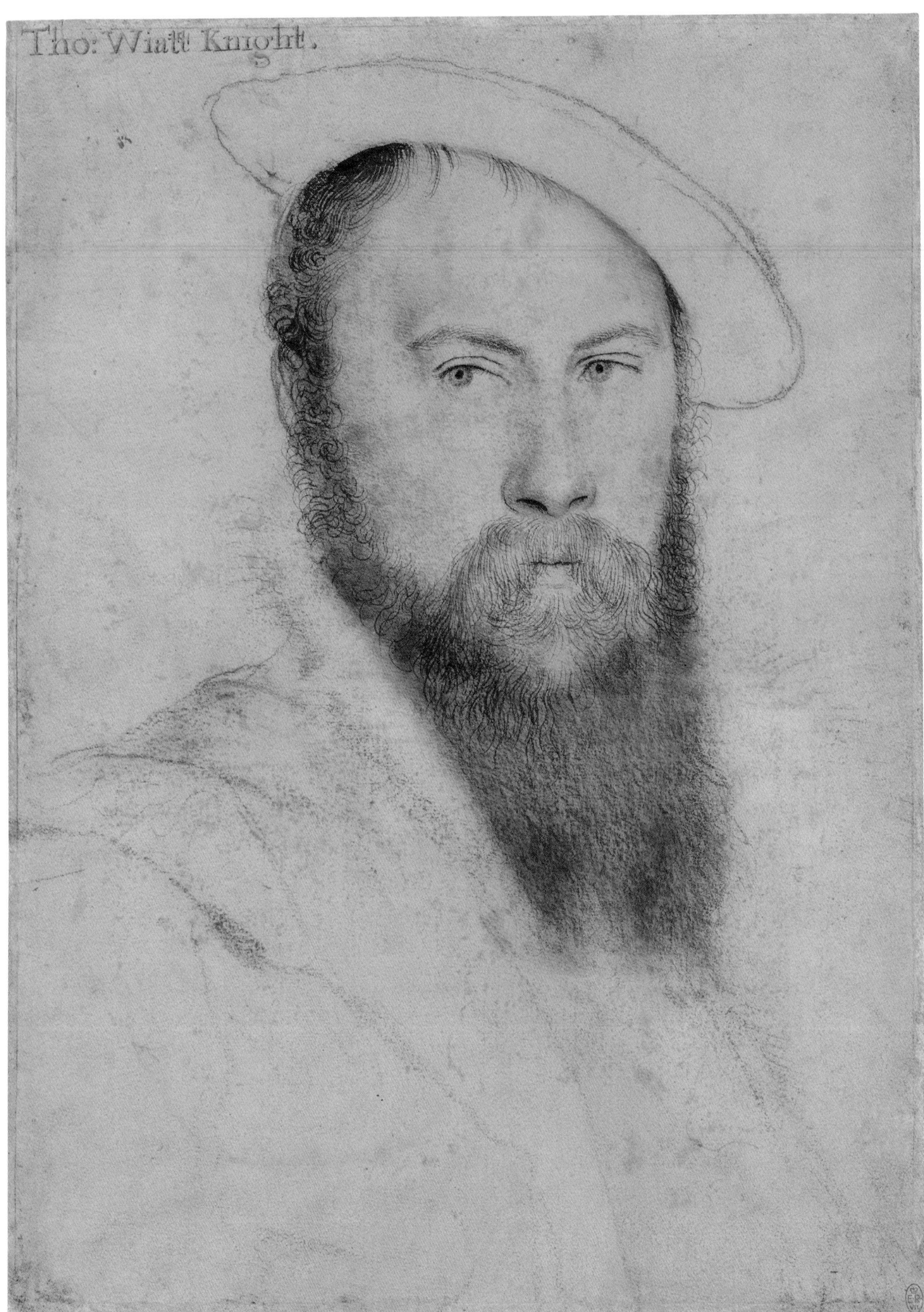
Tho: Wiatt Knight.

Thomas Wyatt (*c.*1503–42)
1532–7?
Black and coloured chalks with ink and watercolour on pink prepared paper
37.2 × 26.9 cm
RCIN 912250

Poet and ambassador, Thomas Wyatt spent much of his life on the road, representing Henry VIII's interests in Italy, France and Spain.[45] In the wake of the king's divorce from Katherine of Aragon, aunt of the emperor Charles V, this was no easy task. Wyatt's success lay in his ability to play the eloquent courtier, a skill that he disparaged in a verse epistle addressed to his friend John Poyntz (p. 60), noting he found it distasteful 'with the nerest vertu to cloke alwey the vice'.[46] Wyatt's poetry was framed by his experiences in Italy, and he brought new literary conventions into English, among them the sonnet. His poems of friendship and love reflect his courtly nature and his circle of friends, among them Sir Henry Guildford (p. 52) and Poyntz. His estranged wife Elizabeth was the sister of George Brooke, Lord Cobham (p. 123). Wyatt's close relationship with Anne Boleyn saw him imprisoned on her downfall; he was released at the instigation of Thomas Cromwell. A second period of imprisonment in 1541 ended when Katherine Howard interceded on his behalf.

Wyatt's peripatetic lifestyle means there were few opportunities when he could have sat to Holbein and this drawing was probably made after Holbein returned to England in 1532, and before Wyatt was sent on embassy in spring 1537. Holbein has concentrated on Wyatt's face, leaving the details of his clothing lightly sketched. Wyatt is shown looking sharply to his right, giving him a restless appearance that was surely unintentional. The pose may indicate that this depiction was to form the basis of a joint 'friendship' portrait: Cardinal Georges d'Armagnac, a fellow ambassador, for example, was depicted in a similar attitude by Titian, in a portrait showing him with his secretary Guillaume Philandrier.[47] If this is the case, such a portrait has not survived.[48] It is tempting, although not supported by any evidence, to imagine Wyatt's friend Poyntz, equally carefully posed, in the position of his companion.

The Wyatt family were significant patrons of Holbein, who also painted Thomas's father Henry and his sister Margaret Lee. The arms and crest of a male member of the Wyatt family appear on the verso of Holbein's drawing of Anne Boleyn (see Fig. 39). Holbein made a second portrait of Wyatt, as a poet, which was praised by the antiquary John Leland after Wyatt's death, in a counterpoint to the inscription on Derich Born's portrait (p. 58):

> Holbein, the chiefest of that curious Art,
> Drew Wyatt's lively Image in each part
> With matchless skill; but no Apelles can
> Portray the wit and spirit of that man.

A close copy of the drawing is also in the Royal Collection, having joined the group by the early eighteenth century.[49]

Anne Boleyn (*c.*1500–36)
1532–6
Black and coloured chalks
on pink prepared paper
28.2 × 19.3 cm

This is apparently one of the few contemporary portraits of Anne Boleyn, second wife of Henry VIII and mother of Elizabeth I. Although the identification of the sitter has been doubted, her informal dress and the presence of an inscription based on an identification made by Sir John Cheke have been cited as convincing evidence that the sitter is the queen.[50] The sitter has the brown eyes described by contemporaries. Her hair was probably built up by Holbein with strokes of different coloured chalks, including yellow, reddish brown and black. Abrasion has removed some pigment from this area of the drawing and Anne's hair may now appear lighter than it did when the drawing was made. Anne wears an informal gown, which has been connected to one given to her as a gift by Henry.[51] It is unclear whether this dress would have been replicated in the finished work, or changed for more formal attire as Holbein did with other of his sitters.[52] In either case, the drawing may have been preparatory work towards a miniature, to be held in the hand rather than displayed upon a wall.

The drawing has a sketch of the Wyatt arms on the verso (Fig. 39). There is nothing to suggest this has any connection with the portrait drawing and it is likely simply to have been made on a spare piece of paper that was to hand. What is interesting is that this is the only one of the Holbein portrait drawings to have any work on the verso, which may indicate the sheet had a different status within Holbein's workshop. Was the sheet reused as a spare piece of paper after the queen's fall rather than being kept with the other portrait drawings, and only returned to the group when sheets were assembled for the book that ended up in royal ownership? If this is the case, the Wyatt arms would date from the period 1536–43 and would be connected with a project either for Henry Wyatt or his son Thomas (p. 62). It may not be a coincidence that Henry Wyatt, who was painted by Holbein, died in November 1536, a few months after Anne's execution and therefore at exactly the time we might expect the sheet to be reused. Could Holbein's sketch be associated with his funeral, or with the chantry chapel he had founded for his commemoration at Milton in Kent?

Anne Boleyn, niece of Thomas Howard, Duke of Norfolk (p. 129), was an intelligent and cultured woman who spent her early life in France. In 1521 she was considered as a potential wife for James Butler, later Earl of Ormond (p. 114). First coming to Henry VIII's attention in 1526, she married the king and was recognised as queen in 1533. In the same year, their daughter Princess Elizabeth was born. Anne was at the centre of a group of young reformers at court, and counted Thomas Wyatt among her friends. She supported the reforming exile Nicholas Bourbon (p. 77), and Mary Shelton (p. 136) was her cousin. This drawing must have been made between Holbein's return to London in 1532 and May 1536 when Anne and a close circle of

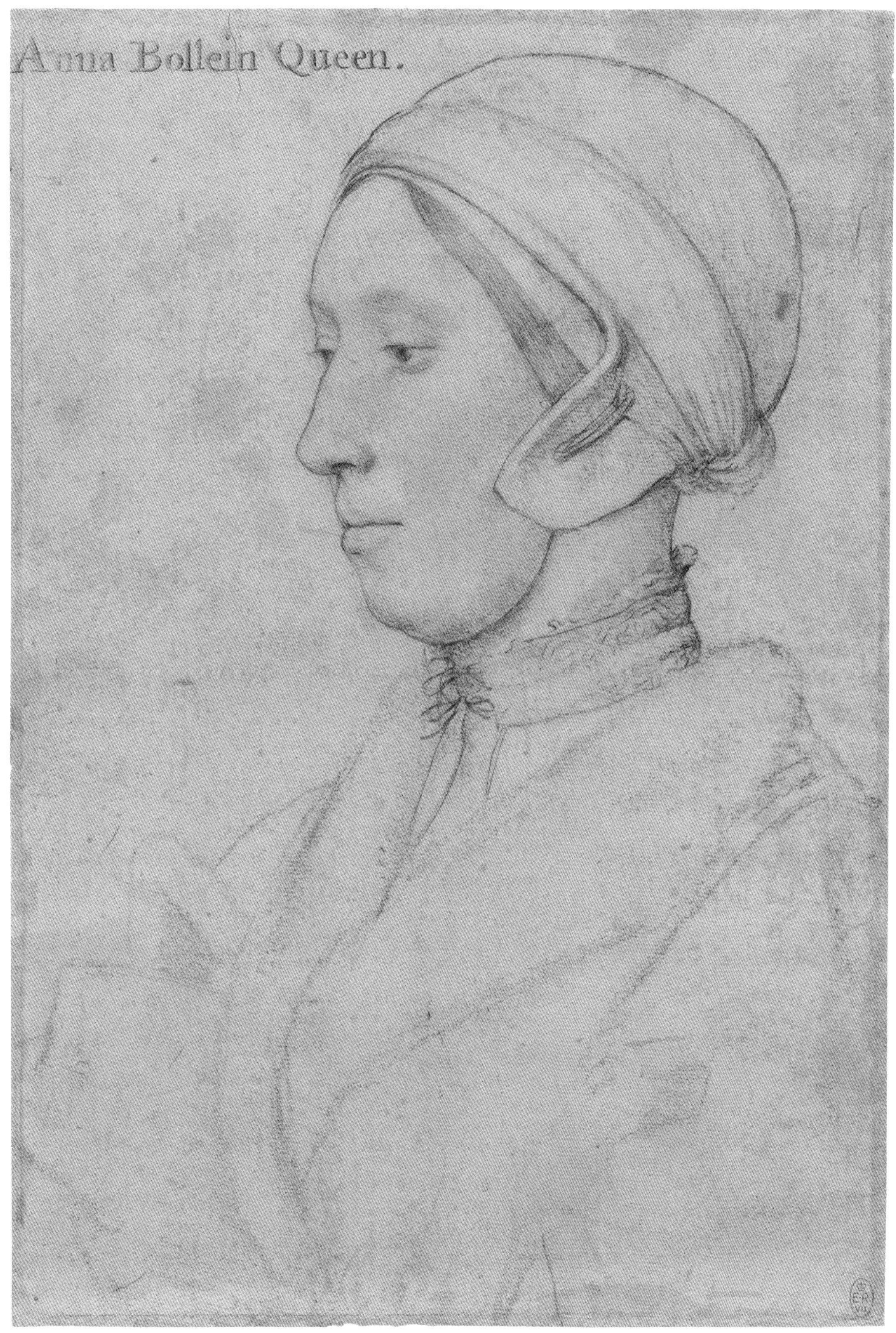
Anna Bollein Queen.

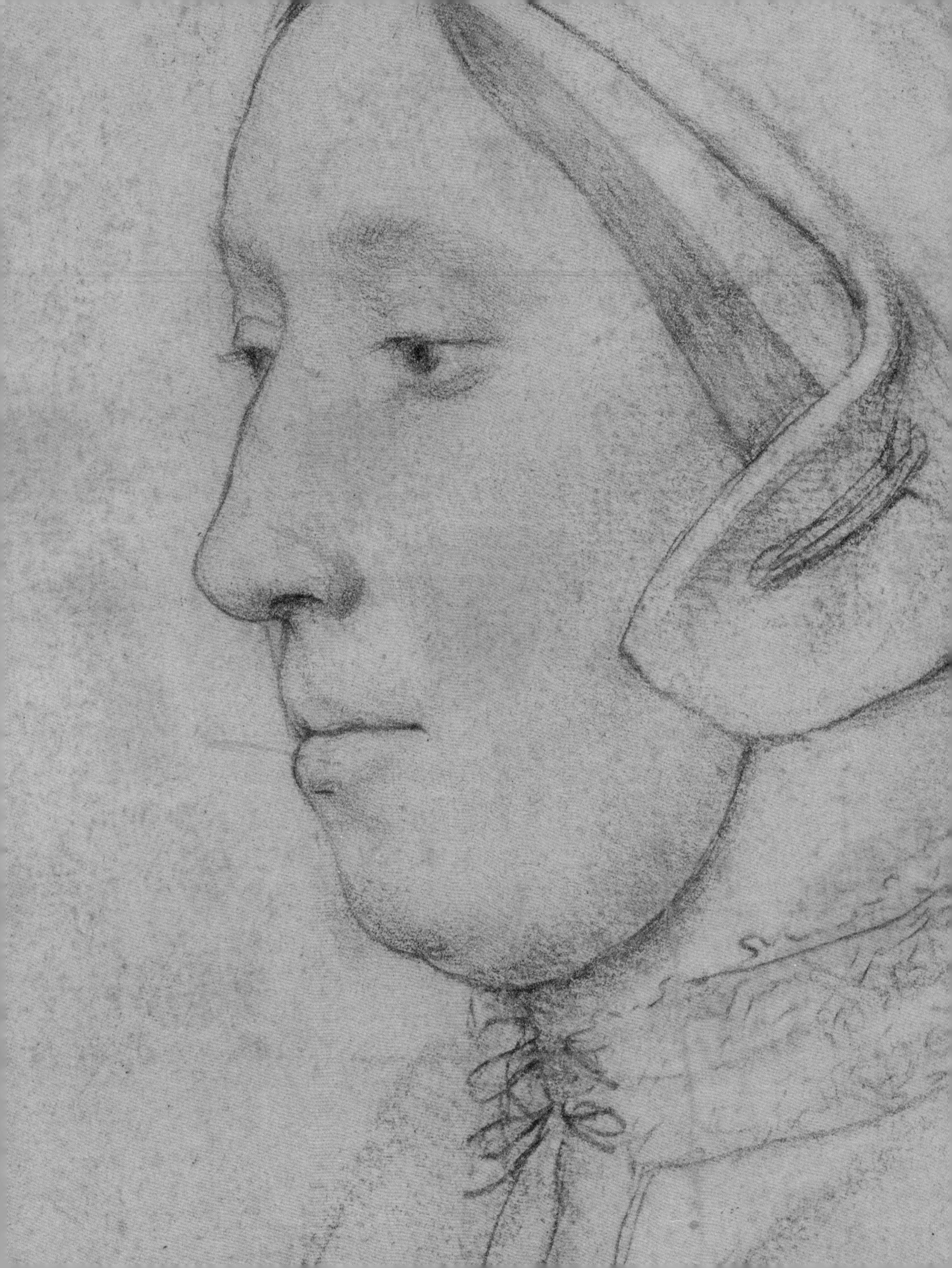

her friends and relatives were arrested on spurious charges of adultery. Anne Boleyn was executed on 19 May 1536.

Anne has been regarded as one of Holbein's earliest patrons after his return from Basel in 1532, but considering our lack of information about his commissions at this date, it is impossible to determine if this was the case.[53] He certainly designed jewellery with an intertwined 'H' and 'A', probably for Henry and Anne, and painted figures of Adam and Eve for the queen, but the latter was undoubtedly work subcontracted to him by the goldsmith Cornelis Hayes and it is unknown who commissioned the jewellery.[54] Holbein also designed a table fountain for Anne to give as a New Year's gift to Henry in 1534, but again this is likely to have been commissioned from the goldsmith who made it, and does not indicate the queen's direct patronage of Holbein. Notably, similar commissions associated with Jane Seymour (p. 105) have been regarded as originating with Henry rather than his queen, illustrating the contrasting ways in which historians have treated the two women.

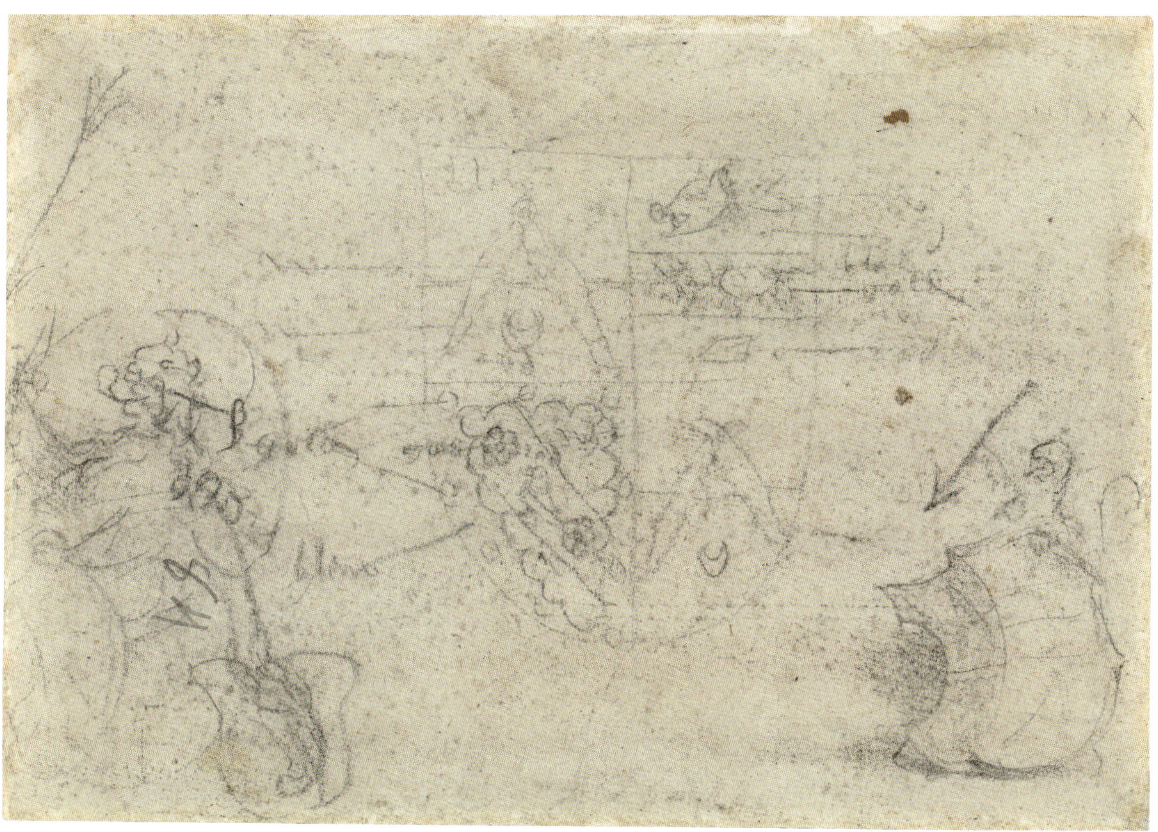

Fig. 39 **Hans Holbein, Wyatt arms, *c*.1536, black chalk**
RCIN 912189 (verso)

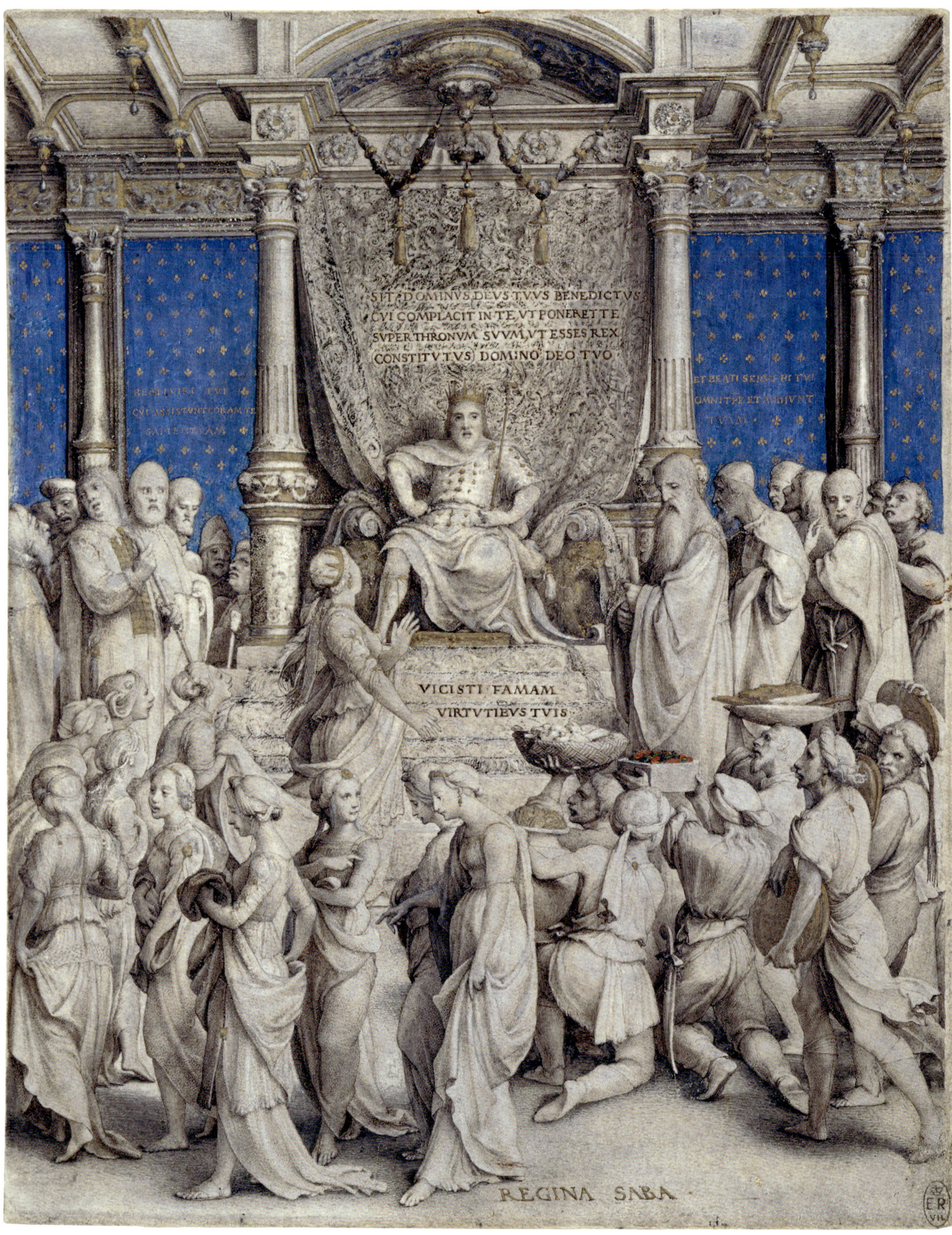
SIT DOMINVS DEVS TVVS BENEDICTVS
CVI COMPLACIT IN TE, VT PONERET TE
SVPER THRONVM SVVM, VT ESSES REX
CONSTITVTVS DOMINO DEO TVO
VICISTI FAMAM
VIRTVTIBVS TVIS
REGINA SABA

Solomon and the Queen of Sheba

*c.*1535
Watercolour, bodycolour and gold paint on vellum laid onto card
22.9 × 18.3 cm
RCIN 912188

Holbein's skill as a miniature painter is apparent in this depiction of the Queen of Sheba paying homage to King Solomon. The Biblical Book of Kings describes how the queen visited Solomon in order to test his reputation as a wise king, and was won over by his wisdom and magnificence. Solomon sits on a throne at the centre, flanked by his advisers. The Queen of Sheba mounts the steps towards him. Behind her follows a retinue of female attendants and she gestures to her male attendants, who offer gifts to the king. The composition owes a debt to an engraving of the subject by Marcantonio Raimondi, although Holbein has turned the scene 90 degrees so that Solomon sits facing the front in an assertion of power.[55]

The work is painted in expensive pigments on vellum, in a manner reminiscent of a manuscript illumination or portrait miniature. It is composed almost entirely in grisaille, set against brilliant blue and gold wall hangings and enlivened by touches of red and green, which colour the strawberries held by one of the queen's attendants.[56] Texts adapted from the second book of Chronicles praise Solomon, among them, on the steps of the throne, '*VICISTI FAMAM / VIRTVTIBVS TVIS*' ('By your virtues you have exceeded your reputation'). A quotation from the Wisdom of Solomon recorded in the eighteenth century may have been inscribed on the frame: 'But the multitude of the wise is the welfare of the world: and a wise king is the upholding of all people'.

The purpose and interpretation of the work have been much debated.[57] The figure of Solomon has long been seen as an allegorical likeness of Henry VIII and there is a clear comparison with the image of the king on the title page Holbein designed for the Coverdale Bible of 1535 (see Fig. 27).[58] That he does not descend to greet the queen but waits for her to climb the steps towards him is an indication of his dominance in the carefully nuanced diplomatic etiquette of the time. The piece may refer to Henry's assertion of his authority over the English Church in the early to mid-1530s.[59] It has been suggested that the Queen of Sheba is an allegory of the English Church, but the work may more simply be a flattering depiction of Henry as the biblical king renowned for his wisdom.[60]

This is not the only allegorical depiction of Henry, who was shown as the biblical King David in an illuminated psalter made for him in 1540.[61]

This is a work intended to be held in the hand and scrutinised closely, and it rewards such close looking with its wealth of detail and the inventive poses of the many figures.[62] It is thought that it was presented to Henry VIII as a gift. Thomas Cromwell and Richard Rich, themselves both portrayed by Holbein, have been suggested as possible donors.[63] Perhaps notably, Rich compared Henry to Solomon in a Parliamentary speech of 1536.[64] Such rhetoric, along with Henry's assumption of supremacy over the Church and the Coverdale Bible of 1535, provides a convincing context for this otherwise enigmatic commission.

Sir Nicholas Poyntz (by 1510–1556)
1535
Black and coloured chalks with black and brown inks and white heightening on pink prepared paper
28.4 × 18.3 cm
RCIN 912234

Sir Nicholas Poyntz was a courtier who owned estates in Gloucestershire.[65] He was the nephew of John Poyntz (p. 60) and an acquaintance of Thomas Wyatt (p. 62), who dedicated to him a satirical poem. Poyntz probably sat to Holbein for this drawing in 1535, the year inscribed on early copies of the portrait and in which he hosted Henry VIII and Anne Boleyn during a progress around the west of England.[66] Poyntz, one of a number of religious reformers chosen to act as hosts during the tour, is chiefly renowned for having built a magnificent new range on his house at Iron Acton to receive the royal party.[67] This was erected in the spring of 1535, and decorated with an antique frieze thought to be by Italian or French artists, while Poyntz bought elegant Italian and Spanish tableware for the use of his guests.[68] He was probably elevated to the knighthood in the same year and perhaps as a result of the visit; Poyntz is shown prominently wearing his chain of knighthood in Holbein's drawing.[69]

Holbein has worked up the sitter's features in ink, as he did with a number of other drawings, but here has employed two inks. One of these, which is deep black, has been used to enlarge Poyntz's goatee into a fuller beard and to make his eyebrows more bushy, as well as to articulate his eyelashes, set the line of his profile and extend the hair at the nape of his neck. Does this represent the result of a second sitting in which Holbein returned to the drawing to make final changes before transferring the design to panel?

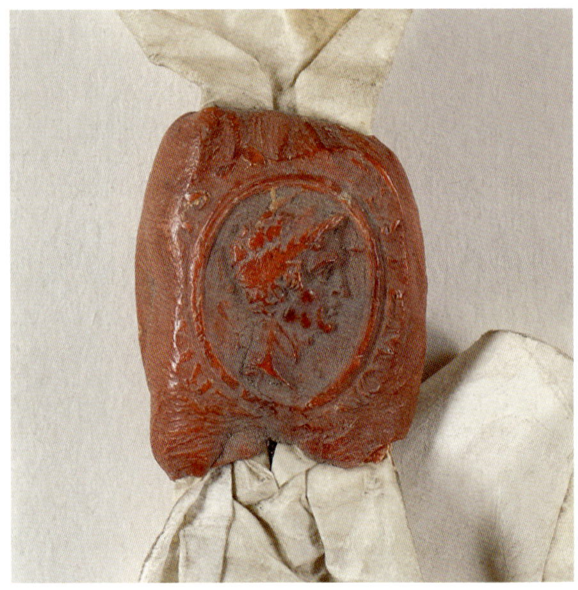

Fig. 40 **Seal of Sir Nicholas Poyntz, 1538**
East Sussex Record Office, SAS/G 21/38

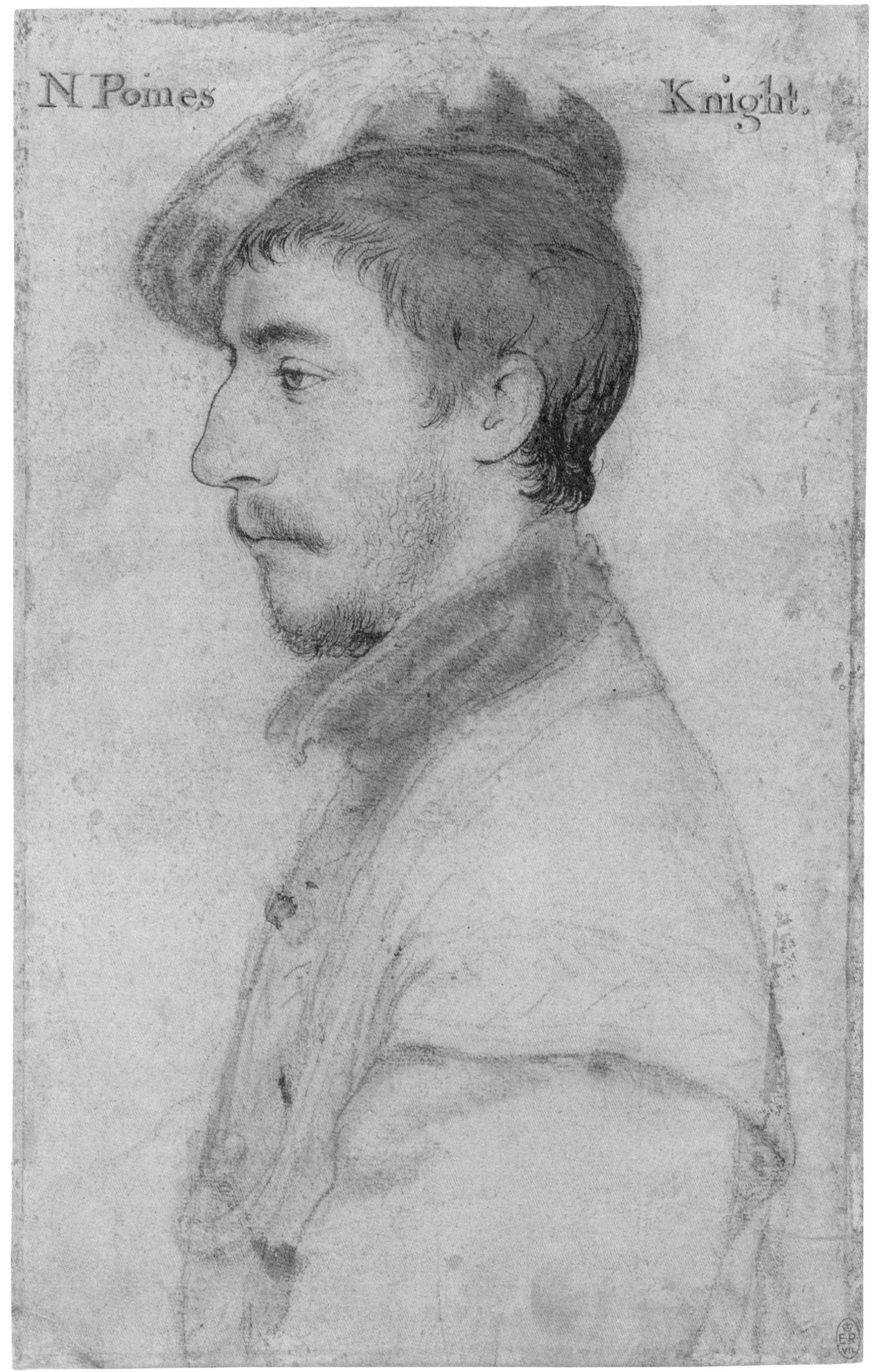
N Poines
Knight.

Poyntz is one of the few sitters shown by Holbein in strict profile, and it has been convincingly suggested that this reflects his interest in classical precedent, which Renaissance patrons often experienced through coins and medals.[70] A direct comparison is found in Poyntz's seal, a Renaissance intaglio of an antique-style male head wearing a helmet, perhaps intended to evoke a classical hero (Fig. 40).[71] No finished portrait by Holbein is known, although there are a number of early copies, which were probably commissioned by Poyntz's numerous children and grandchildren (Fig. 41).[72]

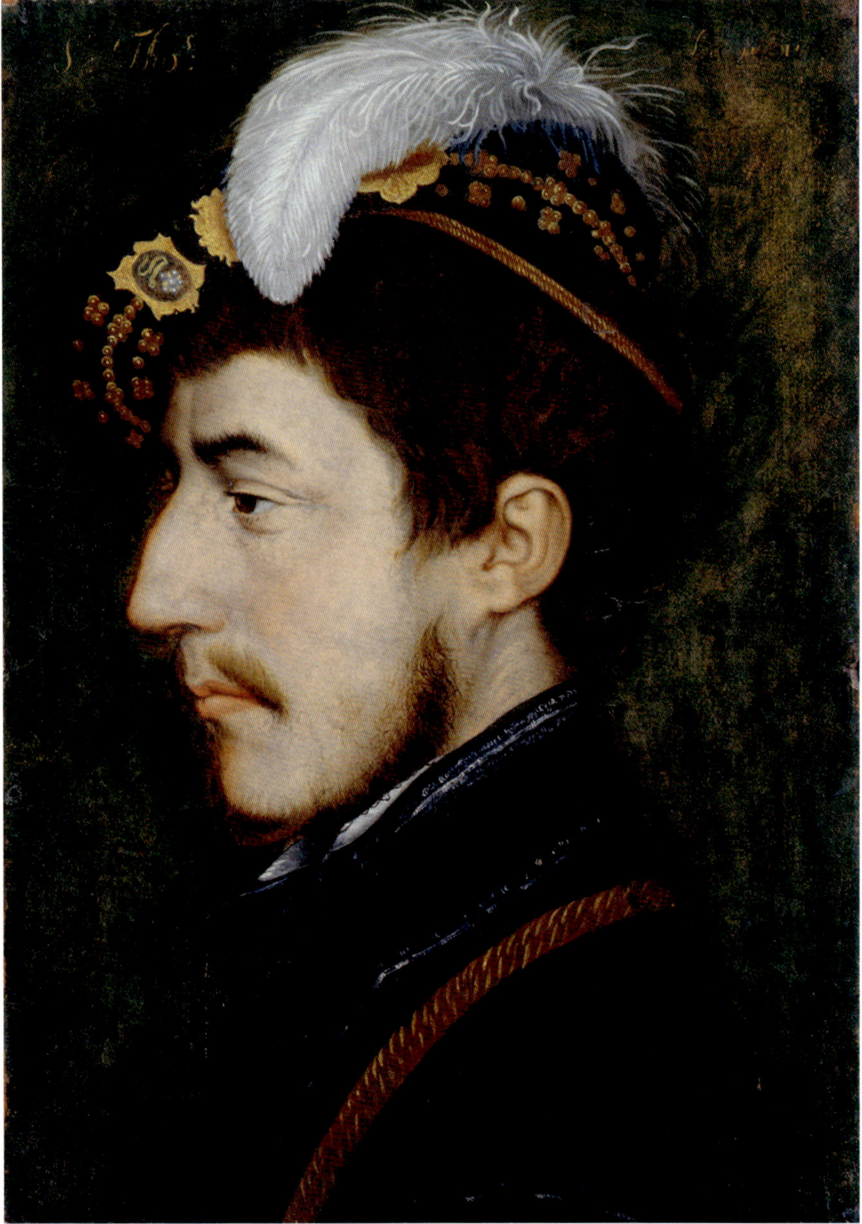

Fig. 41 **After Hans Holbein, *Sir Nicholas Poyntz*, c.1535–99, oil on paper mounted onto panel**
National Portrait Gallery, London, NPG 5583

[PAGE 74]

Margaret, Lady Elyot (d. 1560)
*c.*1535
Black and coloured chalks with black ink and white heightening on pink prepared paper
27.8 × 20.8 cm
RCIN 912204

[PAGE 75]

Sir Thomas Elyot (*c.*1490–1546)
*c.*1535
Black and coloured chalks with black ink and white heightening on pink prepared paper
28.4 × 20.5 cm
RCIN 912203

Sir Thomas Elyot and his wife Margaret were probably drawn by Holbein around 1535, since the paper used for the portrait of Margaret, and possibly also Sir Thomas, is the same as that of the drawing of Sir Nicholas Poyntz (p. 71). The unusual orientation of the sitters, with Margaret on the left (traditionally the placement for the male of a pair), has been remarked on and it has been proposed that her portrait was made first, before Sir Thomas's was added to form a pair.[73] Holbein shows Margaret's head, with only a small section of her dress included. White heightening is used to suggest that her skin is luminous as well as to brighten the whites of her eyes. Her husband's face is similarly delineated in black ink, but his clothing is more comprehensively depicted in coloured chalks, with which Holbein portrays the fur at his neck and a yellow and gold fabric border or chain appearing at the neck of his black gown.

Margaret à Barrow and Thomas Elyot married in 1520. Sir Thomas, who described himself as 'beynge of a cholerike humour myxte with fleume [phlegm]' (that is, of a quick wit and combative spirit, but tending to lethargy), served a term as clerk to the King's Council, and briefly (and without distinction) as ambassador to Charles V (September 1531–March 1532).[74] By 1535, when these drawings were probably made, the couple were largely living in Cambridgeshire. Sir Thomas's main activity in the 1530s was as a humanist author, publishing, among other works, a treatise on governance and education (*The Boke Named the Governour*, 1531) and a popular manual of health (*The Castel of Helth*, *c.*1536) and a well-regarded Latin–English dictionary (1538). Sir Thomas described the political attacks on papal supremacy of the early 1530s in a private letter as 'a great kloude which is likely to be a great storm when it falleth'.[75] His *The Defence of Good Women* (1540) has been interpreted as a homage to Katherine of Aragon, and it may be notable that he is one of the few of Holbein's English sitters to be shown wearing a crucifix.[76]

Although Sir Thomas's activities by the mid-1530s were largely provincial, that he sat to Holbein is unsurprising. He and Margaret were both friends of Sir Thomas More (from whom Elyot felt the need to distance himself after More's disgrace), and Elyot continued to be a correspondent of Thomas Cromwell, another of Holbein's patrons, noting in 1538 that they had been friends for 19 years.[77] He read widely to inform his own writings, and *The Boke Named the Governour* is indebted, among other sources, to Baldassare Castiglione's *The Book of the Courtier* (1528) and the works of Erasmus. Margaret was, with her husband, part of the learned circle around Thomas More in the 1520s, and her husband may have had her qualities in mind when he wrote in *The Defence of Good Women* that 'women, which are prudent in keping, be more excellent than men in reason'.[78]

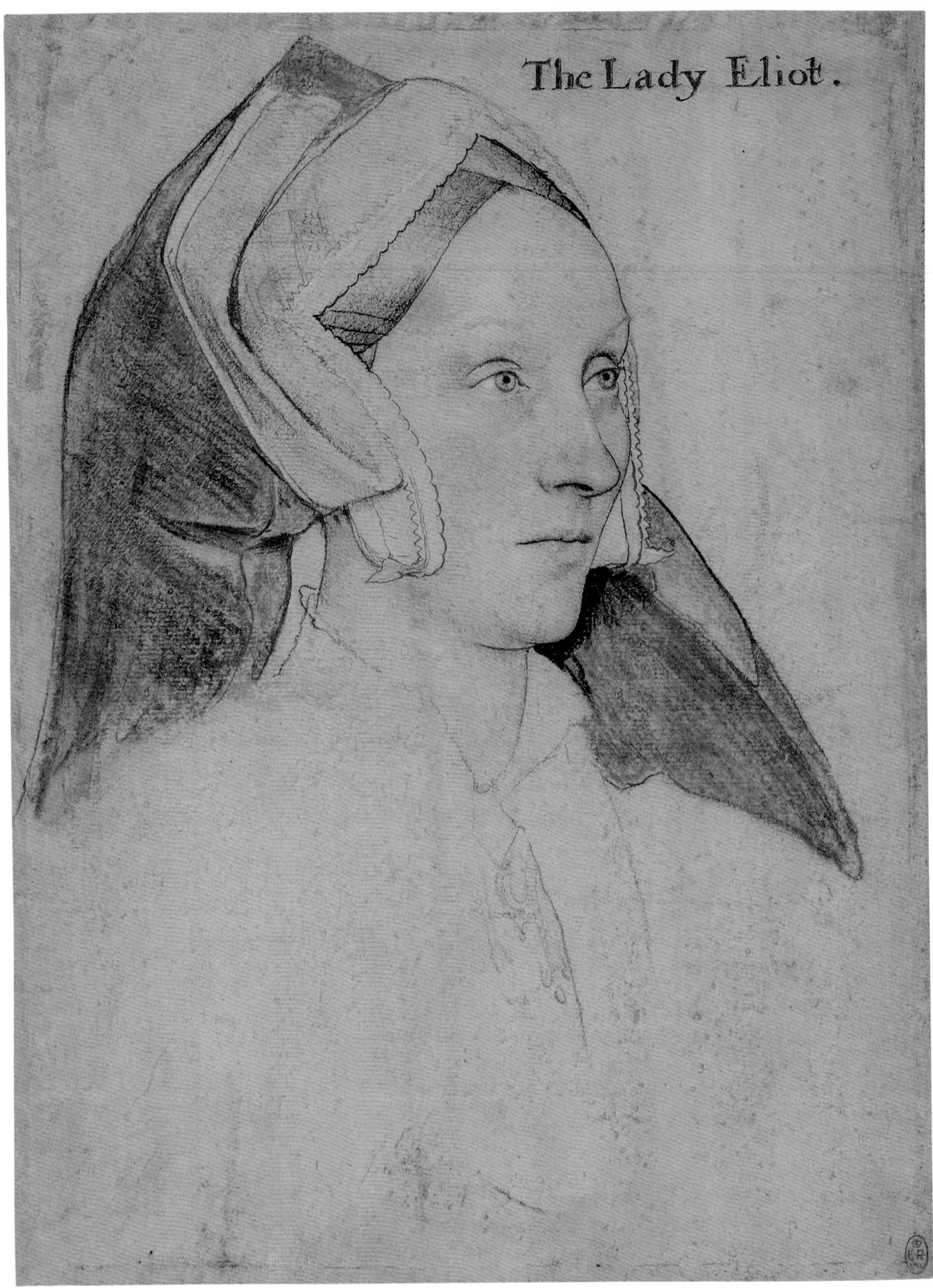
The Lady Eliot.

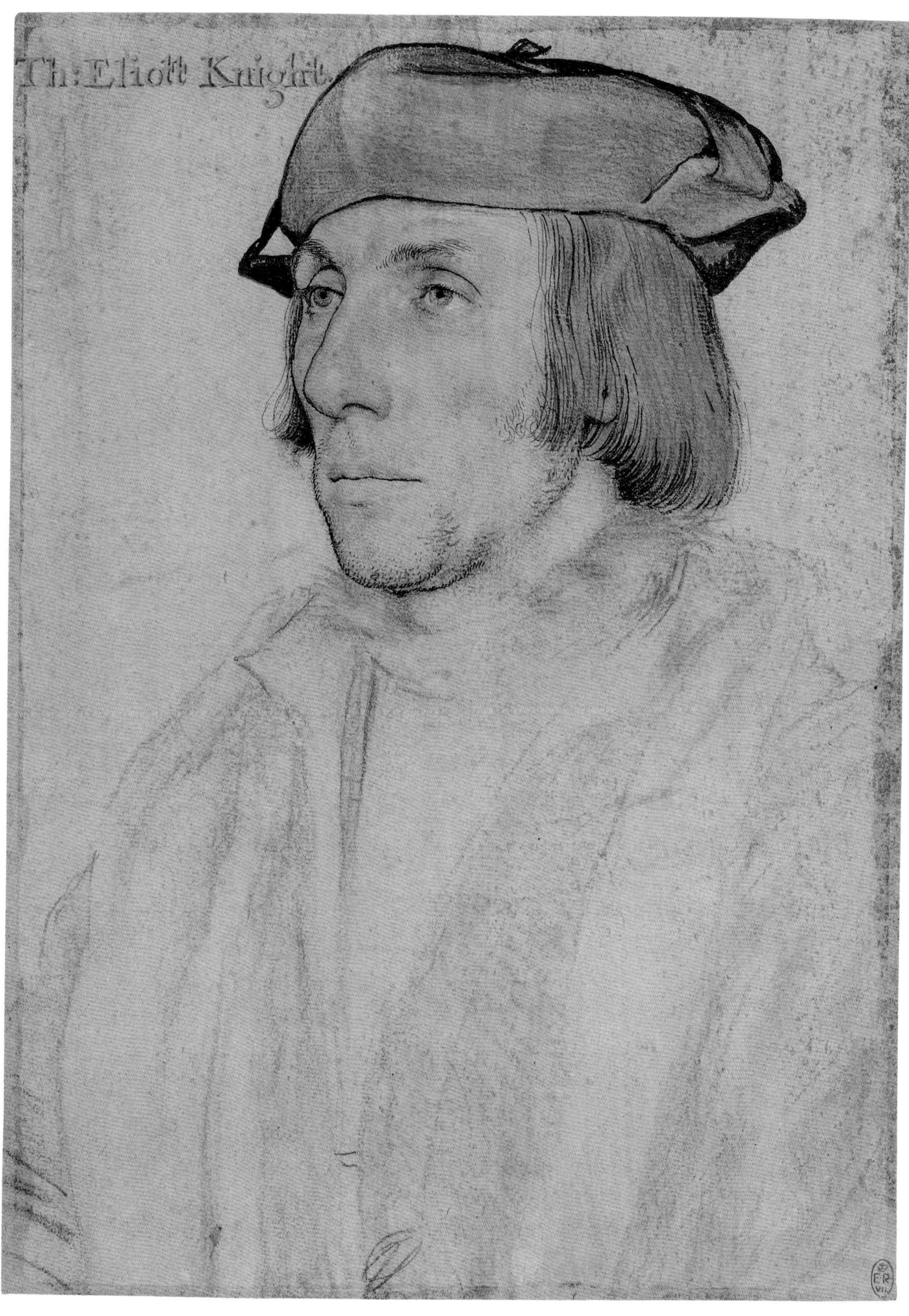
Th: Eliott Knight

Nicholas Bourbon (*c*.1503–49/50)

1535
Black and coloured chalks and black ink on pink prepared paper
30.8 × 25.9 cm
RCIN 912192

The French poet Nicholas Bourbon arrived in London in 1534, where he lodged with Cornelis Hayes, the king's goldsmith and a close contact of Holbein.[79] Bourbon had been imprisoned in France for his reforming views, and appears to have been released after intervention by Anne Boleyn, William Butts and perhaps also the French ambassador Jean de Dinteville, all of whom would sit to Holbein. It was within this group of reforming courtiers and immigrant artists that Bourbon would find support and encouragement during his brief time in London.

Bourbon returned to France in late 1535, giving a short window during which he could have sat for this drawing. He is shown in the act of writing, but looks straight ahead rather than at the sheet of paper in front of him, clearly posing for the artist rather than captured at work. A woodcut after the design was included in the *Paidagogeion*, a group of poems by Bourbon published in 1536 (Fig. 42).[80] It seems unlikely that Holbein's portrait was made specifically as a model for a print since the block-cutter has had to alter the pose to ensure Bourbon is right-handed in the woodcut, not a detail that Holbein, an experienced print designer, is likely to have got wrong. Otherwise, the block-cutter follows Holbein closely, echoing the folds in Bourbon's hat and the shading on his collar. An inscription on the woodcut records that it shows Bourbon in 1535.

In a poem, probably written in response to this portrait, Bourbon described how he had painted Holbein in words, and Holbein, an 'incomparable painter', had captured his likeness on panel. This may suggest the drawing was the basis for a painting, now lost.[81]

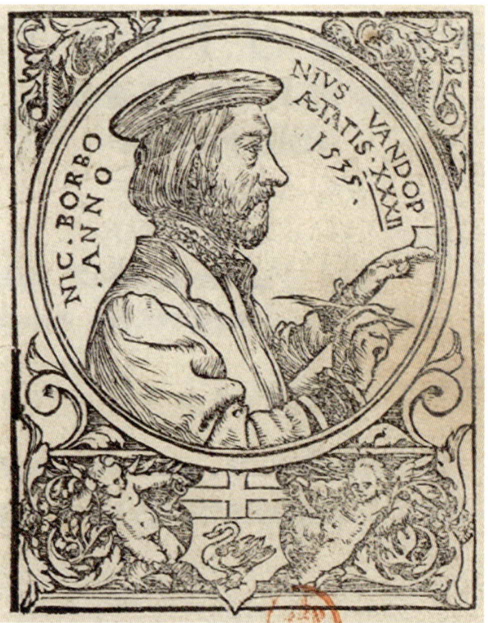

Fig. 42 **Unknown artist after Hans Holbein, *Nicholas Bourbon* from *Opusculum puerile ad pueros de moribus, sive paidagogeion*, 1536, woodcut**
Bibliothèque nationale de France, inv. no. Z-2503

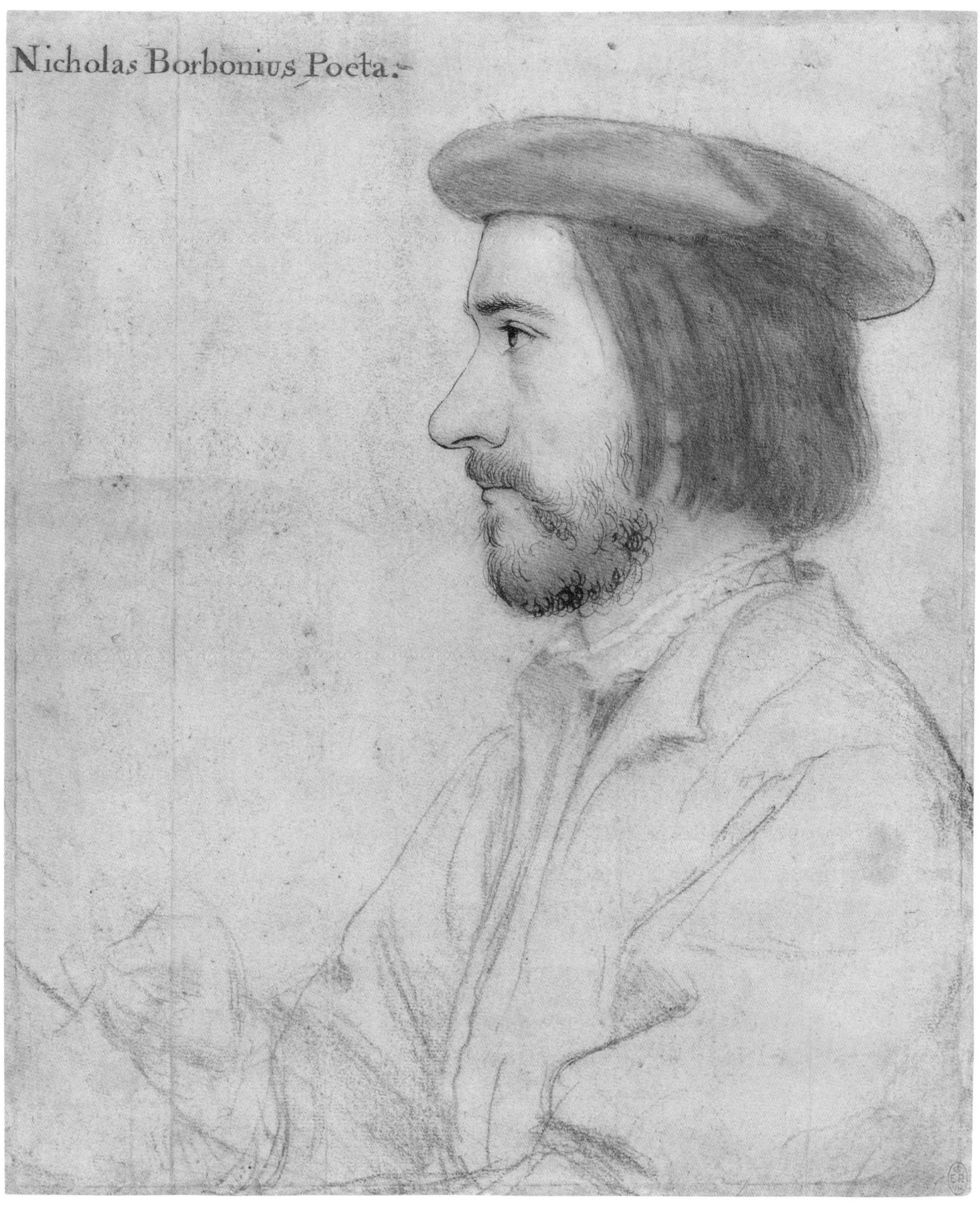
Nicholas Borbonius Poeta.

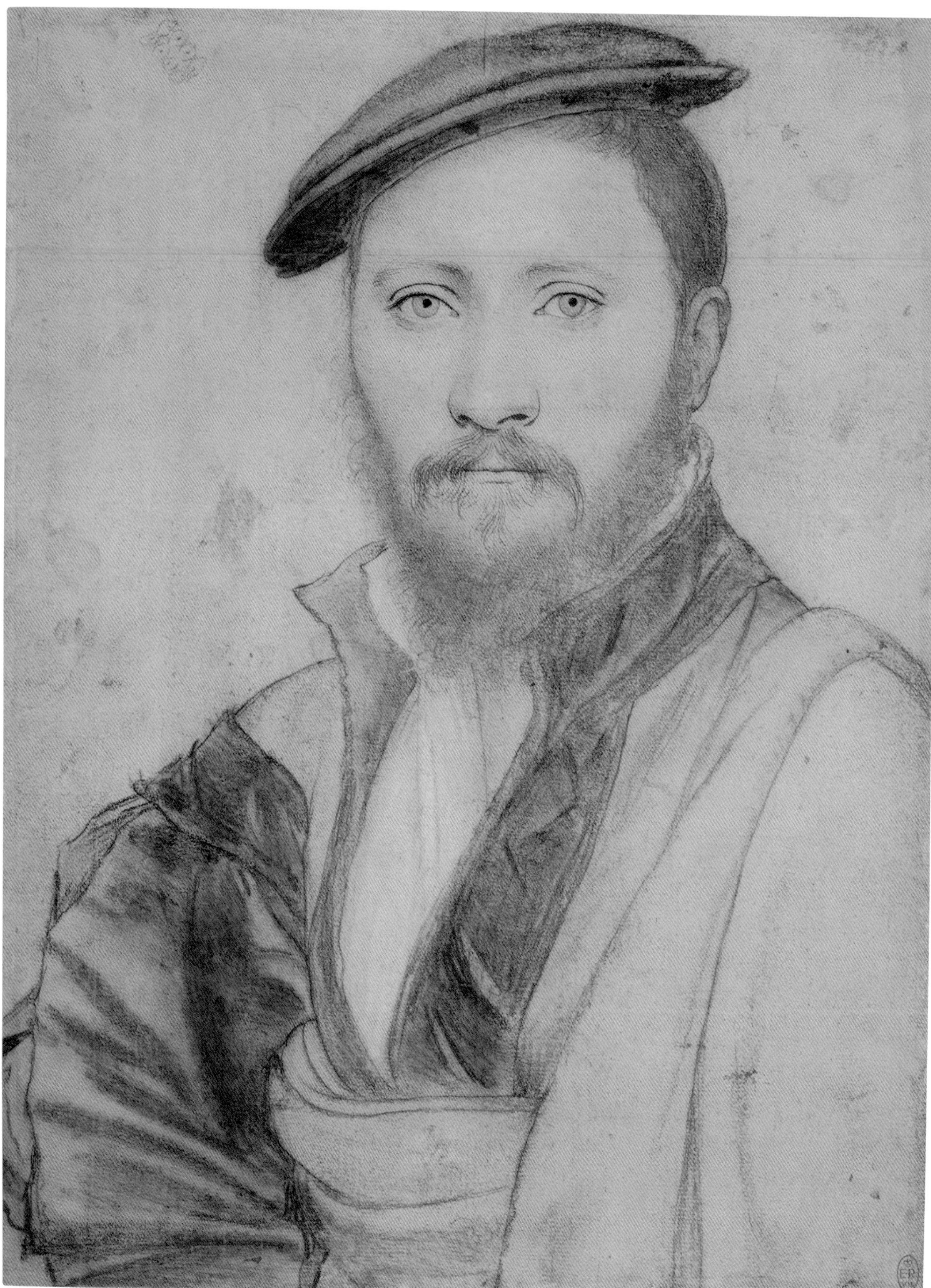

Unidentified man

1535
Black and coloured chalks, white heightening, black and brown inks and blue watercolour on pink prepared paper
29.6 × 22.2 cm
RCIN 912259

This sitter, who turns his head to face the viewer, wears an elegant jacket, with a cloak thrown over his shoulder and wrapped around his waist. Holbein has worked mainly in coloured chalks, with strokes of pen and ink to define the sitter's features and a touch of blue watercolour in the eyes. The texture of the satin and velvet on the sitter's clothing is conveyed through the rubbing of the black chalk to an extent rarely found in Holbein's portrait drawings. A brief pattern in red chalk at the top of the sheet, perhaps recording a textile decoration, bears no relationship to the copy of the finished portrait and may be unrelated to this project.

Although no painting by Holbein is known, a version by an unknown artist, perhaps based on this drawing, is in the Metropolitan Museum of Art (Fig. 43).[82] This bears an inscription with the date 1535, and the sitter's age: 28. On the basis of this, it has been suggested the sitter may be Ralph Sadler (1507–87), a secretary to Thomas Cromwell, who in 1535 was appointed Clerk of the Hanaper of Chancery, responsible for handling documents issued under the Great Seal.[83] If the sitter is Sadler, then the portrait may have been commissioned to mark this appointment, which was the first in a quick succession of promotions that saw him rise to become a diplomat and privy councillor.

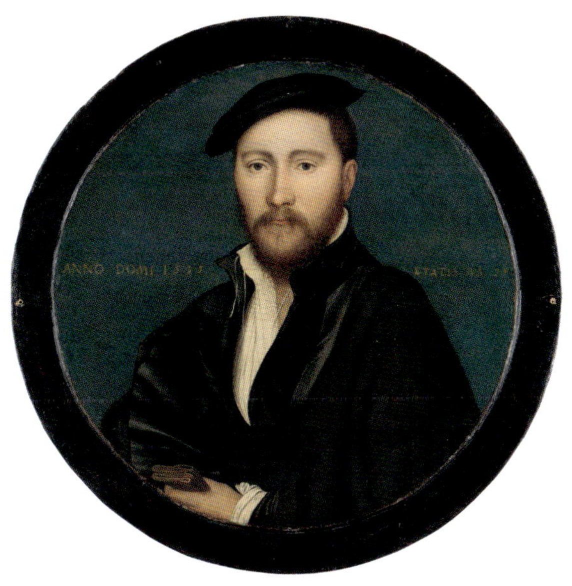

Fig. 43 **After Hans Holbein, *Unidentified man (Ralph Sadler?)*, *c.*1535, oil on panel**
Metropolitan Museum of Art, New York, 49.7.28

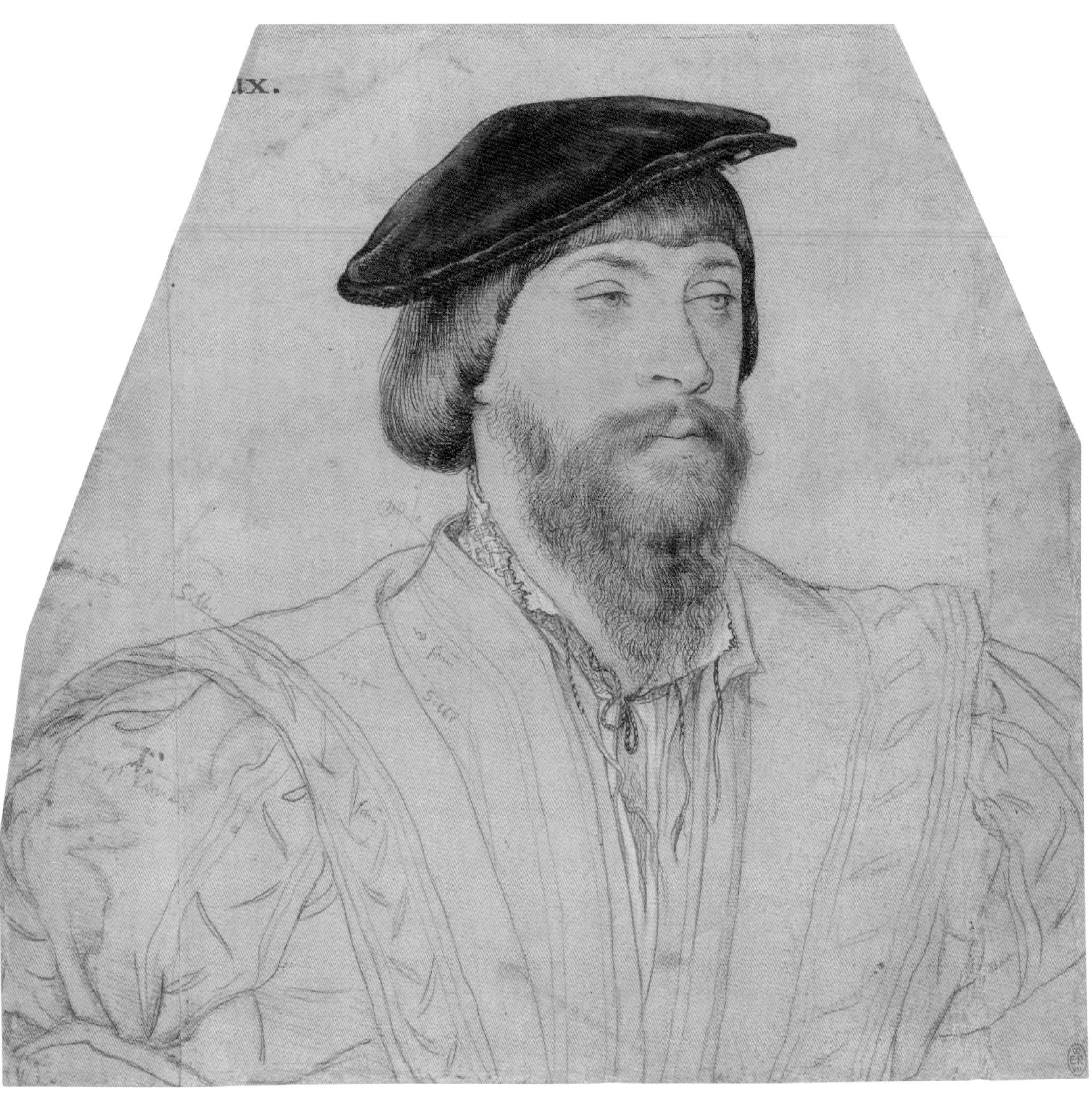

[OPPOSITE]

Thomas Vaux, 2nd Baron Vaux (1509–56)
*c.*1535
Black and coloured chalks with black ink and white heightening on pink prepared paper
27.9 × 29.5 cm
RCIN 912245

[PAGE 83]

Elizabeth, Lady Vaux (*c.*1504–56)
*c.*1535
Black and coloured chalks with metalpoint, black ink and white heightening on pink prepared paper
28.1 × 21.5 cm
RCIN 912247

Thomas Vaux, 2nd Baron Vaux, was a well-connected courtier born into great wealth drawn from estates and sheep farming in Northamptonshire.[84] Vaux married Elizabeth Cheney in 1523 and succeeded his father Nicholas, 1st Baron Vaux, the following year. He was cousin to Sir Henry Guildford and brother-in-law to Sir Thomas Lestrange (p. 99). Despite his connections and prominent position, Vaux, who remained committed to Catholicism, withdrew from court and politics in 1536, apparently unable to reconcile his beliefs with Henry VIII's move to take control of the Church in England. His absence was noticed: on 28 April 1536, he wrote in some consternation to Thomas Cromwell that 'I do parceue [perceive] the kynges hyghnesse nott to be contentyd wt my beyng in kent' and regretting that 'I haue as I perceue a grett many mo foes than frendes'.[85] He was largely absent from court until the accession of the Catholic Queen Mary, whose coronation he attended in October 1553 and under whom he returned to sit in the House of Lords. Baron Vaux died of plague in October 1556, his wife (probably of the same cause) a month later. He is associated with a handful of verses, all published posthumously. Among them is *Of a Contented Mynde*, which may have been written during his retirement in the country, and which celebrates the 'quiet minde' that is 'clere from worldly cares'.[86]

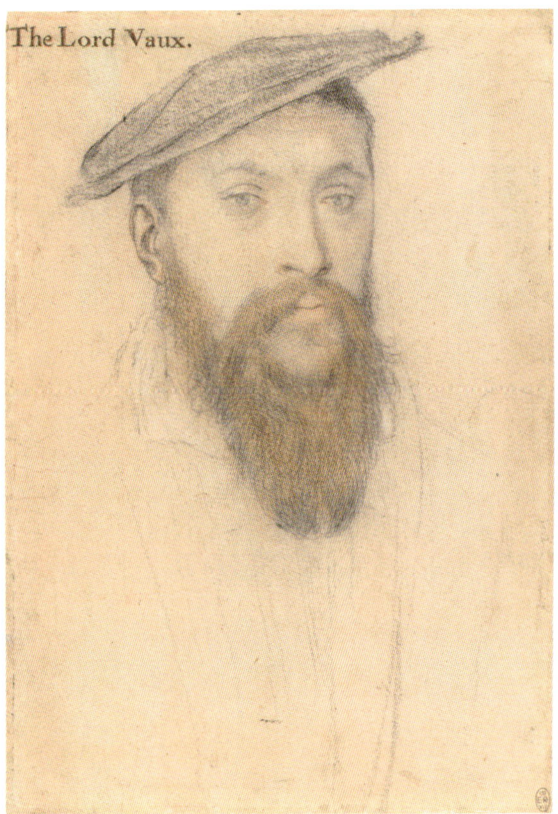

Fig. 44 Hans Holbein, *Thomas Vaux, 2nd Baron Vaux*, *c.*1535, black and coloured chalks on pink prepared paper
RCIN 912246

There are two drawings by Holbein of Thomas Vaux in the Royal Collection and one of Elizabeth. The drawing of Lady Vaux is particularly carefully worked up in the area of her headdress, which has been modelled in stumped chalk and inks. Faint touches of white heightening on her face convey the sheen of her skin. The main outlines have been traced with a stylus, leaving offset lines on the verso of the sheet. On the basis of the paper used, this is probably a pair with the drawing of Sir Thomas, which is entirely in chalks (Fig. 44). These probably date from 1535, shortly before Vaux retired from court, since they are on the same stock of paper as that used for the portrait of Nicholas Bourbon (p. 77), which can be securely dated.[87] The drawing of Sir Thomas worked up in ink is undated, but shows Vaux with longer hair and a less luxuriant beard. This drawing is on two sheets of paper that have been joined by Holbein, apparently to accommodate Vaux's voluminous jacket. A third sheet of paper has been added later (and not by Holbein) to balance the composition. The drawing has been trimmed at the top corners, probably due to damage, sometime between the 1720s (when the inscription was added at top right) and the middle of the eighteenth century when George Vertue recorded the lost corners in his copy, now at Sudeley Castle.[88] No finished portrait of Lord Vaux is known, although an early copy of that of Lady Vaux is in the Royal Collection (Fig. 45).

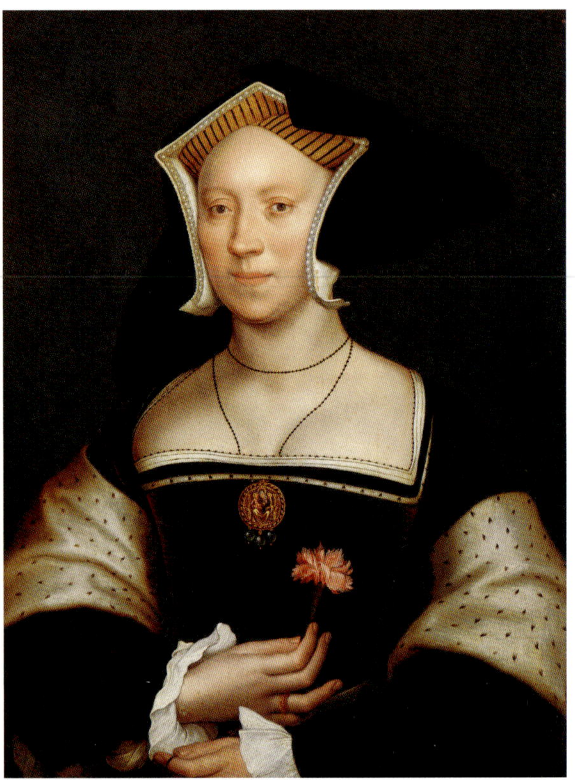

Fig. 45 **After Hans Holbein, *Elizabeth, Lady Vaux*, *c.*1600–30, oil on panel**
RCIN 402953

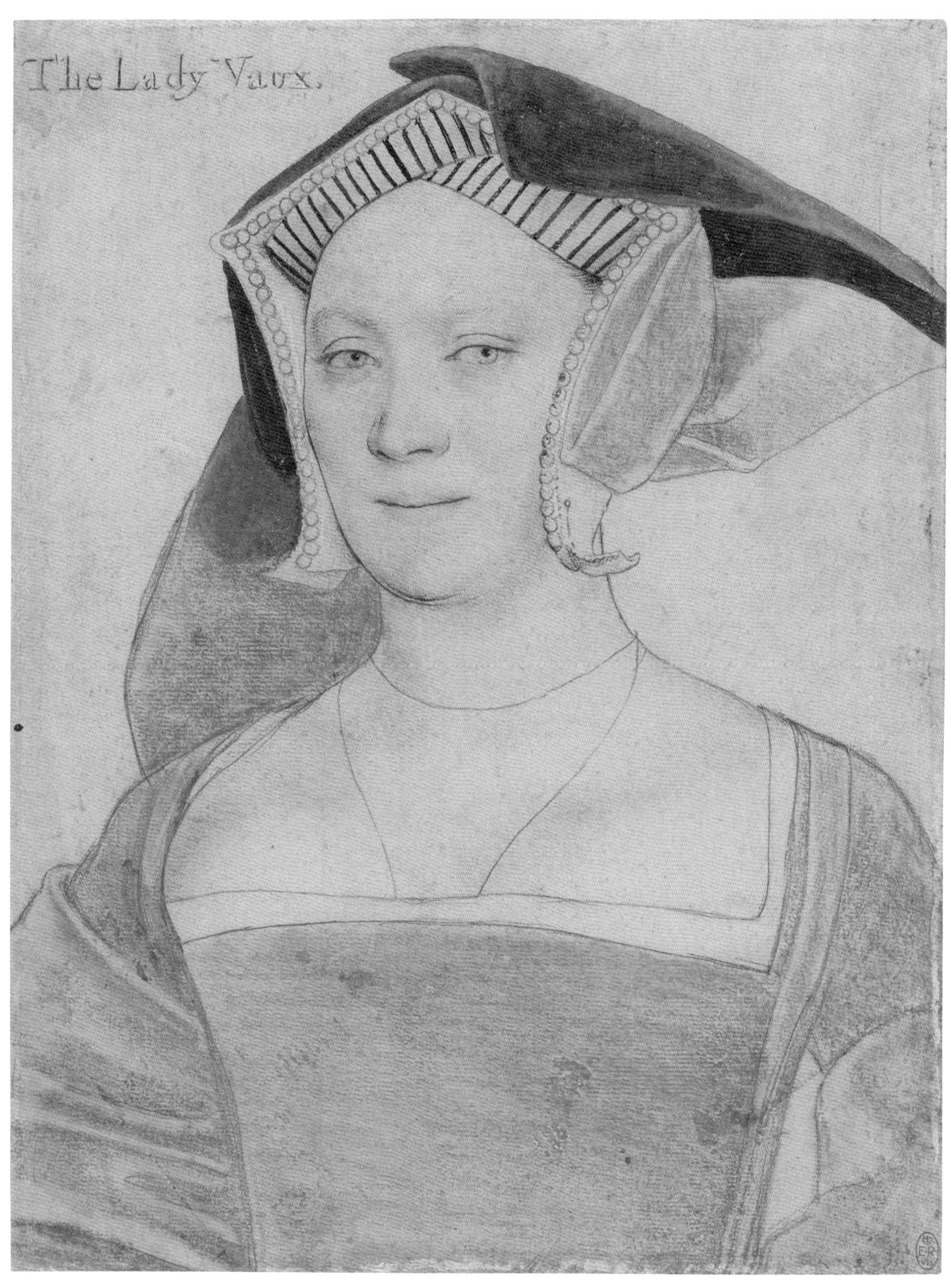
The Lady Vaux.

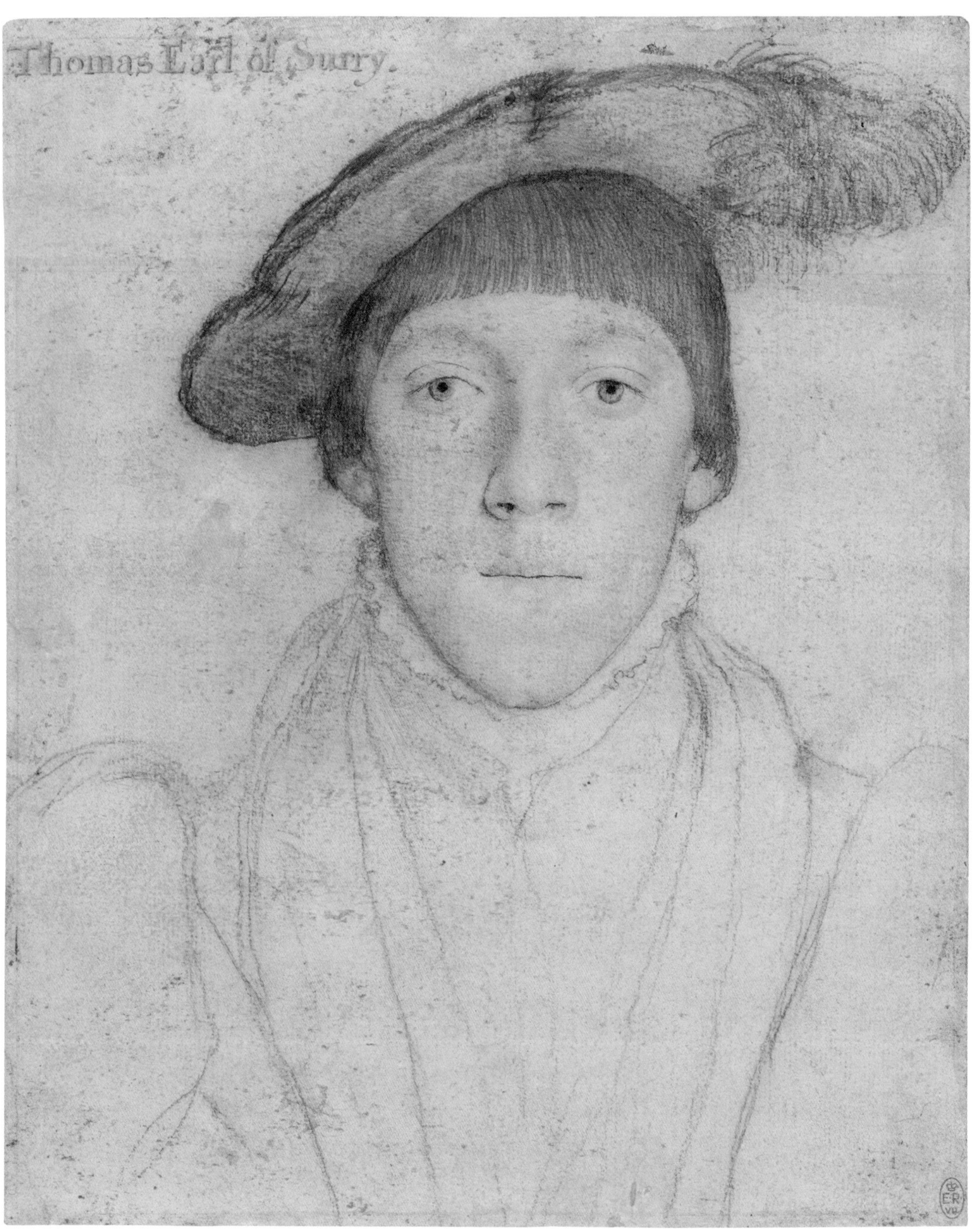
Thomas Earl of Surry.

Henry Howard, Earl of Surrey (1516/17–47)

*c.*1535–6
Black and coloured chalks with black ink on pink prepared paper
24.8 × 20.4 cm
RCIN 912215

Two drawings by Holbein of Henry Howard, Earl of Surrey, are in the Royal Collection. One shows Surrey facing the front left and the other depicts the sitter in three-quarter profile (p. 87). The eighteenth-century inscriptions mistakenly name the sitter as Thomas, but it is generally accepted that the drawings are of Henry Howard, who was the subject of a number of portraits. The full-face portrait appears to be a pair with that of his wife Frances, Countess of Surrey (p. 88), who was drawn at the same scale and in the same pose, and both probably date from 1535–6, when the couple were in their late teens.

The drawings of Henry Howard are likely to have been made at the same time: the sitter wears the same outfit, and any variation between the two is probably due to the different stages of completion of the sheets.[89] The three-quarter profile portrait is less finished: maybe the composition was deemed less successful and was abandoned. Comparison of the two reveals the stages in which Holbein built up the composition, first sketching in the outlines lightly in black chalk, before roughly adding brown chalk to give colour to the hair, and working up the face in chalk and ink. He stopped the profile drawing at this stage (perhaps deciding, as the face developed, that he did not want to proceed with this angle), but in the full-face drawing has carefully added individual strands of hair, and worked up the hat, both in black chalk. Here he has dampened the chalk in places to give a smoothness to what appears to be velvet, and used sharp, hard lines to indicate the long decorative stitches that join the panels of fabric.

Surrey was the oldest son and heir of Thomas Howard, Duke of Norfolk (p. 129).[90] He was educated alongside Henry Fitzroy, Henry VIII's illegitimate son (see Fig. 21). The two became brothers-in-law in 1529, when Fitzroy married Howard's sister Mary (p. 90). Some years after Fitzroy's death, Howard still owned a painting of his friend, which appears to have been displayed in his house in London.[91] A soldier and poet, Surrey was a close friend of Mary Shelton (p. 136). He dedicated verses to Thomas Wyatt, and Sir Nicholas Poyntz, among others. Surrey's prominence and air of confidence won him both praise and suspicion. Charles V described him in a letter to Henry VIII as having 'a gentle heart and dexterity', while Charles's ambassador François van der Delft wrote to the emperor that 'although he has always been so generous to his countrymen, [he] is not beloved by them'.[92] In December 1546, partly on the testimony of Richard Southwell (p. 93), Surrey and his father were arrested on suspicion of plotting to take control of the country while the king was ill at Windsor. Henry Howard was executed on 19 January 1547.

Henry Howard, Earl of Surrey
*c.*1535–6
Black and coloured chalks with black ink
on pink prepared paper
29.0 × 21.0 cm
RCIN 912216

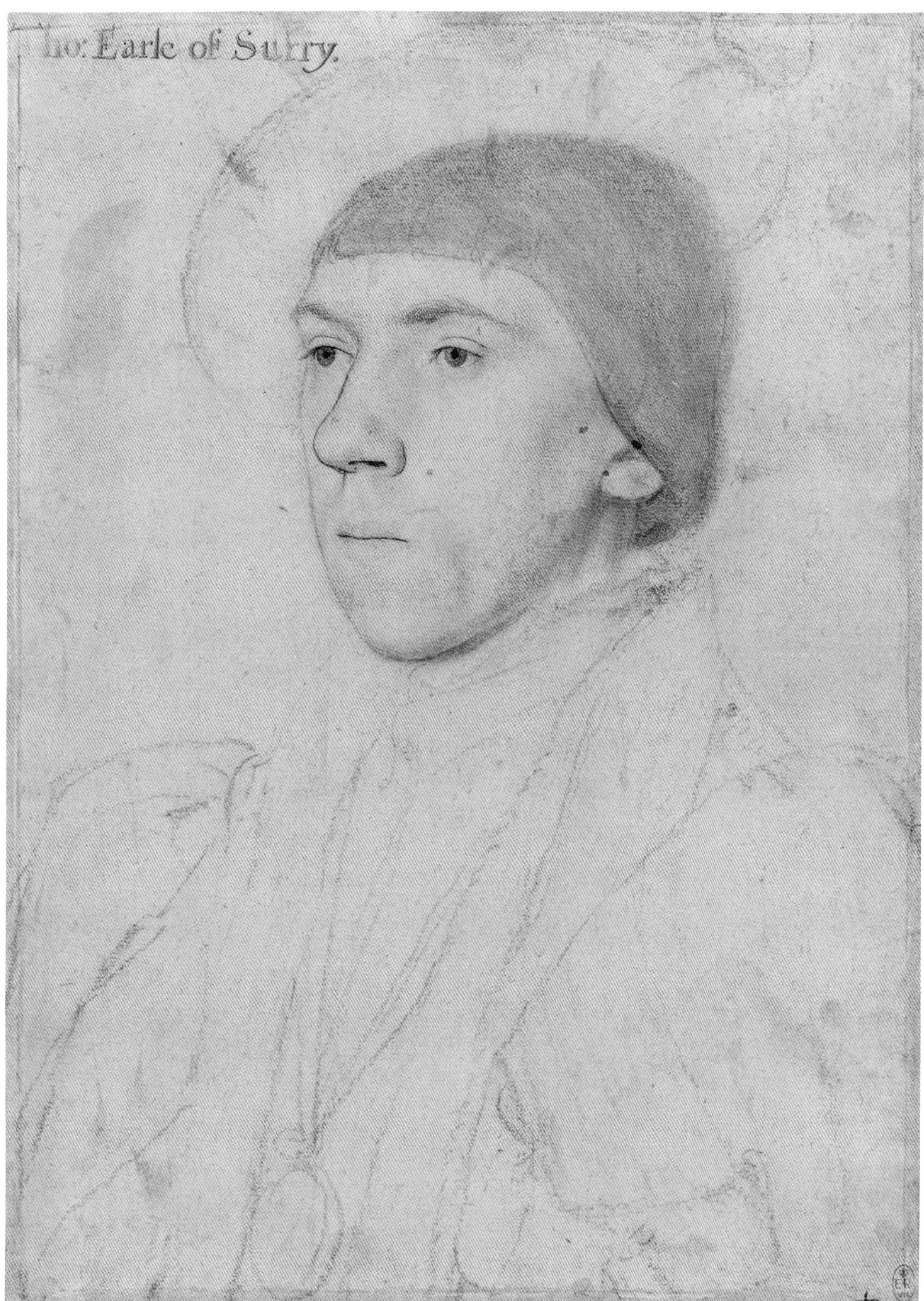
Tho: Earle of Surry.

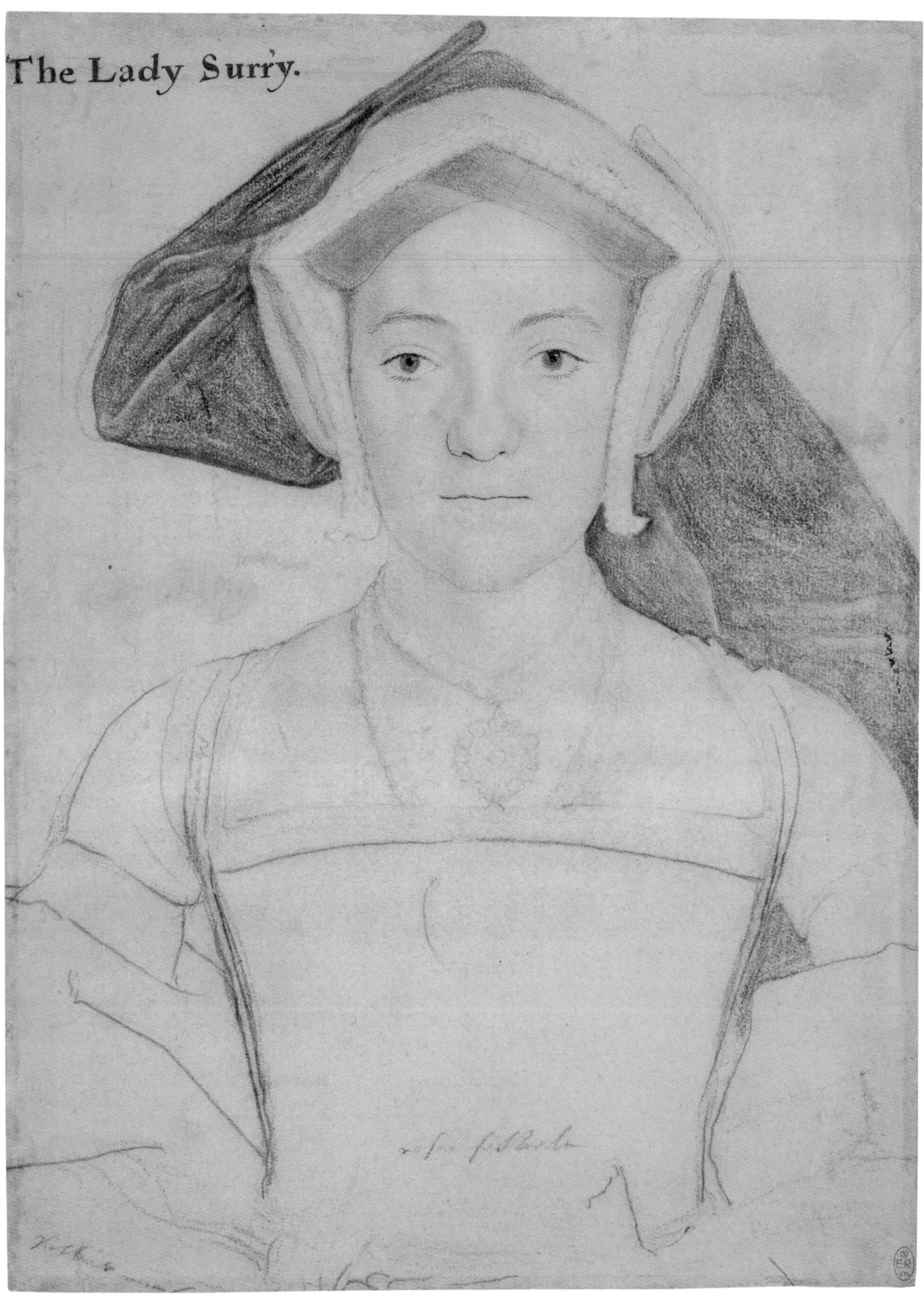
The Lady Surry.

Frances, Countess of Surrey (1517–77)
c.1535–6
Black and coloured chalks with white heightening and touches of black ink on pink prepared paper
31.0 × 23.0 cm
RCIN 912214

Frances de Vere, daughter of John de Vere, Earl of Oxford, was betrothed to Henry Howard, Earl of Surrey and heir to the Duke of Norfolk, in 1532. On hearing the news, Eustace Chapuys, the imperial ambassador, reported that:

> the duke of Norfolk has often said that he should marry his son soon to avoid the suspicion of wishing for the Princess [Mary] for him. He has now performed his word, and must have had some urgent cause; for his son will not be fit for marriage for three years, and the lady has neither great riches nor connections. It is said that the lady Anne [Boleyn] has forced the Duke to do this.[93]

The Earl and Countess of Surrey had five children, who lived with the countess at Kenninghall, the seat of the Dukes of Norfolk, and were tutored by the Dutch humanist Hadrianus Junius, and later by the reformer John Foxe.[94]

The countess is shown facing forward, wearing an English hood and dress with wide sleeves, and clasping her hands before her waist. Her gown is, Holbein notes, of pink velvet ('rosa felbet') and she has a yellow girdle around her waist. Her features are delicately drawn, with tiny strokes of black ink to indicate her eyelashes and touches of white enlivening her eyes. This drawing is on the same paper as that used by Holbein for his portrait of Richard Southwell (and has similar pink priming) and may therefore date to 1535–6 (p. 94).[95] It was probably intended as a pair with that of Frances's husband (p. 87).

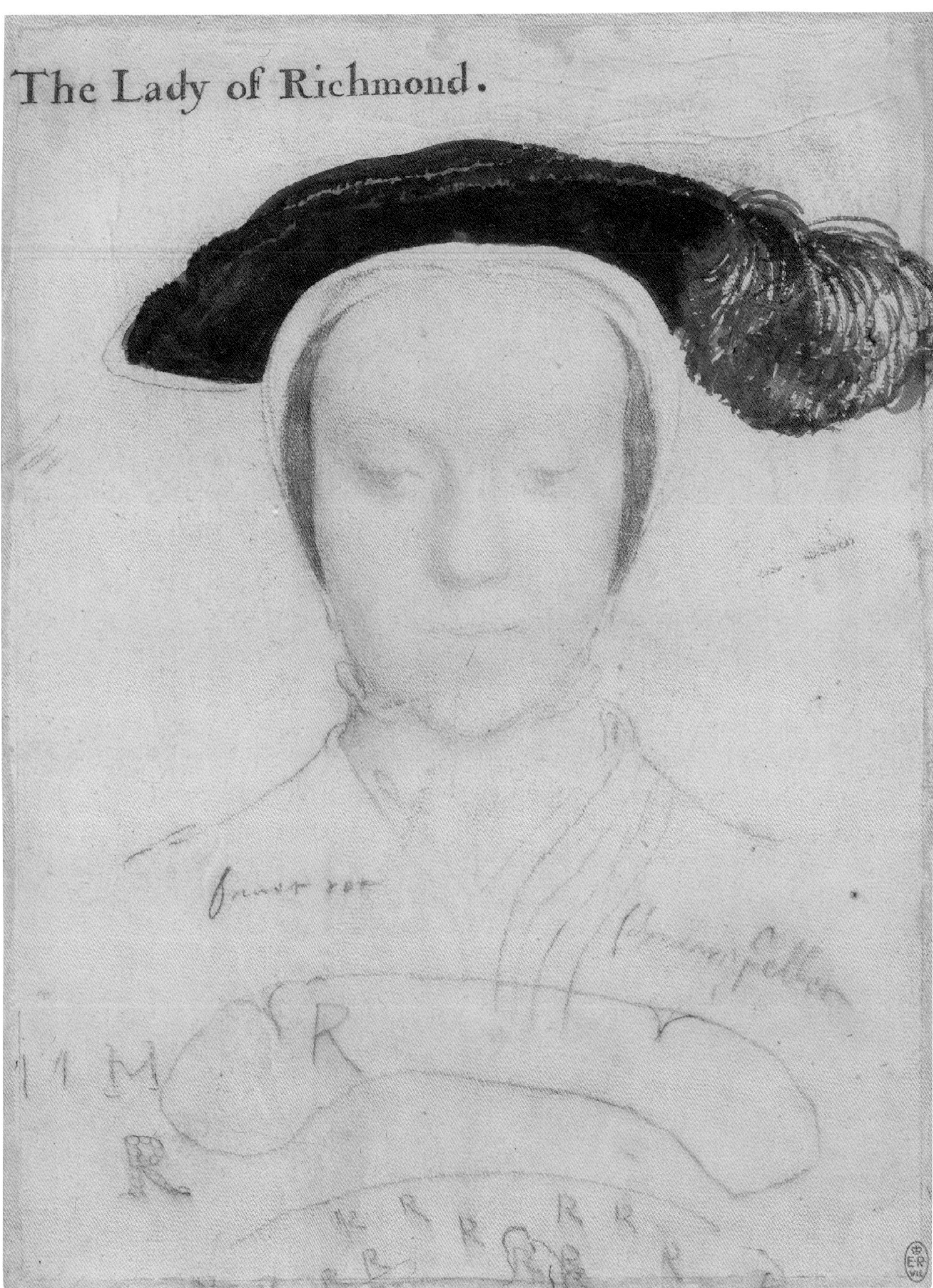
The Lady of Richmond.

Mary Fitzroy, Duchess of Richmond and Somerset (*c*.1519–?55)
c.1535–6
Black and coloured chalks with black ink on pink prepared paper
26.6 × 19.9 cm
RCIN 912212

Unusually among the Windsor drawings, Holbein's focus here is the dress of the sitter, particularly her headwear. Two sketches at the bottom of the sheet show the construction of her black velvet ('schwarz felbet') cap, which is decorated with 'M's and 'R's, for Mary Richmond. Her gown was of red velvet ('samet rot') with gold bordering, which Holbein has recorded with yellow chalk. Holbein has used both an approximation of the English 'velvet' and his native German 'samet' here. The duchess looks down, probably because the artist is not working on her face. This is not modelled, beyond the faint drawing of the features and a touch of red chalk at her lips. A second drawing in the Royal Collection may be a companion study, which was worked up further to portray the sitter's features (Fig. 46, overleaf). This is on the same paper as that used by Holbein for the three-quarter profile portrait of Henry Howard, Earl of Surrey (p. 87), suggesting a similar date. Whether or not the second drawing does show the duchess, the present drawing was clearly abandoned for some reason, Holbein using it as a convenient place to record the details of the sitter's cap.

The drawing may have been made around 1535–6, when Holbein also drew Fitzroy's brother and sister-in-law, the Earl and Countess of Surrey (pp. 87–91). It certainly dates to before the death of the sitter's husband on 23 July 1536, after which she would have been in mourning. The frontal pose has been taken as indication that this is part of a set with other portraits of the Duke of Norfolk's children, although such a group is not listed among the paintings in the duke's residences in the inventories taken at his arrest in 1546.[96] A portrait of the Duchess of Richmond, 'wrought gold' and with her father's arms, likely to be a pair to a depiction of the Duke of Richmond's arms 'wrought wt gold', was recorded at Mendham, the residence of the Duke of Norfolk's mistress Elizabeth Holland in December 1547.[97] These probably related to her marriage in 1529 and seem unlikely to be connected to Holbein's drawing.

Mary Howard was betrothed to Henry Fitzroy, Duke of Richmond and Somerset and illegitimate son of Henry VIII, when she was around ten years old. After the duke's death in 1536, Mary was left without income for many years. In letters pleading her cause, she described herself as an 'unwoorthe desolate widowe', while her father, who was supposed to be furthering her case at court, scoffed that she was 'to[o] wise for a woman'.[98] In 1538 Henry VIII considered marrying her, along with the similarly widowed Lady Margaret Douglas and his daughter Princess Elizabeth, to Italian princes as a means of furthering his foreign policy. But this alliance did not take place and the duchess's plight became apparent at dawn on 14 December 1546 when Richard Southwell, John Gates and Wyndham Carew arrived at Kenninghall, the residence of the Howard family, to break the news that her father and her brother, Thomas and Henry Howard, had been arrested for treason and to search the house. Writing to the king, they described how 'wee found the duchesse a woman sore perplexed trembling and like to fall downe',[99] although she was quickly able to recover her composure and speak in support of her father and brother. On searching her room, the men were clearly shocked, describing finding 'her coofers and chamber soo bare as your maiestie wold hardlie think',[100] and noting that she had sold or pawned all her jewellery to pay her debts. On moving to the rooms of Elizabeth Holland, the duke's mistress, they found them in contrast full of jewels and costly clothing.

Despite the duchess's precarious circumstances, this 'too wise woman' was, with Mary Shelton (p. 136) and Lady Margaret Douglas, one of the inventive compilers of the Devonshire Manuscript, which includes poetry by Thomas Wyatt and Henry Howard, Earl of Surrey. She was a committed Protestant, who supported reforming preachers in East Anglia and who encouraged the evangelicals John Bale and John Foxe (appointing the latter to teach her nephews and nieces). After her father's arrest, careful provision was made for her by those administering the seizure and confiscation of his goods.[101] The date of her death is not known, but was probably around 1555, when she was about 35 years old.

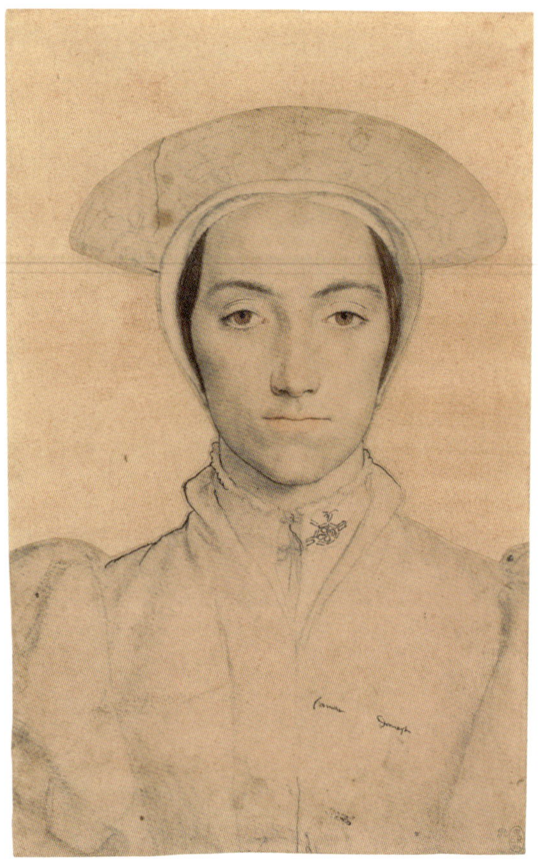

Fig. 46 **Hans Holbein, *Unidentified woman*, *c.*1535–6, black and coloured chalks with ink on pink prepared paper**
RCIN 912190

Richard Southwell (1502/3–64)
1536
Black and coloured chalks and black ink on pink prepared paper
36.6 × 27.7 cm
RCIN 912242

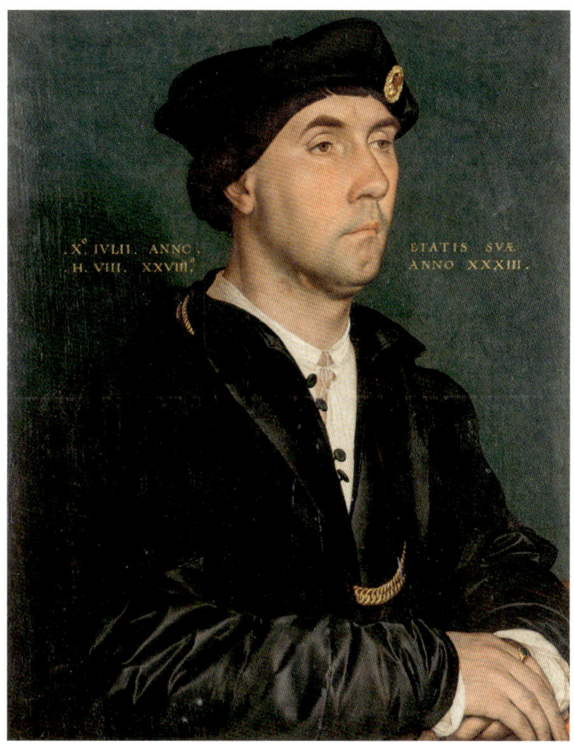

Fig. 47 **Hans Holbein, *Richard Southwell*, 1536, oil on panel**
Uffizi Gallery, Florence, 1890,1087

In 1536, when this portrait was taken, Richard Southwell was a rising star. Recently appointed Sheriff of Norfolk and Suffolk, and one of the Receivers in the Court of Augmentations (established to oversee the confiscation and redistribution of monastic wealth), Southwell was beginning to amass money, land and power, much of it based on the assets of religious foundations in East Anglia, which he had been responsible for seizing. As a close associate of Thomas Howard, Duke of Norfolk, and his family, Southwell was a figure of influence in the East Anglian community, which included Sir Thomas Lestrange (see p. 99), whose daughter was married to his brother, Anthony. In 1532 Southwell was among a group of men responsible for the murder of Sir William Pennington, for which he later obtained a pardon. He spoke against his close associates Sir Thomas More, Sir Thomas Cromwell and Henry Howard, Earl of Surrey, each of whom would be executed for their supposed disloyalty to the king. In 1540 Southwell was knighted and had soon made himself so indispensable to Henry VIII that he was one of those who received a £200 bequest in the king's will for their 'speciall love and favour' towards the monarch.[102]

According to an inscription, the portrait (overleaf) shows Southwell at the age of 33. Holbein does not usually include such lettering on his drawings and this may have been added at the sitter's request, either to record the wording

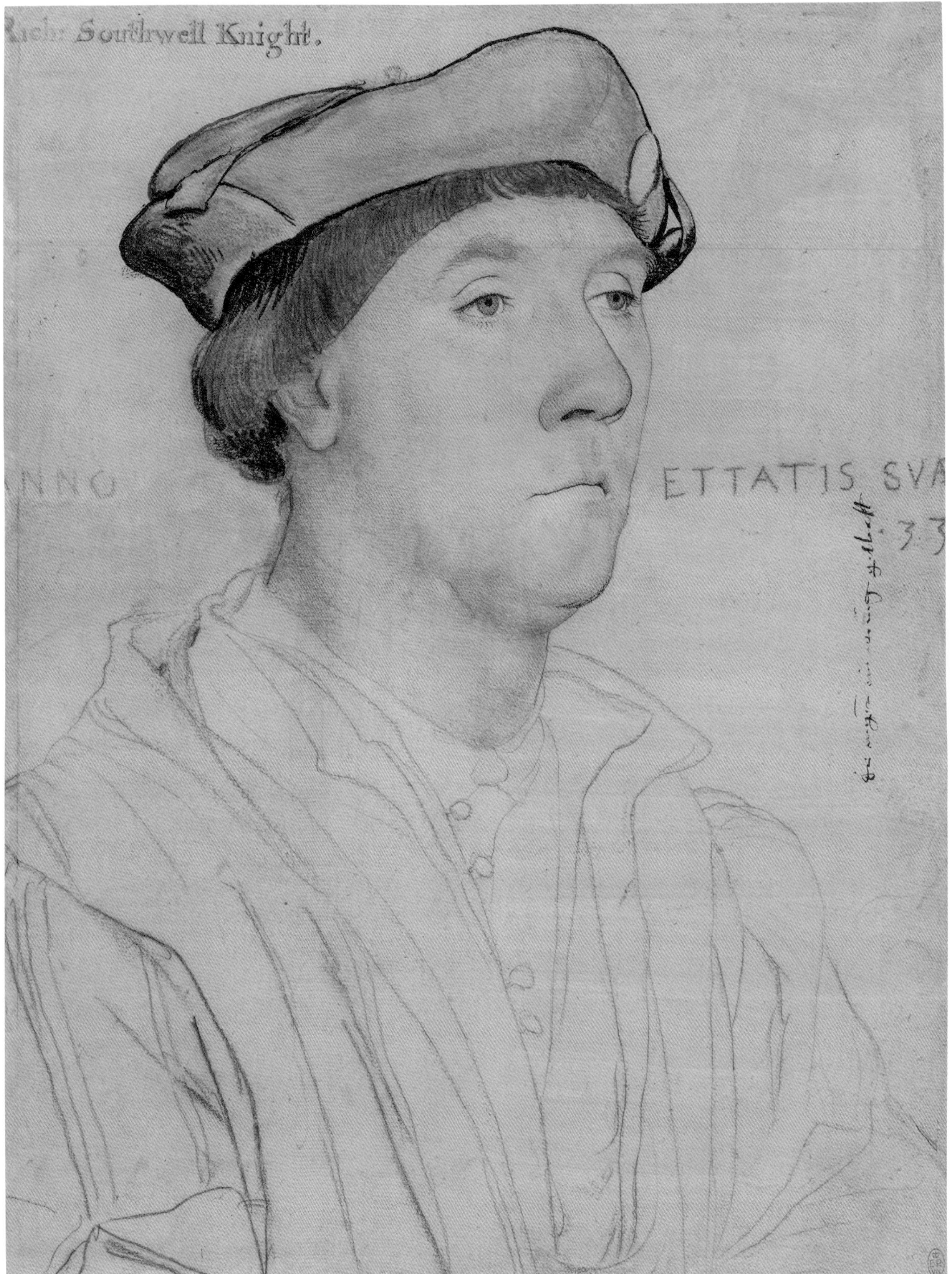
Southwell Knight.
ETTATIS SVA
33

he required, or to show how the letters would be placed, although these differ on the finished portrait. This, now in the Uffizi Gallery in Florence, is precisely dated to 10 July 1536, suggesting this date has a significance that has not been discovered (Fig. 47).[103] The scars on Southwell's neck and face are carefully shown, as are the lines of embroidery indicated in red chalk on his jacket, which match those on the finished portrait. Holbein has recorded the yellowish tinge of Southwell's eyes in an inscription (*Die augen ein wenig gelbatt*) on the right-hand side of the drawing.

Southwell's commissioning of Holbein at this moment reflects his confidence in his growing status, and his increasing disposable wealth. The list of bequests in his will of 1561 indicates a man who revelled in the accumulation of ostentatious goods of the finest quality. He owned woven hangings and armour made for him by Erasmus Kyrkenar, the master armourer. His sizeable collection of plate included items previously owned by William Fitzwilliam, Earl of Southampton, and Cardinal Wolsey, as well as pieces purchased from Antonio Buonvisi, a merchant from Lucca resident in London who supplied the most senior courtiers with luxury goods.[104] Among his extensive collection of 'bookes of scripture, prophane stories and other lattein authors and my bookes of lawe and statue'[105] were three religious manuscripts that survive today, each bearing Southwell's motto *Sapit qui sustinet* ('He who provides support is prudent'). The fact that Southwell benefited from the attacks on papal authority in England while remaining until his death a religious conservative (described in a Spanish briefing document in 1558 as 'a good man and devoted'[106]) is testament to his ability to put aside his own beliefs and act as was required to advance.

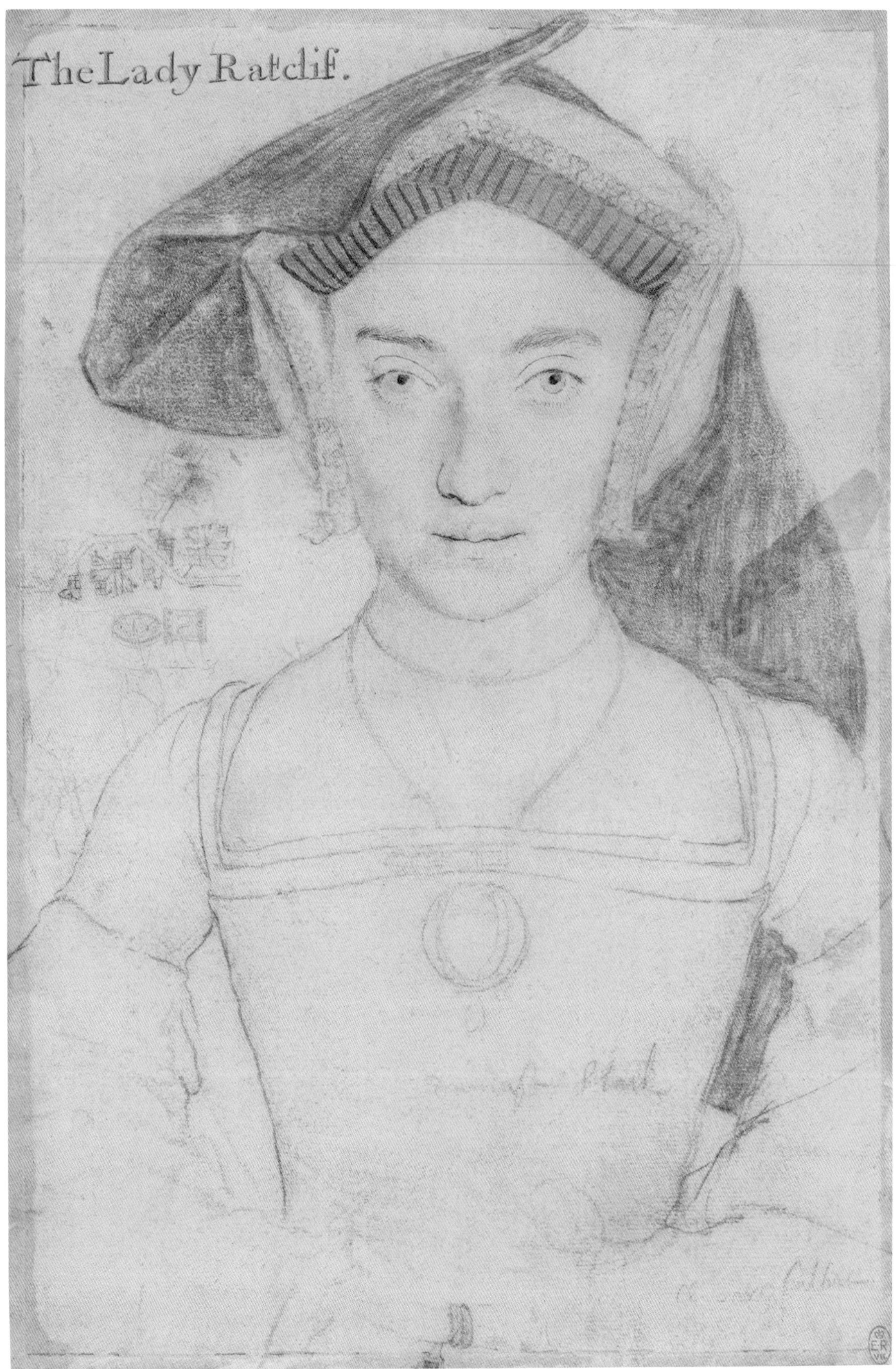
The Lady Ratclif.

Lady Ratcliffe
*c.*1536
Black and coloured chalks with black and brown ink and metalpoint on pink prepared paper
30.1 × 20.3 cm
RCIN 912236

The sitter faces the viewer in a pose adopted by a number of women in Holbein's drawings. As well as modelling her face, Holbein has taken trouble to record the decoration on her bodice in the spare space to the left of her cheek and to note the black damask ('damast black') and velvet ('schwarz felbet') in a hybrid of German and English. Her hood has a floral border and a network of red over the yellow band. To the left of her head are studies of embroidered patterns in black chalk and metalpoint. These include a band of alternating oval and rectangular lozenges at the top of her bodice, which incorporate the letter 'S'. The position of a second band of stylised foliage is not clear. The sitter's hands have been partially trimmed from the sheet; she is shown wearing three rings.

Despite the inscription on the drawing, the identity of the sitter is unclear. 'Lady Ratcliffe' could refer to Margaret Stanley (d. ?1534) or Mary Arundell (d. 1557), who married Sir Robert Ratcliffe, Earl of Sussex, in 1532 and 1537 respectively, or to the wife of the earl's son, Sir Humphrey Ratcliffe, whose name was either Isabel or Elizabeth (d. 1594).[107] The 'S' on the sitter's bodice may refer to the Sussex family.[108] The drawing dates from the mid-1530s, when it was the fashion for women to pin up one side of their hoods, as seen in the portraits of Elizabeth, Lady Vaux (p. 83), Frances, Countess of Surrey (p. 88), and Jane Seymour (p. 105).[109]

Sir Thomas Lestrange (*c.*1490–1545)
*c.*1536
Black and coloured chalks with blue watercolour on pink prepared paper
24.4 × 21.2 cm
RCIN 912244

This drawing shows Sir Thomas Lestrange, a courtier and Norfolk landowner whose main residence was Hunstanton Hall, near the north Norfolk coast. Holbein has captured the sitter's slim, elegant features with sharp black chalk. Touches of white chalk indicate the shine on the sitter's hair, the white linen of his shirt and the ties that fall from the nearside of his collar. Two paintings of Lestrange, both probably copies of Holbein's original, were recorded in his descendants' collection in the early twentieth century.[110] One of these previously bore an inscription dating the portrait to 1536.[111] It shows the sitter facing the viewer rather than to the left, suggesting that changes were made, as so often by Holbein, between the drawing and the finished portrait. This may once have been a pair with a lost portrait of Anne, Lady Lestrange, who was described as wearing a black cap and holding in her left hand a black velvet bag embroidered with a medallion.[112]

The meticulous accounts kept by Sir Thomas and his wife over the course of many years reflect the close-knit East Anglian community that would be among Holbein's most enthusiastic patrons.[113] The Lestranges were close to the Lovell and Southwell families, and exchanged regular gifts and correspondence with Sir Richard Southwell (p. 94), described in the accounts as 'cosyn'. They were frequent visitors to Kenninghall as guests of both Thomas Howard, Duke of Norfolk (p. 129), and Henry Howard, Earl of Surrey (p. 84). Through the Norfolks, the Lestranges also socialised with the Boleyn family: Lady Elizabeth Boleyn, mother of the future queen, was a guest at Hunstanton Hall on a number of occasions in 1527, as was Anne Shelton, mother of the poet Mary Shelton (see p. 136). Their invitation to visit may have resulted from Anne Boleyn's increasing prominence at court. Sir Thomas rented lands from Charles Brandon, Duke of Suffolk, paying his fee to the duke's trustee and cousin, Sir Humphrey Wingfield, uncle of Charles Wingfield of Kimbolton (p. 120).

Betrothal to Anne Vaux in 1501 brought Sir Thomas into the world of the Vaux and Parr families.[114] William Parr (p. 127) was Lady Lestrange's nephew and the Lestranges bought wine for him in Lynn on a number of occasions, perhaps indicating that Parr had a taste for the French wine traded into this major port.[115] The Vaux were newly created Barons of Harrowden, and also patrons of Holbein, who drew two portraits of Anne's brother Thomas, 2nd Baron Vaux, and one of his wife, Elizabeth (pp. 80–3). The paired drawings of Thomas and Elizabeth Vaux date from around 1535, shortly before it seems Lestrange sat for this drawing. Was it the Vaux commission that prompted Lestrange to request his own portrait?

The accounts give the impression of a lively and sociable household, with payments of hunting expenses, gambling debts and, in 1543, to a juggler sent from Henry Ratcliffe, Earl of Sussex. The duke

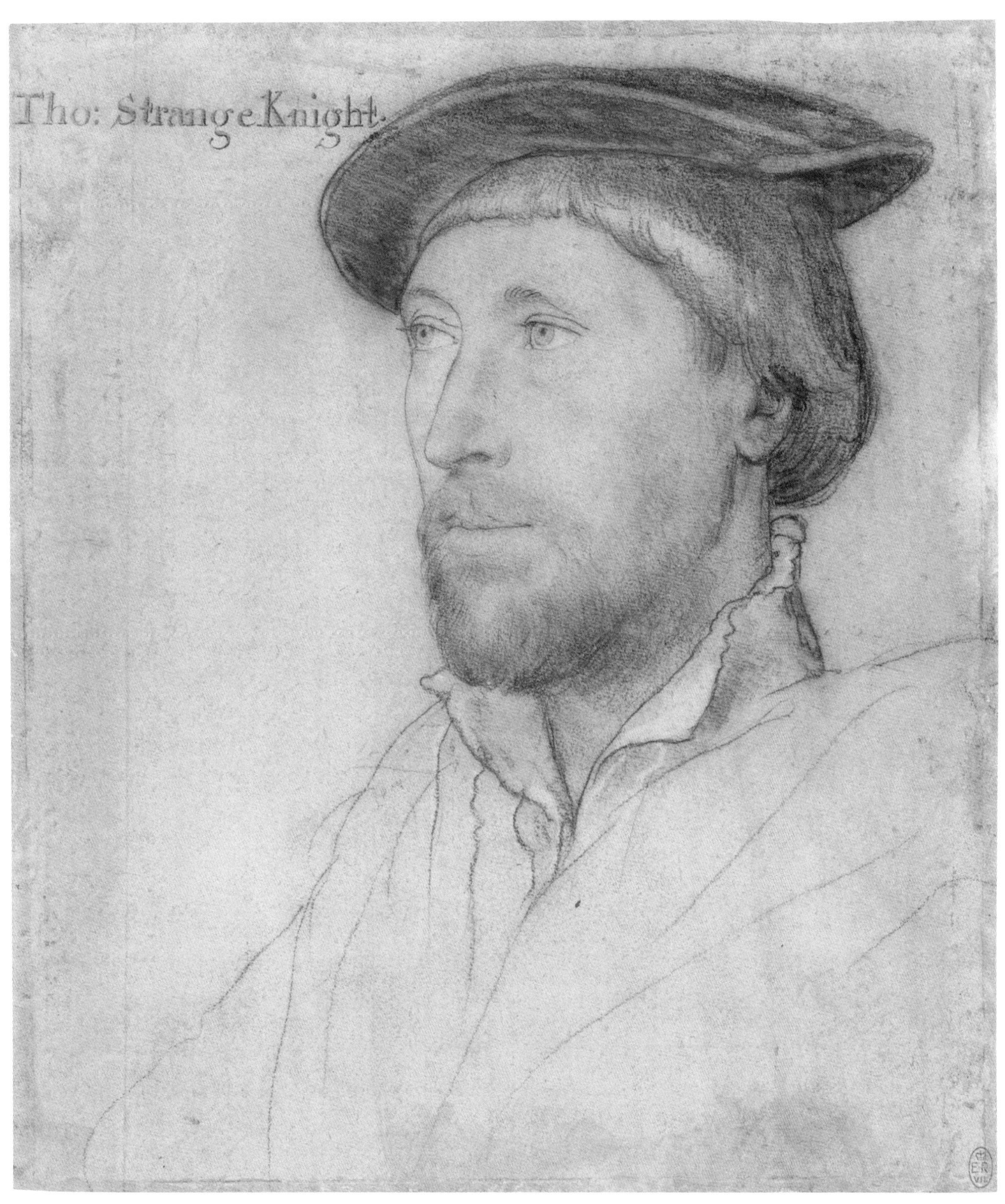
Tho: Strange Knight.

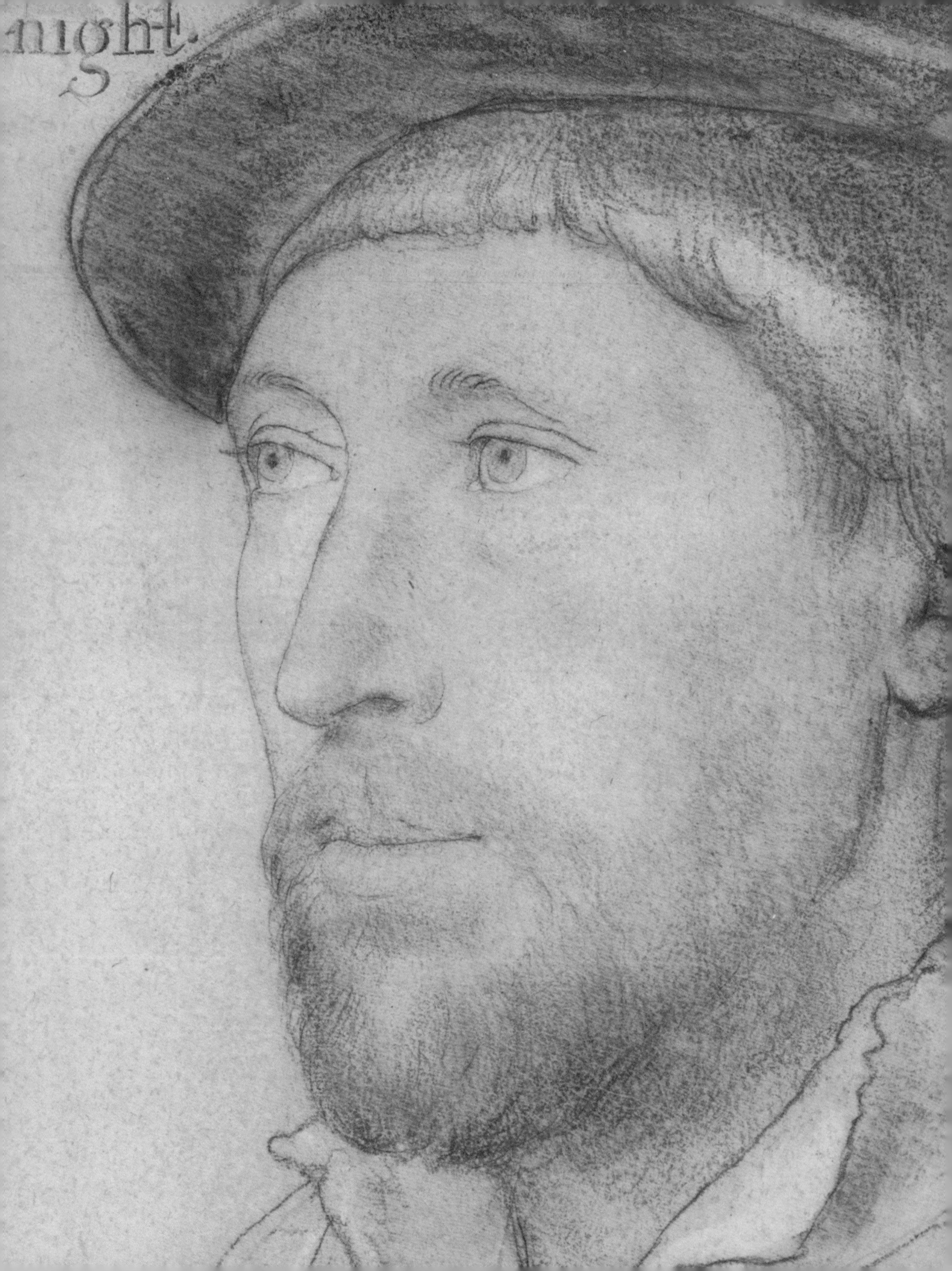
night

of Suffolk's trumpeters entertained the Lestranges in May 1530 and his wife Mary's troupe of players performed before the household in 1531. Other entertainments at Hunstanton included minstrel groups associated with the king, Sir Thomas Boleyn and Henry Parker, Lord Morley (did Lestrange know the portrait that Albrecht Dürer had made of Morley in 1523, surely a prized possession?).

Alongside the amusements, Sir Thomas was a busy courtier, engaged on the king's business. He was among those who travelled to Calais for the grand diplomatic meeting between Francis I and Henry VIII known as the Field of the Cloth of Gold. In July 1525 he was recorded hiring boats to take him, probably carrying messages, between Thomas, Cardinal Wolsey in London and the king at Greenwich. He remained largely in Norfolk from the 1530s, when payments for the entertainments described above are mostly concentrated. In 1544 he was among the Norfolk landowners listed in the 'Vantguard' for the invasion of France, accompanied by ten foot soldiers. Whether he travelled to France is uncertain and he died in January 1545, having suffered from ill health for a few years previously.[116]

M. Zouch

1536–43

Black and coloured chalks with black ink, blue watercolour and white heightening on pink prepared paper

29.4 × 20.1 cm

RCIN 912252

Holbein has here used a number of different coloured chalks to capture the sitter's hair and headdress and gently model the contours of her face. Her eyes are painted in blue watercolour and white heightening, with thin black penstrokes for her eyelashes: her left eyelid droops very slightly. The different bands of her hood are delineated in yellow, black, red and salmon chalks, with the same salmon used for her lips. Her gown is of black velvet ('black felbet') with a white border and she holds a flower, perhaps a pink. A medallion at her breast appears to show an ascending figure, perhaps Fortune.[117] The drawing is on a paper bearing a watermark with the coat of arms of Zurich, which seems to have been in use after 1536, and which is found on four of the other portrait drawings in the Royal Collection, three of them by Holbein and one apparently by an artist associated with him.[118]

Despite the inscription 'M Souch', the sitter in this drawing is unidentified and could be any of a number of women with the surname Zouch at the Tudor court.[119] One of these was Mary Zouch, lady-in-waiting to Jane Seymour (the 'M' of the inscription is more likely to stand for 'Mistress' than 'Mary'). Other suggestions include Anne Zouche, née Gainsford, a lady-in-waiting to Anne Boleyn, or Margaret, second wife of Richard Zouche.[120] Just as likely is the Mistress Souch who was gentlewoman to Mary, Duchess of Richmond (p. 90); it may be notable that the duchess was shown by Holbein in the same frontal pose as the sitter here.[121]

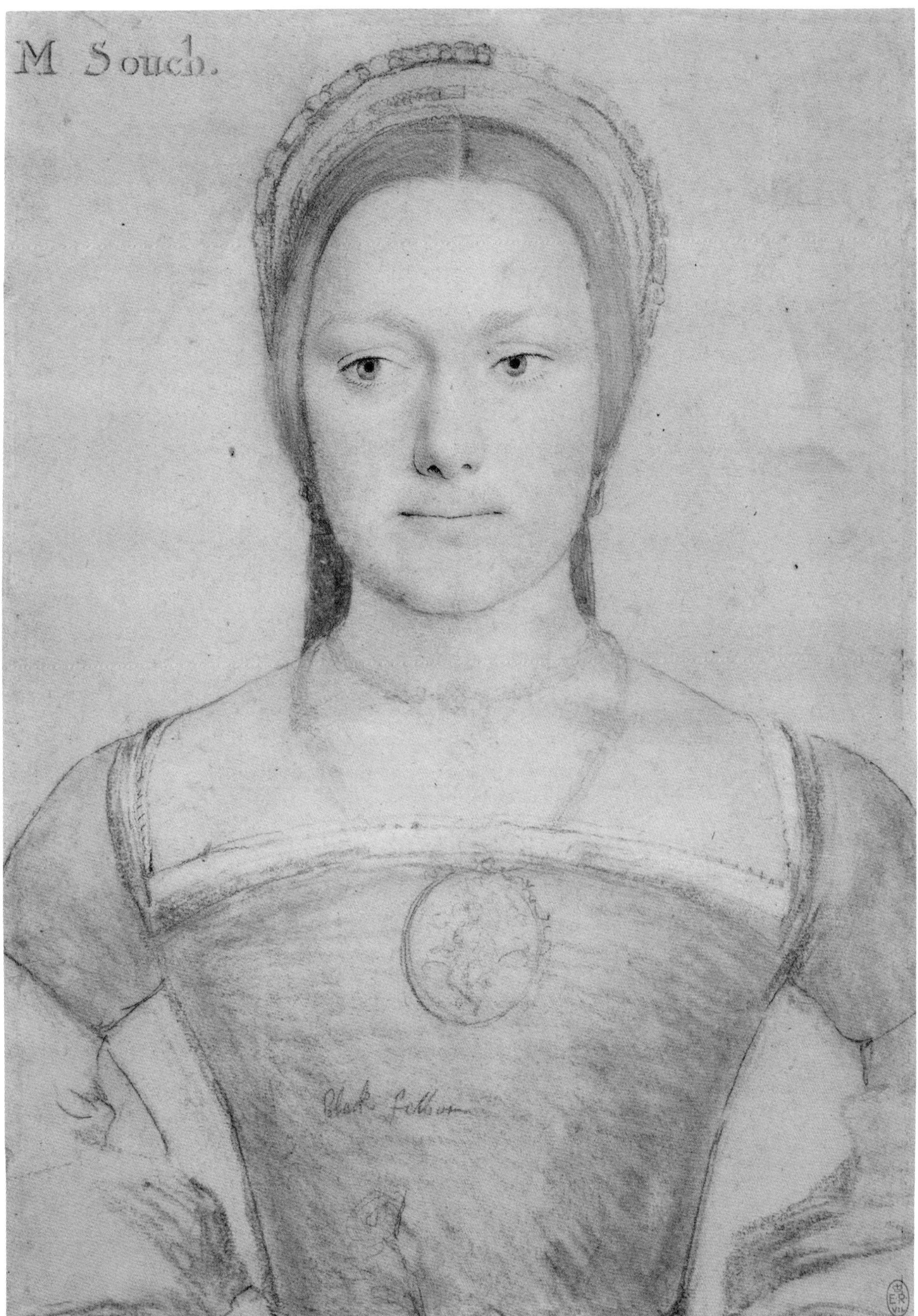
M Souch.

Jane Seymour (1508/9–37)
1536–7
Black and coloured chalks with pen and ink and green watercolour on pink prepared paper
50.0 × 28.5 cm
RCIN 912267

Jane Seymour was lady-in-waiting to Katherine of Aragon and Anne Boleyn. She married Henry VIII on 30 May 1536 and died in October 1537, shortly after giving birth to his son Prince Edward. This portrait appears to have been taken before, or early in, her pregnancy, perhaps in late 1536 or early 1537, possibly with a panel painting in mind.[122] The queen is shown standing, with her hands clasped in front of her. Although Holbein has included the flowers on the frame of her headdress, the drawing provides very little detail about the fabrics and decoration of her outfit, and there may have been other studies recording these details which no longer survive.

Jane's status as the mother of the future king Edward VI ensured her portrait was circulated widely and the sheet shows signs of reuse as a pattern for portraits. Another sheet has been added at the bottom to lengthen the composition and the sheet is also intersected with drawn and folded lines to act as a guide for portraits in other formats.[123] Many of these portraits were by other artists, but one in Vienna is by Holbein himself (Fig. 48) and he may also have painted a portrait of the queen for her brother Edward in 1542.[124] Jane was shown in this pose, perhaps posthumously, in the Whitehall mural, which celebrates the Tudor dynasty, and the present drawing may have been used to make a full-size cartoon like that which survives for the figures of Henry VII and Henry VIII. Holbein carried out other work connected with Jane during her short period as queen. Among these are items of jewellery and a design for a magnificent standing cup with antique ornament that may have been a gift from the king.[125]

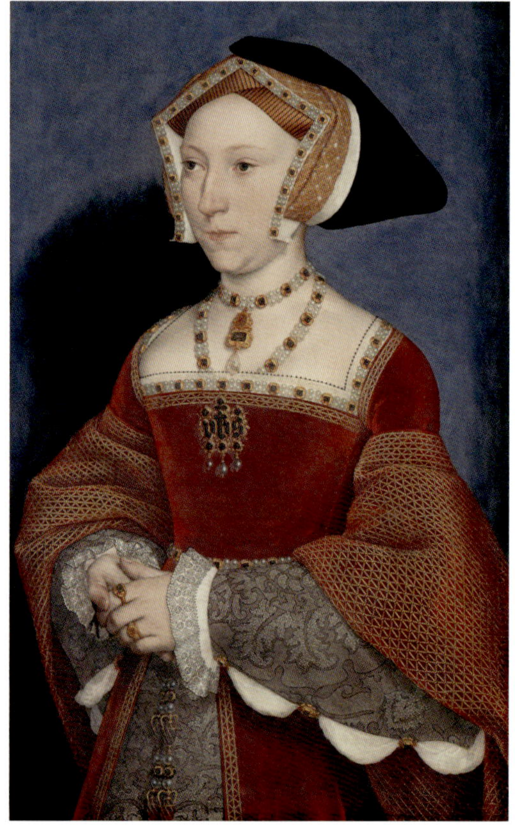

Fig. 48 **Hans Holbein, *Jane Seymour*, *c.*1536–7, oil on panel**
Kunsthistorisches Museum, Vienna, Gemäldegalerie 881

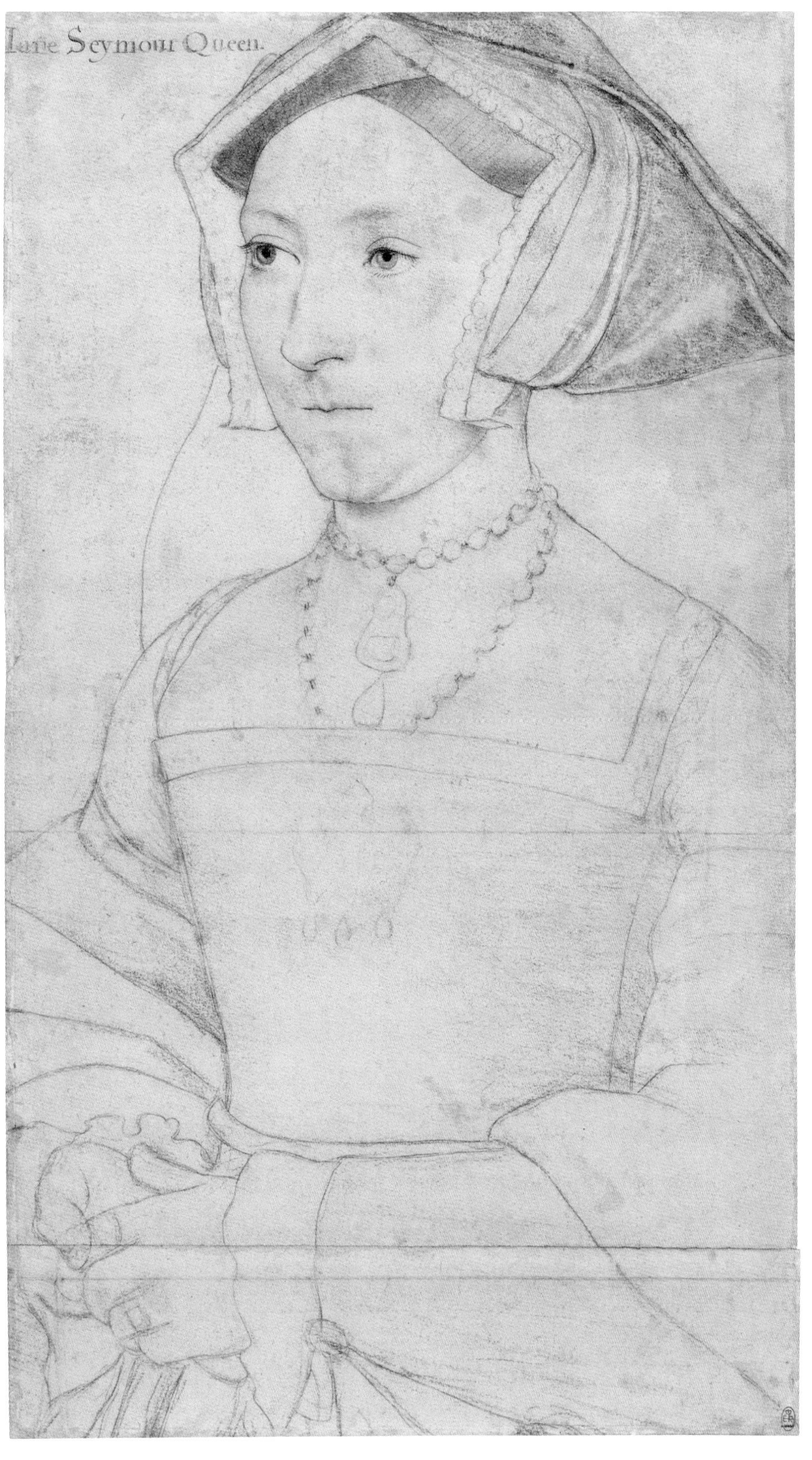
Iane Seymour Queen.

William Reskimer (d. 1552)
*c.*1536–9
Black and coloured chalks with watercolour on pink prepared paper
29.0 × 21.0 cm
RCIN 912237

Both Holbein's drawing (right) and the finished painting of William Reskimer (p. 109) are in the Royal Collection, the latter presented to Charles I by Reskimer's descendant, Sir Robert Killigrew.[126] Holbein's drawing is almost entirely in chalk, which he has sharpened and smudged to create different textures. There is a touch of greenish watercolour in the eyes.[127] As well as black, red and yellow, he has used a reddish-brown chalk to catch the colour of the fur that appears under the collar at the sitter's neck. Since in the finished painting this fur is almost the same tone as Reskimer's beard, Holbein may have been using the different colours to denote the different textures. These details have been carried through into the painting, which follows the drawing closely. For this, Holbein reused a panel that had previously been painted with red and grey layers, perhaps intended to create a decorative marbled effect.[128] On top of this Holbein added a pink priming, and carefully traced over the outlines of his drawing, leaving indentations on the paper.[129] He then worked up the composition further on the panel, with hatching on the hands that is comparable to that found on the drawing of John Godsalve (Fig. 49, left, and see p. 138). In both the drawing and the panel, Holbein has made several attempts to capture the profile of the nose, and it is possible that he returned to the drawing to resolve this area with the panel in front of him, amending the sheet of paper simultaneously with the panel. A similar area of uncertainty in both drawing and painting is found in the back of the sitter's head, which is not coloured with brown chalk in the drawing, and which is tentatively delineated in the painting (Fig. 49, right).

William Reskimer was the younger brother of John Reskimer, Sheriff of Cornwall (who has also, less convincingly, been suggested as the subject of the portrait).[130] By 1526 he had been appointed one of the pages of the king's Bedchamber, at a salary of 26s 8d and with livery provided, and subsequently was promoted to the position of gentleman usher in or shortly after 1546.[131] As page, he was the recipient of a series of grants of lucrative offices: in November 1532 he was appointed bailiff of Sheriff Hutton; in February 1538 he received grants of office for lands in Warwickshire; and in 1543 he was appointed Keeper of the Ports of the Duchy of Cornwall.[132] In 1542 he was granted lodgings in the recently dissolved Blackfriars Priory, where his neighbours included George Brooke, Lord Cobham (p. 123), and Giovanni Portinari, an Italian military engineer.[133] Amid these formal grants are glimpses of Reskimer's increasing confidence as his fortunes grew. Around 1532 he took legal action over the ownership of a gold chain, which he had pledged to Anthony Vyvoll, a merchant of Genoa, undoubtedly in exchange for imported goods.[134] In February 1539 he pledged to marry Alice, daughter of John Densell, serjeant-at-law, a match

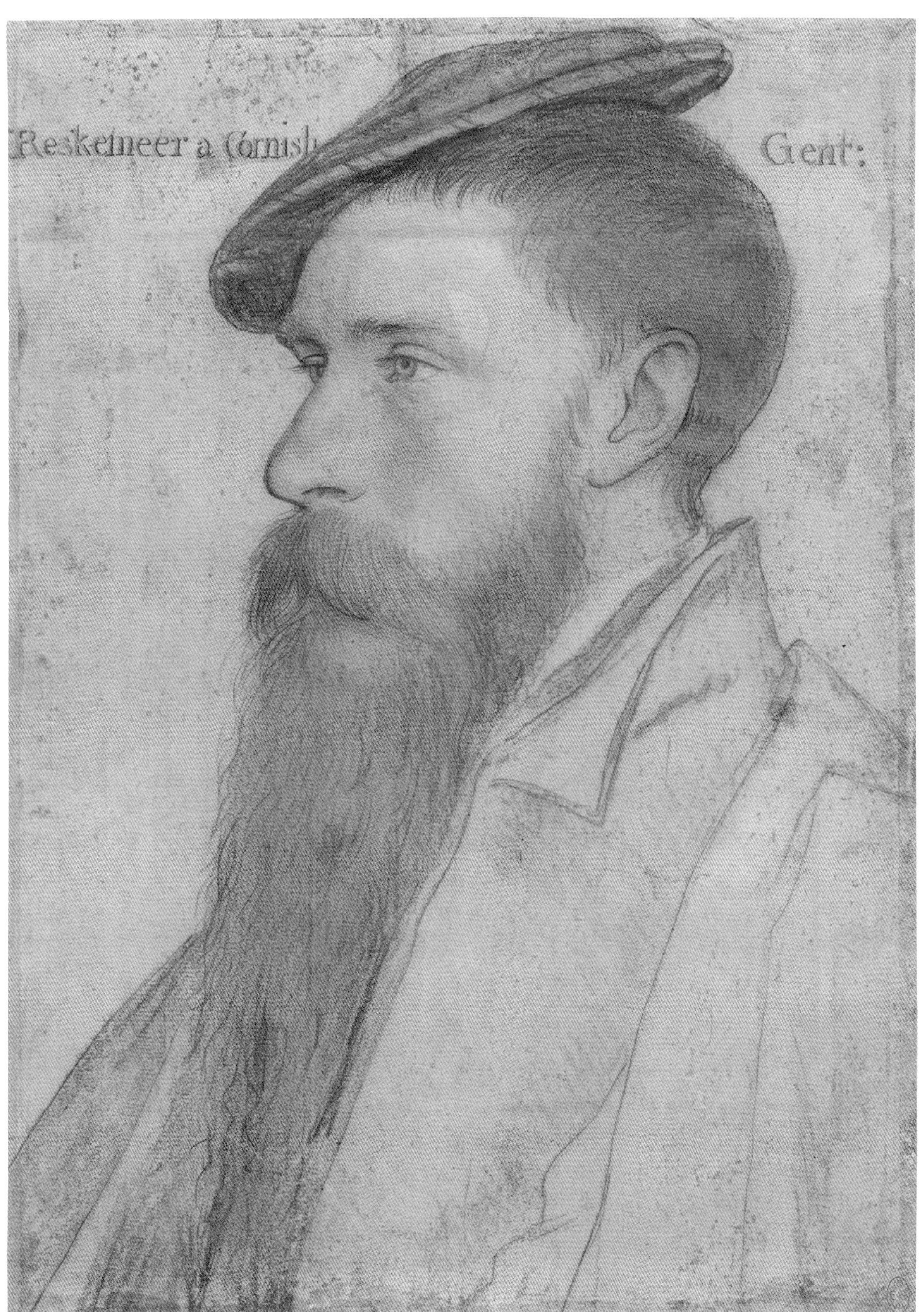
Reskemeer a Cornish
Gent:

that brought him lands and rights over tin mines in Cornwall.[135] The couple had four daughters who survived into adulthood.[136]

The portrait has traditionally been dated to *c.*1532–4 due to the vine leaves that appear in the background of the painting, which are also found on a number of Holbein's paintings in the late 1520s and early 1530s.[137] But on the basis of Reskimer's biography, a date in the mid- to late 1530s, as commissions for Holbein portraits increased among courtiers, seems more likely. At this time, Reskimer's own prosperity was growing and it might be expected that he sought to mark his success with a portrait by the favoured Holbein.

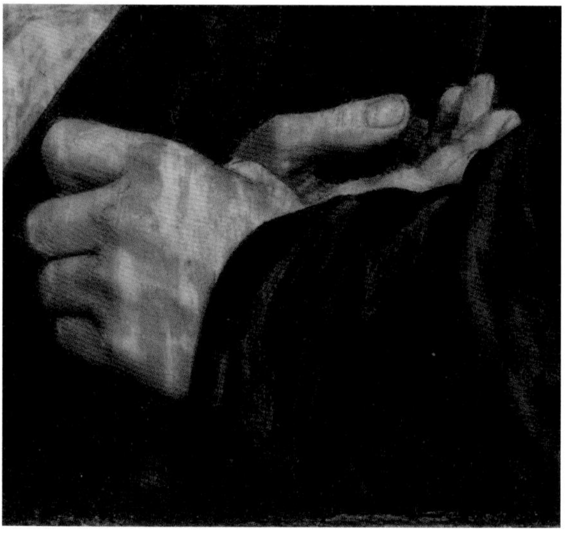

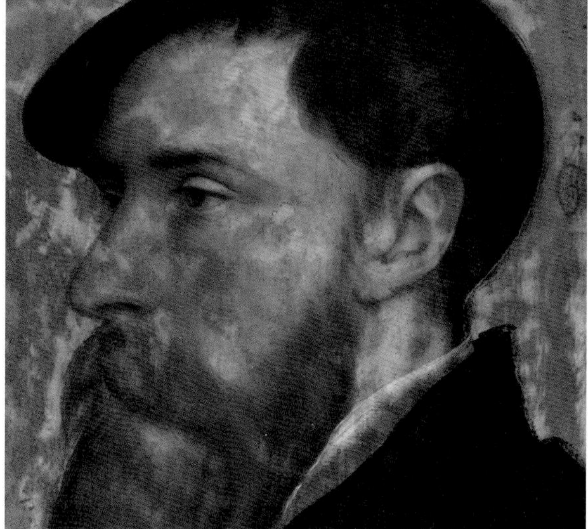

Fig. 49 **Hans Holbein, *William Reskimer*, details of infrared photograph**

William Reskimer
*c.*1536–9
Oil on panel
46.0 × 33.5 cm
RCIN 404422

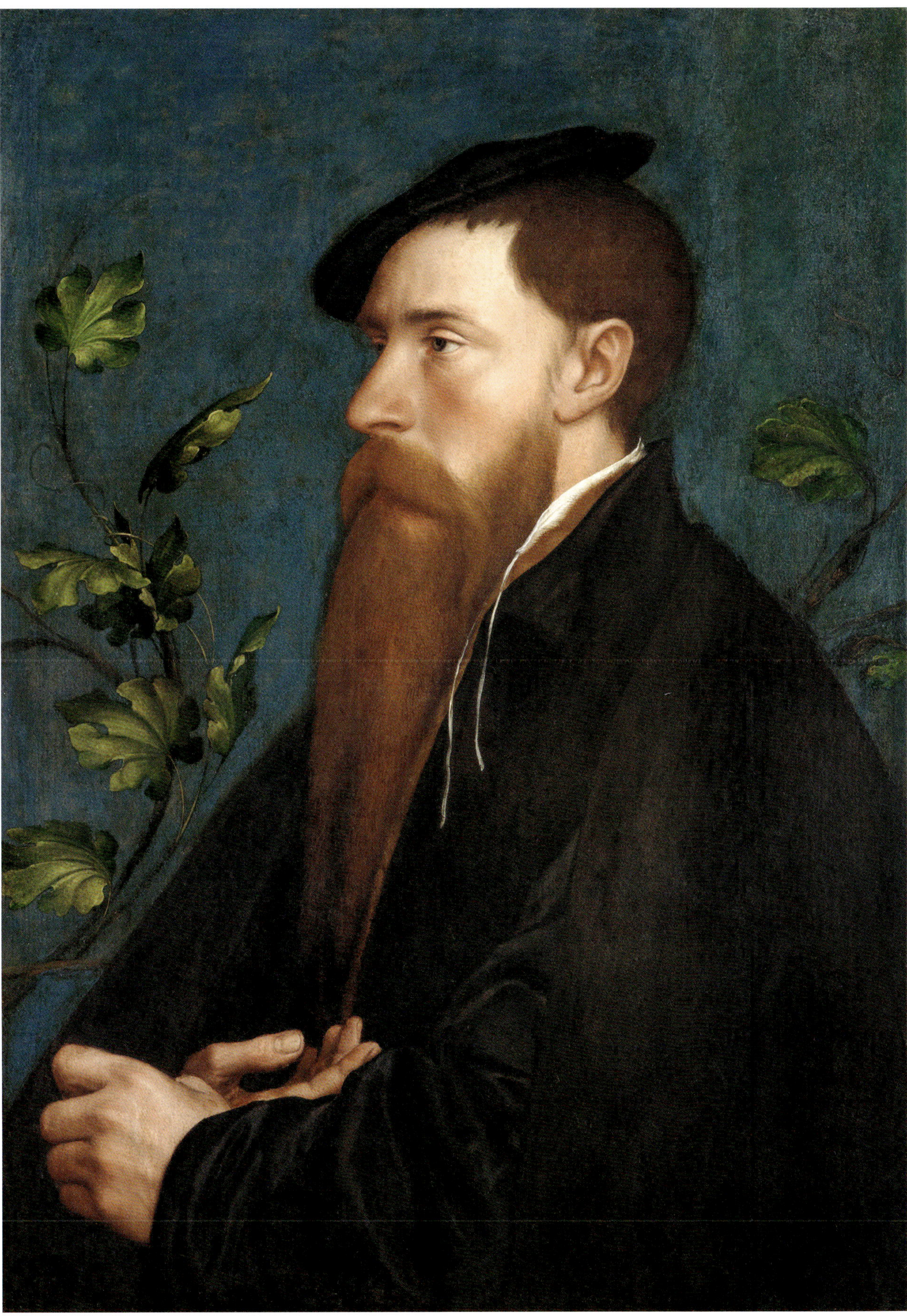

Princess Mary (1516–58)
1537–43
Black and coloured chalks with black ink and blue watercolour on pink prepared paper
38.6 × 29.1 cm
RCIN 912220

The identity of this sitter has been questioned, but there seems little reason to doubt it shows Princess Mary, the future Mary I. She would have been well known to Sir John Cheke, the probable source of the identification inscribed on the drawing.[138] The princess was the only child of Henry VIII and Katherine of Aragon to survive into adulthood.[139] From 1518, she was offered by her father to a series of prospective husbands as a means of cementing foreign alliances; during one such negotiation she was described as 'admirable by reason of her great and uncommon mental endowments', and she received a wide-ranging education, learning Latin and reading works by Erasmus and Sir Thomas More.[140] From the mid-1520s, the king's affection for Anne Boleyn alienated her from her father, and from 1531 she was forcibly separated from her mother. After the birth of her half-sister in 1533, Mary was stripped of much of her status and exiled to Hatfield House in Hertfordshire, and she was declared illegitimate by the 1534 Act of Succession. She returned to her father's favour after Anne's execution, and was godmother to Prince Edward, the son born to Henry and Jane Seymour in 1537. She was particularly close to her father's last wife, Katherine Parr, who had been one of her ladies-in-waiting before marrying the king. Her father's will restored her to her place in the succession after Edward. From her brother's accession, Mary, who remained a Catholic, became the focus for opposition to reform. Despite attempts to prevent her accession, she was proclaimed queen after Edward's death in 1553, and ruled until her death in 1558.

The drawing must date from after Mary's return to favour in 1537. In that year, she paid Hans of Antwerp, Holbein's acquaintance, for unspecified 'goldsmythe's workes', but it is not possible to tell whether she was the moving force behind Holbein's portrait or if the commission came from another source.[141] It is badly rubbed and has lost much of its chalk modelling, but it is nonetheless possible to make out the sitter's blue eyes, the yellow of her pendant and the chain onto which her pearls are strung, and the shading on her hood. No resulting painting or miniature is known.[142]

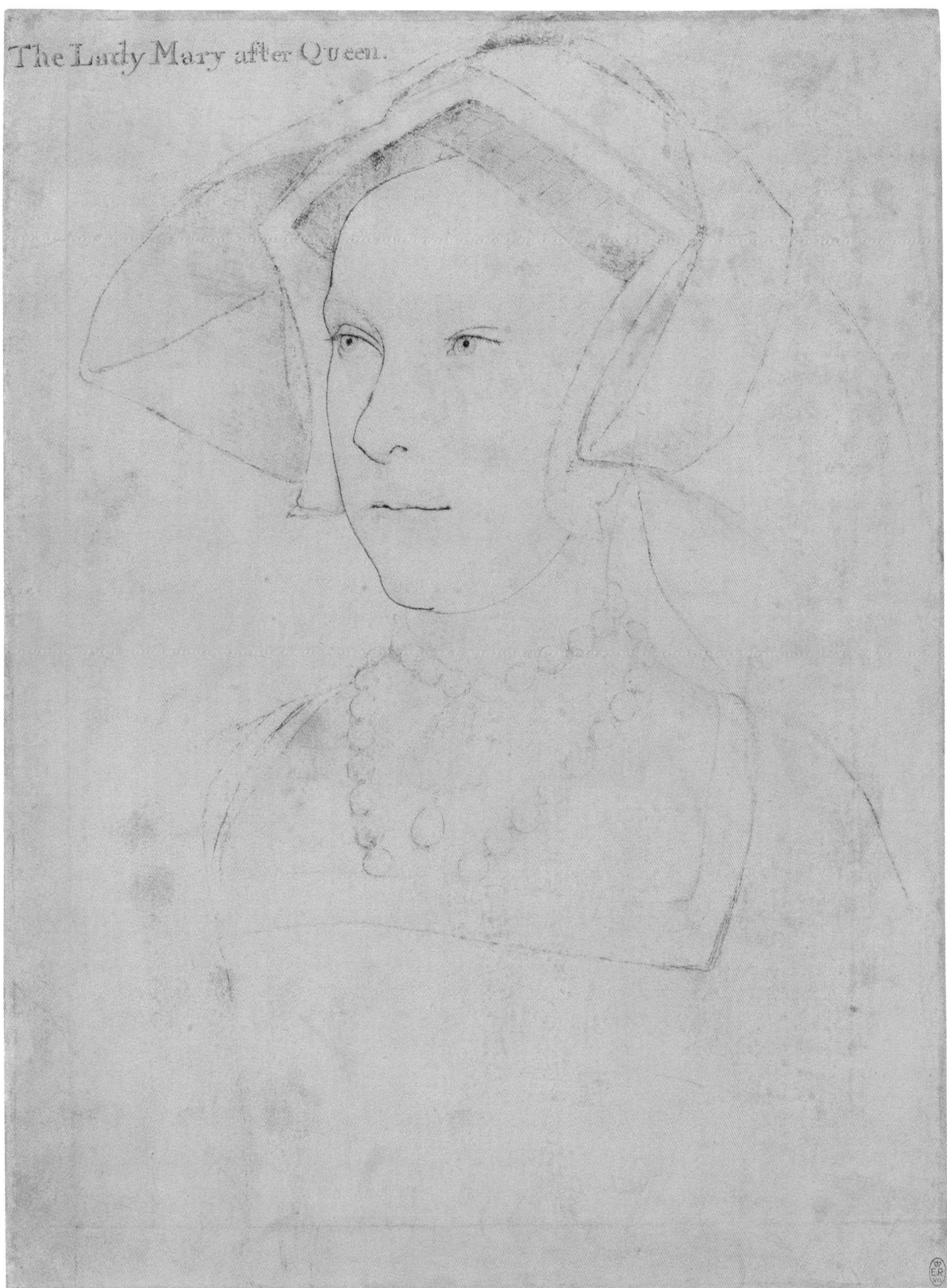
The Lady Mary after Queen.

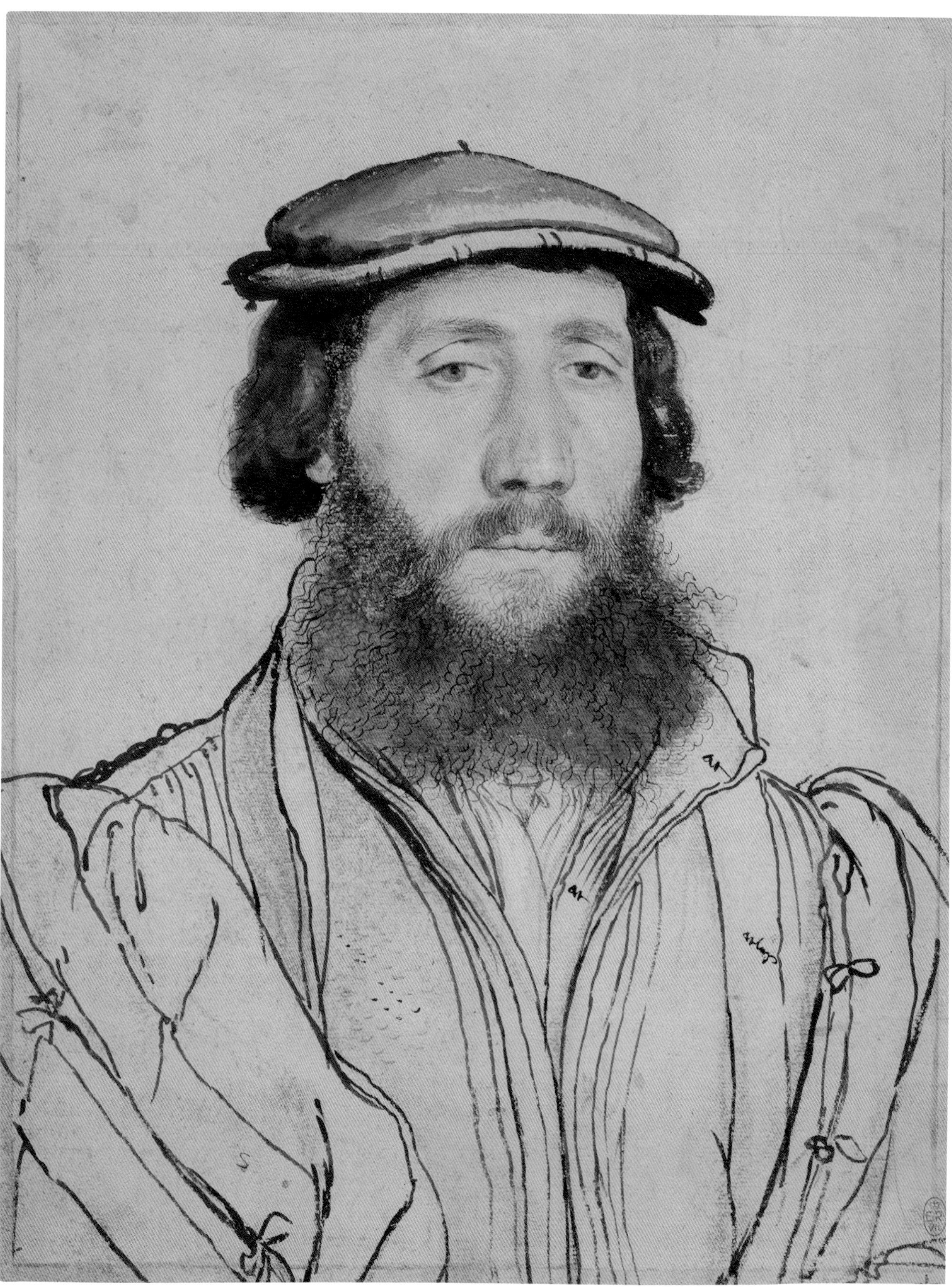

Unidentified man

*c.*1537
Black inks over black and coloured chalks with white heightening on pink prepared paper
27.2 × 21.0 cm
RCIN 912258

The sitter in this striking drawing has not been identified, although many possibilities have been suggested, from Charles Brandon, Duke of Suffolk (*c.*1484–1545), to Jean de Dinteville (1504–55), the French ambassador who was painted by Holbein in 1533 (see Fig. 17).[143] None of the suggestions so far offered is convincing. The drawing probably dates from around 1537, since it is on the same type of paper as that used by Holbein for William Fitzwilliam, Earl of Southampton, and James Butler, later Earl of Ormond (p. 114).

Holbein started this drawing, as usual, in black chalk, but worked it up heavily in two dilutions of ink, one deep black, the other grey. The grey was used first, and the black added afterwards to refine the composition, enlarging the puff of the sitter's left shoulder, defining the outline of his collar and extending his facial hair. The second ink was employed to note the satin ('atlass' or 'at') of the sitter's jacket.[144] Although the drawing is dominated by the ink lines, the delicate treatment of the sitter's face is equally notable, with red and black chalks used alongside voids and white heightening to model the nose, and red and brown chalk suggesting the sitter's tired eyes.

No painting after this drawing is known today, but a print by Wenceslaus Hollar suggests that the finished portrait was in a roundel, like the painting of the man holding a carnation now in the Städel Museum (see Fig. 51).[145] At this time the painting was in the collection of Thomas Howard, Earl of Arundel, and may be one of the two portraits of a man in a black cap listed in the earl's inventory.[146] If so, the sitter's identity was already lost.

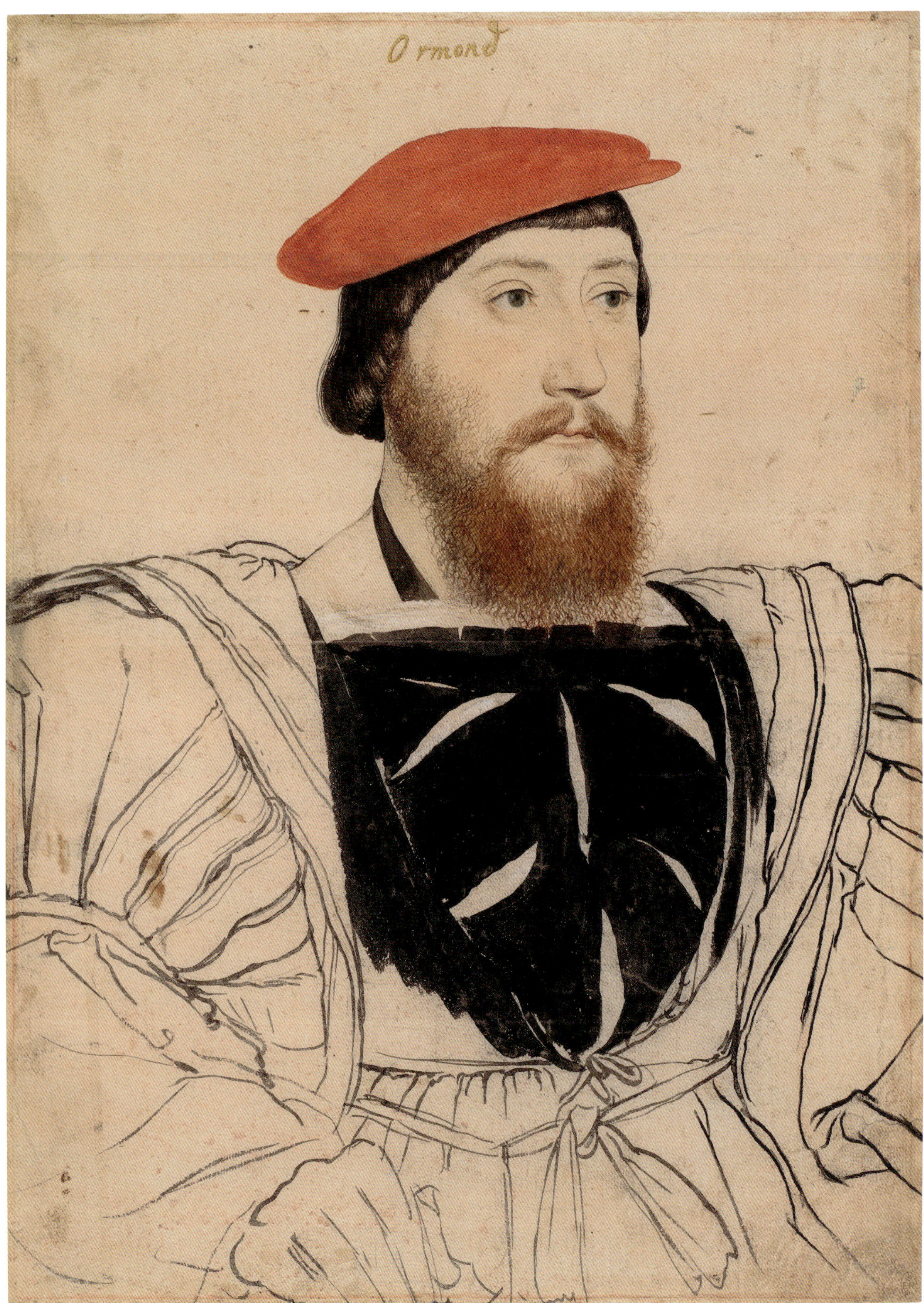
Ormond

James Butler,
later 9th Earl of Ormond (*c.*1496–1546)
1537–8
Black and coloured chalks with black ink, red and blue watercolour and white heightening on pink prepared paper
40.1 × 29.2 cm
RCIN 912263

Although once identified as Sir Thomas Boleyn (1476/7–1539), father of Anne Boleyn, the sitter in this drawing is now agreed, on the basis of age, to be James Butler, who became Earl of Ormond on his father's death in 1539.[147] This drawing must date from either the period August 1537 to early 1538, or July 1543 when Butler, normally resident in Ireland, was in England. The earlier date seems more likely on the grounds of the outfit Butler wears, which has been compared to that worn by Henry VIII in the Whitehall mural (see Fig. 22).[148] Butler, who had fought at Thérouanne in 1513 and spent time in the household of Cardinal Wolsey, was judged 'valiant and active' by the cardinal in 1528.[149] He was considered as a possible husband for Anne Boleyn, but the match did not proceed. In 1532, known to be loyal to the king, he was appointed Lord Treasurer of Ireland. He died (probably accidentally) by poisoning in October 1546.

Holbein has used extensive ink and watercolour to show the magnificence of Butler's dress, with chalk concentrated around the face in an approach similar to that employed for William Parr, Marquess of Northampton (p. 127), and the unidentified man with a beard (p. 112). The latter drawing is on the same paper that Holbein has used here, suggesting they are close in date, and both have the doublet sketched out in a greyish ink then reinforced and worked up in a darker black ink. It has been proposed that this drawing was originally intended to be fully painted in colours like the portrait of John Godsalve (p. 138), but considering the very summary treatment of the hands, this seems unlikely. Black watercolour may simply have been quicker than black chalk to record the expanse of the sitter's slashed doublet, and red watercolour more appropriate to catch the vibrant scarlet of the sitter's hat.

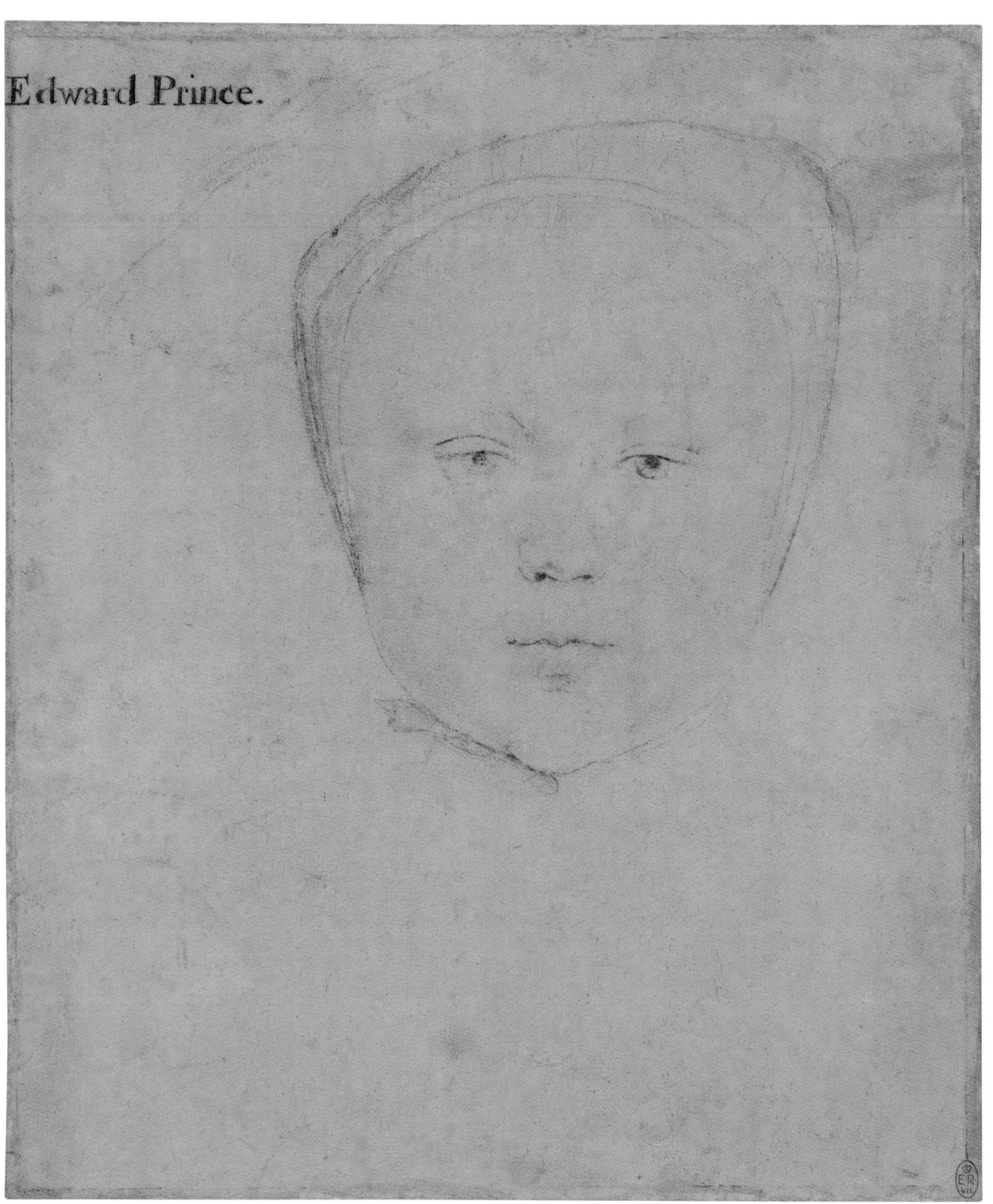
Edward Prince.

Prince Edward (1537–53)

1538
Black and red chalks with blue watercolour and black ink on pink prepared paper
26.4 × 22.4 cm
RCIN 912200

On New Year's Day 1539, Holbein presented Henry VIII with a portrait of the one-year-old Prince Edward, the king's longed-for son. This is now in Washington DC, and shows the prince three-quarter length, holding a rattle, set against a blue ground which has discoloured to brown (Fig. 50). Beneath, verses by Richard Morison are inscribed on a fictive parchment sheet.[150] The current drawing was made as part of the preparation for the portrait.[151] The surface has been greatly rubbed, but it is clear that it was always slightly drawn: it has been suggested the young prince would not have sat still long enough to take a more detailed portrait.[152] As with the portrait of Sir Henry Guildford (p. 52), Holbein has thinned the child's face in the finished portrait, making him appear more mature, in keeping with the verses, which celebrate Edward as his father's heir.[153]

Prince Edward was born to Henry VIII and Jane Seymour in October 1537. He succeeded his father as Edward VI in 1547. He owned the book of Holbein drawings that included this depiction of his younger self and of his mother (p. 105).[154] It seems that he looked through, and was curious about, the drawings since names of the sitters were added to the volume by his tutor, Sir John Cheke, presumably for his instruction. Certainly, on 12 November 1549, it was recorded that Edward, then king, had 'taken' the book of Holbein drawings from the study where they were stored.[155]

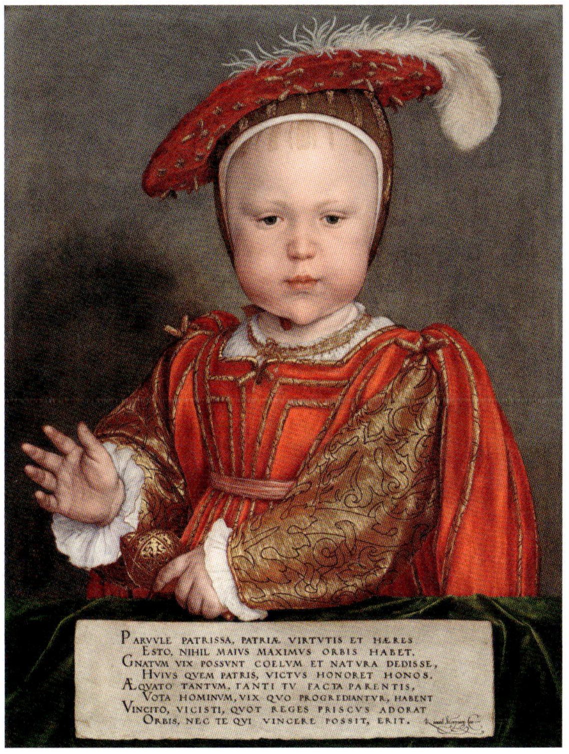

Fig. 50 **Hans Holbein, *Edward, Prince of Wales*, 1538, oil on panel**
National Gallery of Art, Washington DC, 1937.1.64

The Lady Audley.

Elizabeth, Lady Audley (d. 1557)
*c.*1538
Black and coloured chalks with black ink and blue watercolour on pink prepared paper
29.3 × 20.8 cm
RCIN 912191

Elizabeth, Lady Audley
*c.*1538
Watercolour on vellum laid on playing card
5.6 cm (diameter)
RCIN 422292

Elizabeth, Lady Audley, married Thomas, Baron Audley of Walden, as his second wife in April 1538.[156] He was a senior courtier and Sir Thomas More's successor as Chancellor; she was the daughter of Thomas Grey, Marquess of Dorset. In December 1539 Audley explained that he had married at the king's request, 'but yet I repent never a whytt my mareage, but have gret cause to thanke the kynges majeste for enducyng me to it; ffir assuredly I have happened of oone moche to my contentacion and honeste'.[157] Elizabeth Audley's mother had also sat to Holbein and it is possible that the commission for Elizabeth's portrait came from the Grey family rather than from Audley. It may even pre-date her marriage.

Both Holbein's drawing and his finished portrait of Lady Audley, a miniature (see right), are in the Royal Collection, the miniature probably acquired by Charles II. Holbein was largely focused on the sitter's face when making the drawing, using only brief annotations, drawn and written, to indicate important aspects of her outfit such as the form of her jewels, and the colour of her gown, which is noted as being of velvet and red damask ('samet / rot damast'). The proper left eye has caused the artist some trouble and a number of lines have been used to set the position of the iris. It has been suggested that the very slight black chalk sketch of a female bust at top right is a study for a classicising architectural detail, perhaps for a lost portrait after this work.[158]

The ink lines that delineate the sitter's features in the drawing, notably the shape of her nose, are replicated in the miniature, at a tiny scale. The details of the dress are minutely painted to convey the texture of the woven and embroidered fabrics that she wears. A few details appear differently, notably the brooch pinned to Lady Audley's breast, which takes a simpler form.[159] This may be an aesthetic choice, since the smaller-scale brooch shown in the miniature, while still magnificent, is in harmony with the red velvet of the bodice and does not distract from Lady Audley's face.

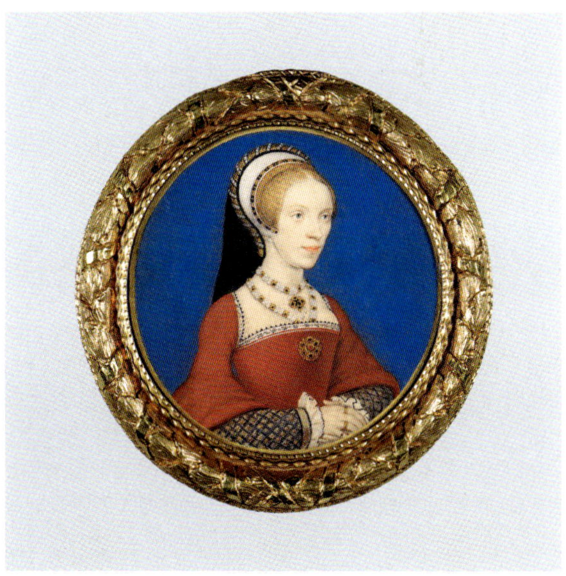

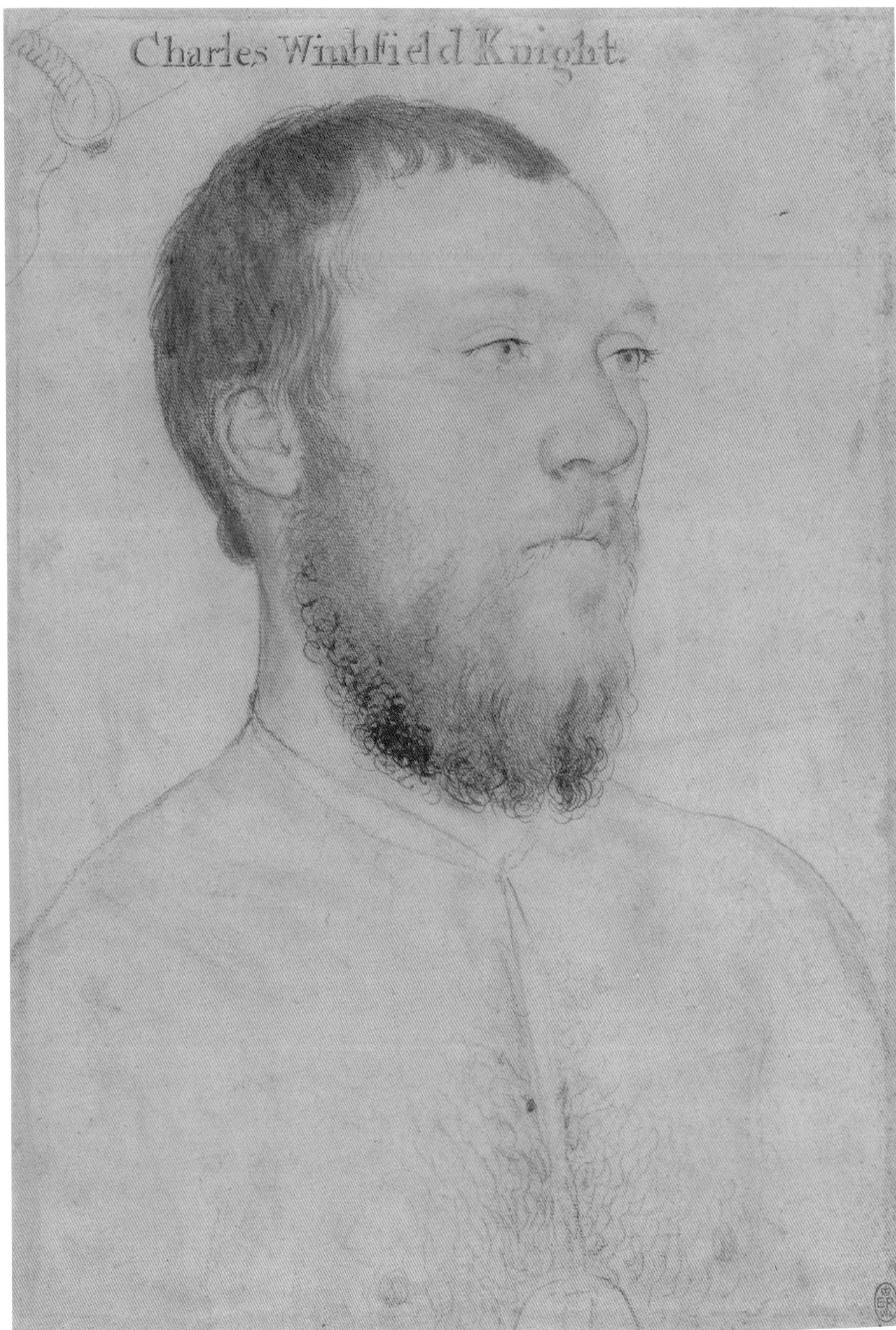
Charles Winhfield Knight.

Charles Wingfield (1513–40)
c.1538–9
Black and coloured chalks with black and brown ink on pink prepared paper
28.6 × 19.8 cm
RCIN 912249

This drawing raises more questions than it provides answers. The sitter is traditionally identified, following the annotation, as Charles Wingfield, the son of Sir Richard Wingfield, a prominent ambassador to the Habsburg court.[160] But little is known about Charles, who is not believed to have been knighted. The Wingfields were a large family and it is possible that another member is depicted here.

Equally perplexingly, the sitter is shown bare-chested, wearing a medallion around his neck and, unusually, appears without headgear. A brief sketch at top left of the sheet seems to show a bracelet through which is threaded a ring set with a single stone. Although the drawing of Wingfield's body is slight, Holbein has nonetheless taken the time and effort to draw the details of the torso, and it is possible that these were to be reflected in the final portrait. The context of the depiction is not known, but may commemorate an achievement on the sitter's part, perhaps a victory at some form of entertainment or competition. Again, no such achievement of Charles Wingfield's is recorded, although a 'Mr Jno [John] Wingfield', probably Charles's cousin, was among those who participated in the Westminster Tournament of June 1540.[161] The drawing is on the same paper as that used by Holbein for the portrait of Lord Cobham (p. 123); while the date of neither is certain, the late 1530s seems likely. If this is Charles Wingfield, he would therefore be shown around the age of 25.

No portrait after this drawing is known. A copy in the Boijmans Van Beuningen Museum, Rotterdam, was probably once in the collection of Lady Elizabeth Germain.[162] An early inscription on the verso of the Rotterdam sheet – 'Charles Winkfield Knight' – suggests that 'Winhfield' on the Royal Collection drawing is a misreading of the original inscription. A portrait of 'Charles Wingfield Knight' was included among the pictures in the collection of the artist Benjamin van der Gucht, sold in 1796, but this was accompanied by a coloured chalk drawing of Katherine, Duchess of Suffolk, and is more likely to be the drawing now in Rotterdam than a painting.[163]

George Brooke,
9th Baron Cobham (*c.*1497–1558)
*c.*1538–9
Black and coloured chalks with a touch of black ink on pink prepared paper
28.9 × 20.3 cm
RCIN 912195

Holbein's drawing shows George Brooke, 9th Baron Cobham, dressed in an open shirt, perhaps with a fur thrown over his shoulders, his clothing indicated with a handful of strokes. This is probably as he appeared before Holbein for his sitting. Although the drawing initially seems simple in execution, Holbein has taken great pains over the modelling of Cobham's face, using black and red chalks to delineate his high cheekbones and the curve of his eye sockets. The soft velvet of the hat is suggested by a softening of the chalk: to do this, Holbein may have worked it with a damp brush. The drawing is on the same paper as that used by Holbein for his drawing of Charles Wingfield (p. 120).

George Brooke succeeded his father as Baron Cobham in 1529.[164] A prominent landowner, he pursued a military career in France and Scotland. From June 1544 he was Deputy of Calais, where he oversaw the provisioning of the garrison, gathered information from travellers and spies, and engaged in courteous negotiations with French diplomats. A month after he took up his position, Henry VIII laid siege to Boulogne and for the next two years Cobham played a key role in the English military campaign. He was a committed Protestant: in October 1538 he wrote with apparent glee to his brother-in-law Thomas Wyatt, then on a diplomatic mission in Spain, that 'I trust that there shall be never oone frere [friar] lefte in Englonde before yor commyng home agayne', while in 1543 he and Edward Fiennes, Lord Clinton (another of Holbein's sitters), were brought before the Privy Council accused of eating meat during Lent. Both men were in good enough standing to be 'wyth a good leasson dismissed' rather than punished.[165]

Cobham appears with frequency in government papers of the 1540s and 1550s, and amid the official correspondence there are glimpses of his character and interests. In 1541 William Paget, Clerk of the Privy Council, reported overhearing a council debate about Thomas Fiennes, Baron Dacre, who was accused of treason 'notwithstanding two doores shut betwene us' (it is hard to escape the image of Paget crouched at the intervening keyhole). The discussion was heated and Paget recounted that 'among the rest that could not agre to wilful murder, the lord of Cobham, as I tooke hym by his voyce, was very vehement and stiff'.[166]

But if Cobham could be 'vehement' in debate and brave on the battlefield (as Edward Seymour, Earl of Hertford, noted of his service in Scotland), there are indications of a lighter side to his character. He sponsored a troupe of players and in 1545 purchased silver bowls and candlesticks from the merchant Stephen Vaughan in Antwerp. Although these do not survive, the candlesticks were attractive enough that Paget was urged to follow the same design some months later when ordering his own set. Cobham seems to have had a particular interest in Italy: two of his sons travelled there to study, and he chose the London-based

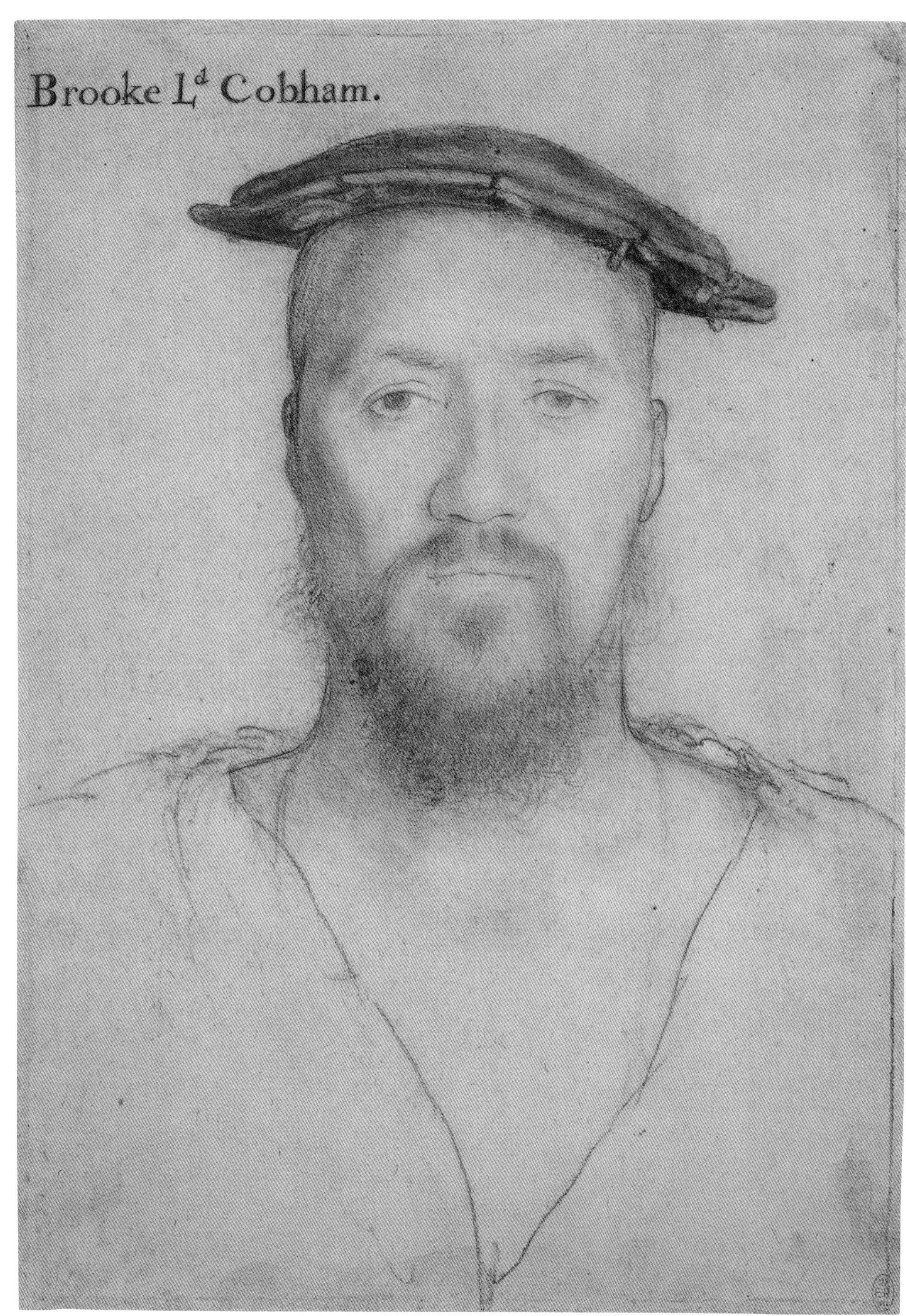
Brooke Ld Cobham.

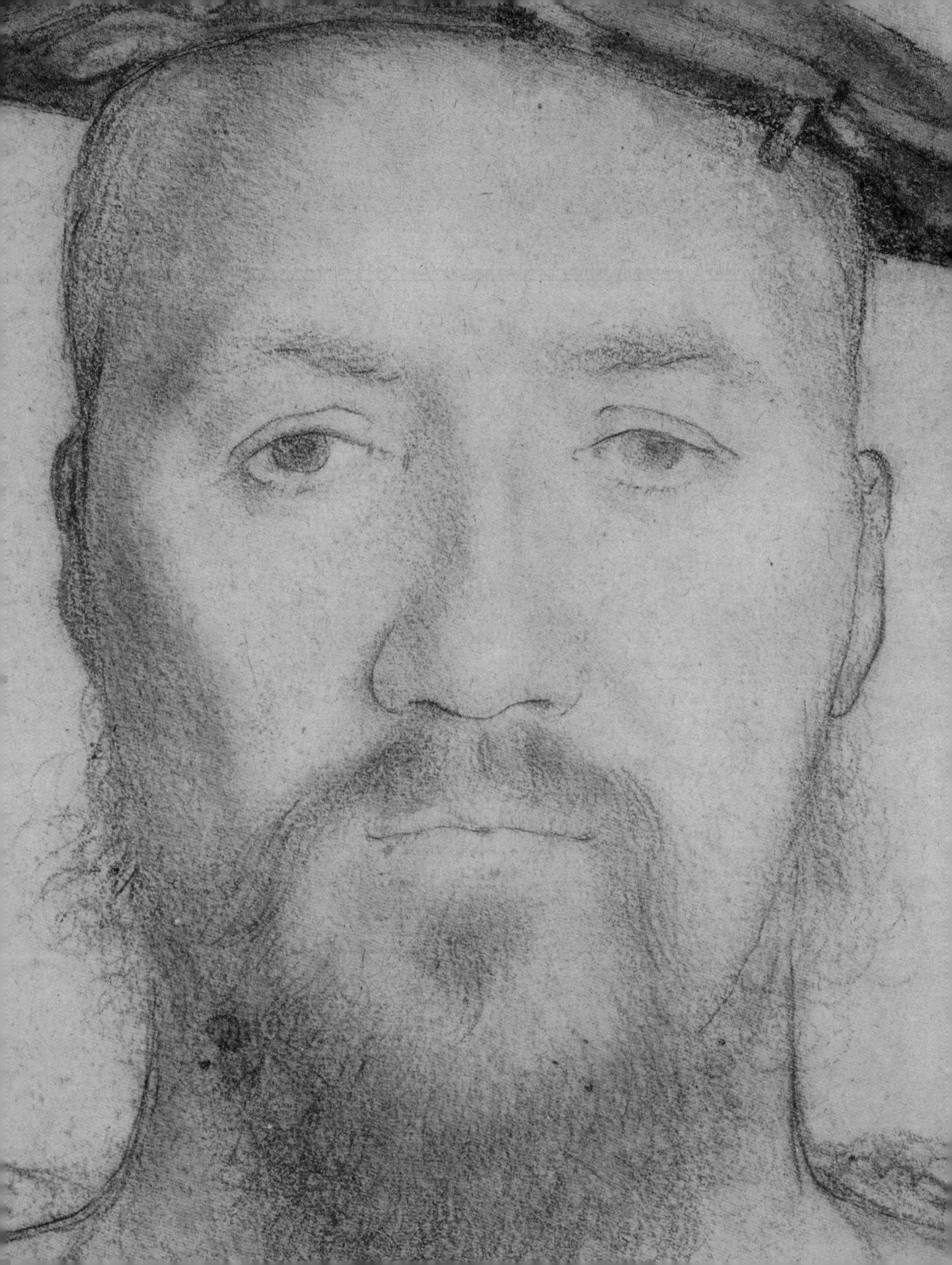

Italian merchant Benedict Spinola as one of the executors of his will.[167] While in Calais, he acted as a conduit for Italians seeking employment in London, earning him a rebuke from Paget who wrote in frustration in June 1545:

> I have receyved your lordships letters written in the commendation of John Baptista de Beni da Gobio, and marvail nott a litl, forasmuch as you have ben the occasion of the coming hither of so many as allready coom over wyth the whiche we are here all weryed (wearied), [that] you mean to contynew the sending of them dayly over, which we woll nott faile hereafter to sende as faste backe to you agayne. And towching this man for whome you have written unto me … Iff you can fynde any place for him there, in the name of godde do as you shall thinke goode, whome as you have sent … by your letters hither I have thowght to retourne wythe my letters from where he came accordingly.[168]

On Cobham's death in 1558 he left his insignia of the Order of the Garter and other gold chains (perhaps including the one he wears in Holbein's drawing), along with a vast portfolio of lands, to his oldest son, William.

Although a painting of Cobham by Holbein is not known to survive, a later copy showing him in a white undershirt and black jacket is in a private collection.[169] This was probably commissioned while his son William was baron and is a roundel, which may reflect the format of the original. Numerous 'picktures' were recorded hanging in the 'old gallerye' at Cobham Hall in Kent when it was in the ownership of Henry Brooke, Cobham's grandson, but these are not itemised and it is impossible to tell whether a portrait by Holbein was among them.[170]

William Parr,
later Marquess of Northampton (1513–71)
1538–9
Black and coloured chalks with black ink and white heightening on pink prepared paper
31.7 × 21.1 cm
RCIN 912231

Described by the sixteenth-century antiquary William Camden as 'a man much conversant and well read in delectable studies of Musicke, and intertainment of Lovers, and other courtly jucundities', William Parr was educated with Henry Fitzroy, illegitimate son of Henry VIII (Fig. 21).[171] His older sister Katherine became Henry VIII's sixth and final queen in July 1543; writing to inform her brother of her forthcoming marriage, she asked him to 'let her sometimes hear of his health as friendly as if she had not been called to this honor'.[172] His knighting in 1538 or his creation as Baron Parr in 1539 may have been the occasion for the commissioning of this portrait. He was made Marquess of Northampton in 1547. Parr's accounts reveal a man who dined from plate provided by the royal goldsmith, who enjoyed playing cards and tennis (he had his own court) and kept a troupe of players.[173] He owned 'a payer of regalles wt virgenalles' (both keyboard instruments) and was a patron of the Bassano family, musicians from Venice who immigrated to England: in September 1542, John Godsalve (p. 138) prepared a passport for 'Casper Bassione, musician, his horse and xvli in redye money', which he handed to Parr as Bassano's patron.[174]

Starting with a brief sketch in black chalk, Holbein has worked up this drawing in black ink, which he has used to record the outlines of the face, dress and hat, annotations of colour and fabric, and the details of Parr's hat badge or medallion and aiglets.[175] Black ink diluted as wash and brown and red chalks are used to add colour to the face and tiny touches of white enliven the sitter's eyes. Parr's clothing must have been magnificent, with white and purple velvet and white satin alongside the fur and gold jewellery. The hat badge appears to show a figure holding a sword aloft. The word 'MORS' on one of the jewellery studies has been interpreted as a memento mori, but may alternatively refer to Parr's motto, *Amour Avecque Loiaulte* ('Love with Loyalty'), which is found on his stall plate as Knight of the Garter.[176] The purpose of the scale drawn at the left-hand edge has not been understood.

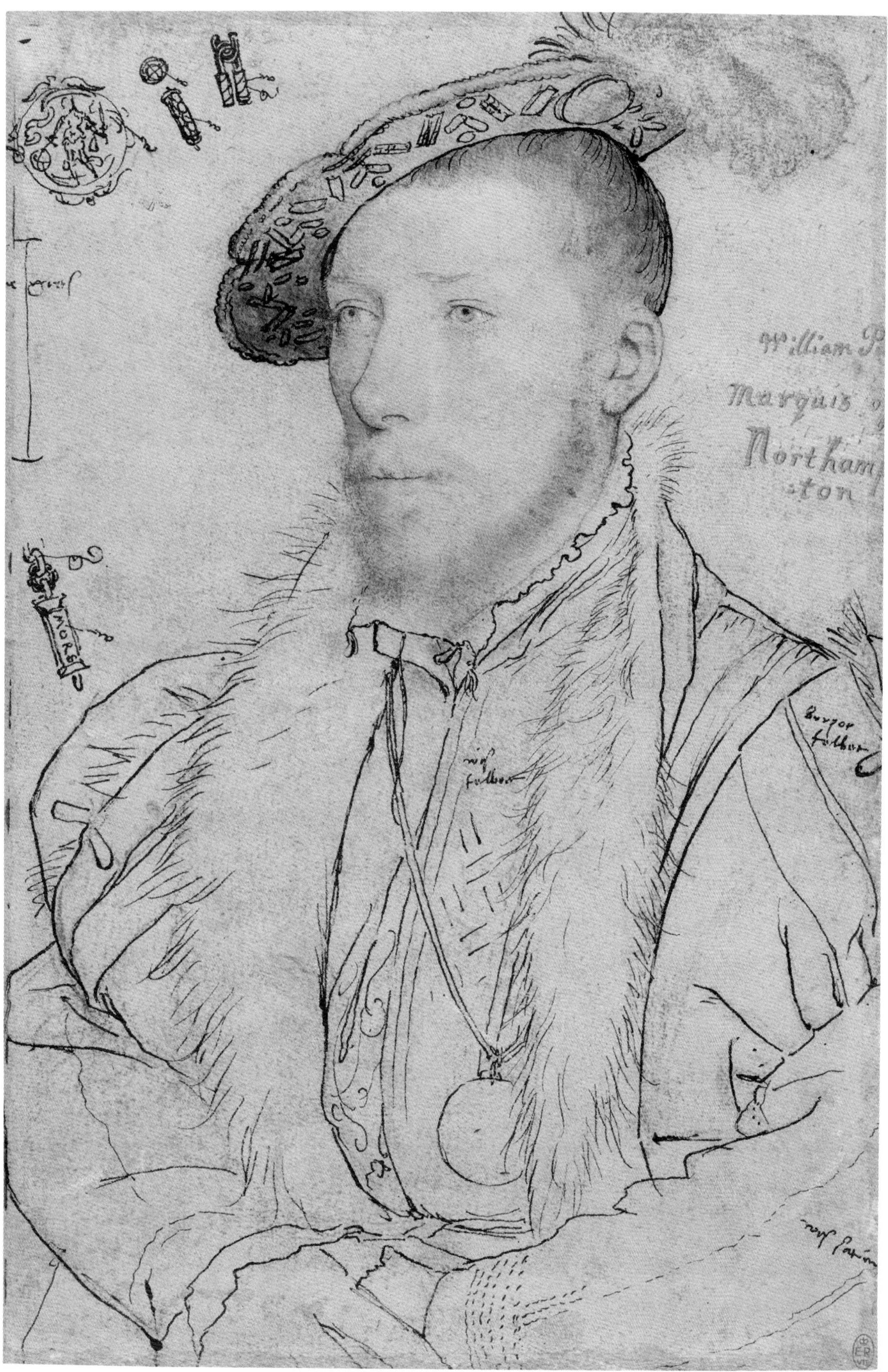
William P
Marquis o
Northamp
ton
MORS

Thomas Howard,
3rd Duke of Norfolk (1473–1554)
*c.*1539
Oil on panel
80.1 × 61.4 cm
RCIN 404439

Thomas Howard, Duke of Norfolk, was thus described by Mario Savorgnano, the Venetian ambassador, in November 1531: 'every employment devolves to him. He is prudent, liberal, affable and astute, associates with everybody, has very great experience in political government, discusses the affairs of the world admirably, aspires to greater elevation, and bears ill-will to foreigners, especially to our Venetian nation. He is 58 years old; small and spare in person, and his hair is black'.[177] After distinguished military service in Scotland, Norfolk became a prominent courtier, working to facilitate Henry VIII's divorce from Katherine of Aragon in favour of Norfolk's niece, Anne Boleyn. Made Earl Marshal in 1533, Norfolk presided over the trial in 1536 that led to Anne Boleyn's execution. In 1540 he advanced the claims of another niece, Katherine Howard, upon the king's affections. Her fall and execution in 1542 threatened Norfolk's influence, but he was able to ride out the storm and served as one of the senior military commanders during the French campaign of 1544.

Norfolk's position was precarious as he remained a religious conservative, at odds with reforming courtiers such as Thomas Cromwell and the Seymours. By 1546 the Seymours were in the ascendant and Norfolk and his son Henry Howard, Earl of Surrey, were committed to the Tower. Surrey was executed and Norfolk escaped only because of Henry VIII's death on 28 January 1547. He was released from captivity in 1553 and died in 1554.

Holbein shows Norfolk with the white baton of the Lord Treasurer (a post he had held since 1522) and the gold baton of the Earl Marshal.[178] He wears the collar of the Order of the Garter, probably that described in an inventory of 1546 as 'a Coller of thorder of saincte George hauing liiij Garthers and knottes wherunto was depending a George set wt diamondes and oon Rubye'.[179] That these were potent symbols is illustrated by the report of François van der Delft, Charles V's ambassador, that on the duke's arrest in 1546, the stripping of his staff of office and Garter collar was taken as proof that there was no hope for his reprieve.[180] Holbein has excelled in the depiction of the textures of the duke's clothing, from the black velvet gown lined with lynx fur to his red satin doublet.[181] Unusually for Holbein's sitters, the duke does not wear any rings and his hat is bare of aiglets or badges.

Holbein's portrait of the duke may have hung at one of his residences. A number of paintings were listed in the Long Gallery at Kenninghall in 1547. This picture is unlikely to have been among them, however, as the portraits in this space were described as 'demonstrating' the 'vizyanamies of sundry estates being in dyuers countries', suggesting they were a series depicting supposed national 'types'.[182] It has been suggested that this portrait, or a contemporary copy, may have been the 'pictor' of the duke recorded on Norfolk's arrest as hanging in Mendham, the home of his mistress Elizabeth Holland.[183]

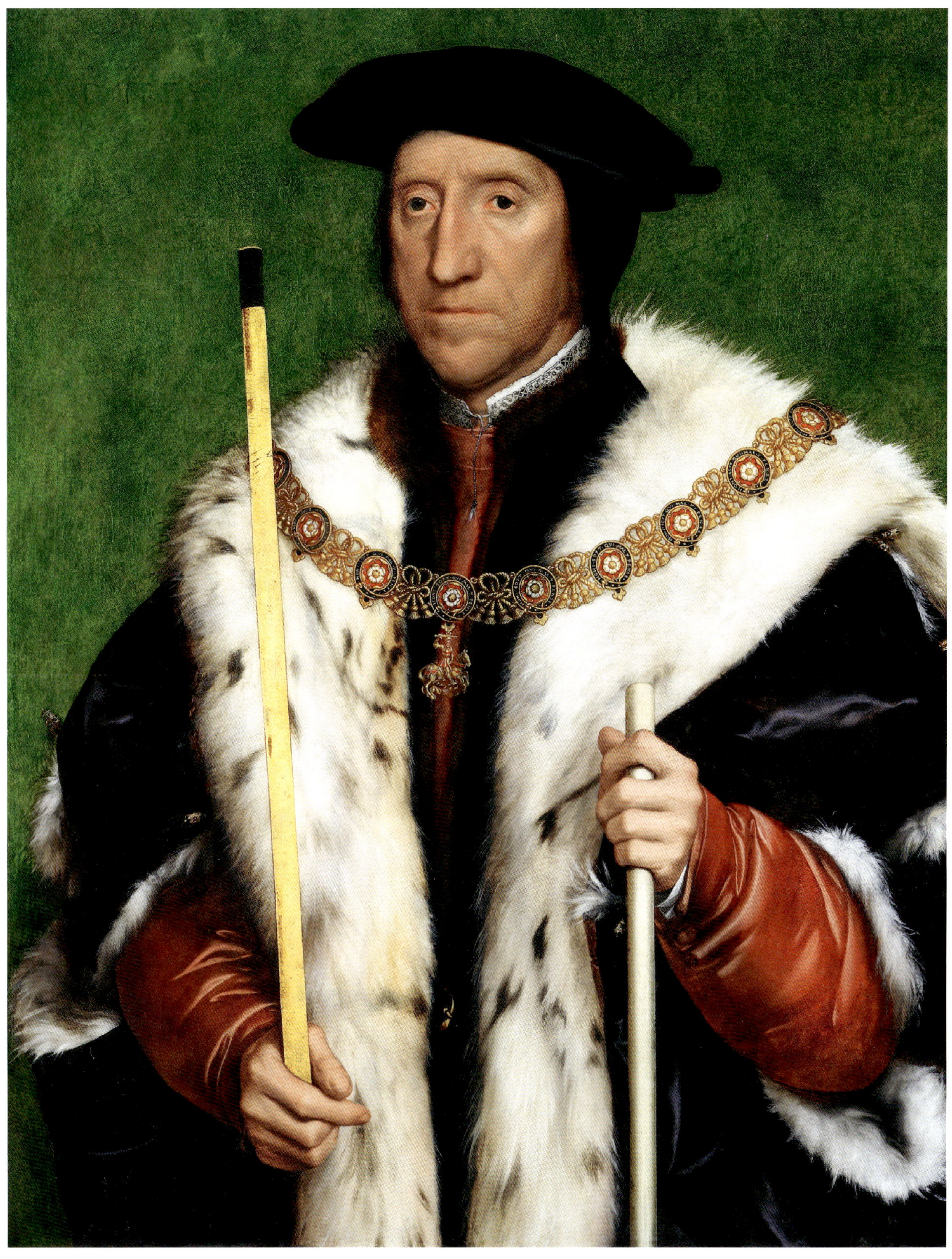

A woman, traditionally identified as Katherine Howard (*c.*1524–42)

*c.*1540
Watercolour on vellum laid on playing card (the four of diamonds)
6.3 cm (diameter)
RCIN 422293

The identity of the sitter in this miniature is the subject of much debate.[184] A second version of the miniature in the Buccleuch collection was described as showing Katherine Howard, Henry VIII's fifth queen, in a print of *c.*1740 by Jacobus Houbraken. The present miniature was first identified as showing Katherine Howard in around 1837, perhaps on the basis of the Houbraken print. More recent alternative suggestions include Mary, Lady Monteagle (1510–before 1544), daughter of the duke of Suffolk, Lady Margaret Douglas (1515–78), Henry VIII's niece, and Anne of Cleves (1515–57), Henry's fourth wife.[185]

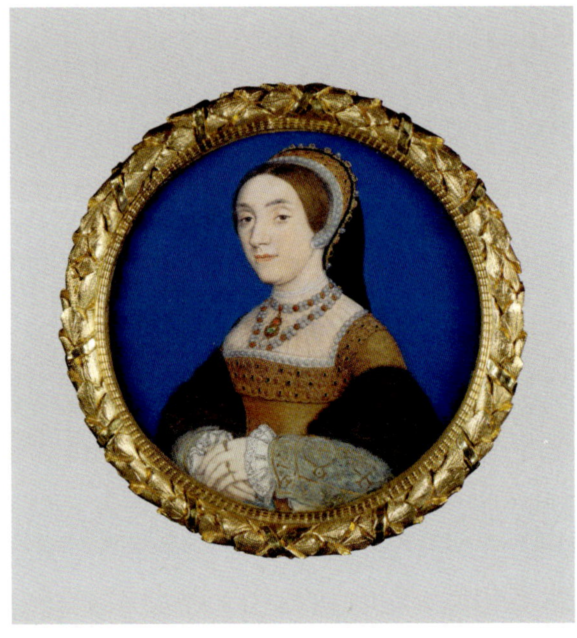

Comparison with known portraits of these three sitters is not convincing enough to make the identification and, since no confirmed portrait of Katherine Howard is known, the name of the woman depicted here must remain a mystery. Katherine, like Anne Boleyn a niece of the duke of Norfolk, married Henry VIII in July 1540 and was executed on 12 February 1542.

Much has been made of the jewels worn by the sitter. These have been identified with ones owned by Jane Seymour, Henry's third wife, and given to Katherine Howard, although Jane's jewels were passed on to other court ladies as well as Katherine.[186] A number of royal sitters are shown wearing similar pendants, among them Katherine Parr and Mary I. Perhaps more compelling is the fur of the sitter's sleeve, which it has been proposed is sable, the wearing of which was restricted to immediate members of the royal family after 1533.[187] This would add weight to the suggestion that the sitter is one of Henry's wives. The depiction of this fur and other aspects of the sitter's dress, in particular, is exquisite, demonstrating Holbein's ready mastery of the art of miniature painting to which he had apparently only recently been introduced.

Henry Brandon,
later 2nd Duke of Suffolk (1535–51)
1541
Watercolour on vellum laid on playing card
5.6 cm (diameter)
RCIN 422294

Charles Brandon,
later 3rd Duke of Suffolk (1537–51)
1541
Watercolour on vellum laid on playing card
(the ace of clubs)
5.5 cm (diameter)
RCIN 422295

These two miniatures were in the collection of Charles I and, although sold after his execution, were reacquired by Charles II, who displayed them in his closet at Whitehall Palace.[188] They show the two sons of Charles Brandon, Duke of Suffolk, and his fourth wife Katherine, whose drawing (overleaf) by Holbein may have been preparatory to a companion miniature. The two boys were educated with Henry VIII's son, later Edward VI. Henry Brandon inherited the dukedom of Suffolk from his father in 1545, and died of sweating sickness in 1551, half an hour before his brother Charles.

The two boys are shown half-length. The elder, Henry, leans his elbow on a table beside him, on which is inscribed his age – five – and the date, 6 September 1535. His birth date is generally thought to have been 16 or 18 September 1535, and it is unclear if the date on the miniature is a misunderstanding by Holbein.[189] The shimmering shot silk of his sleeves is particularly beautifully depicted.[190] It is probable that his bonnet was originally decorated all over with gold aiglets, only a few of which remain today.

His younger brother Charles, shown aged three, holds a piece of paper on which is inscribed the date 10 March – probably his date of birth – and year 1541, which is believed to be the year in which these miniatures were painted. His face is finely worked, and his grey jacket with red panels would have appeared even more luxurious, but has suffered small losses and retouching that have obscured the articulation of the fabric.

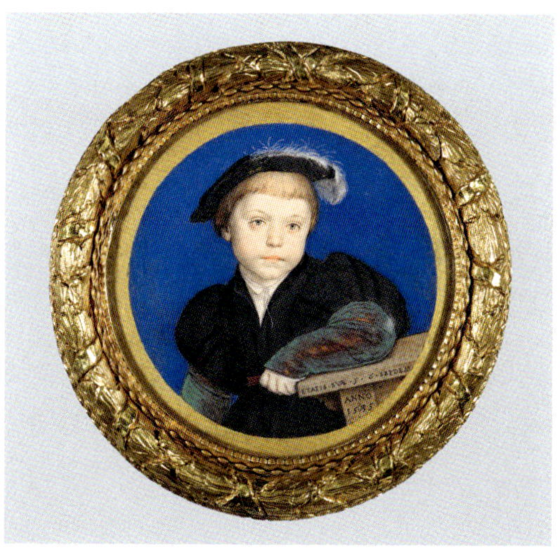

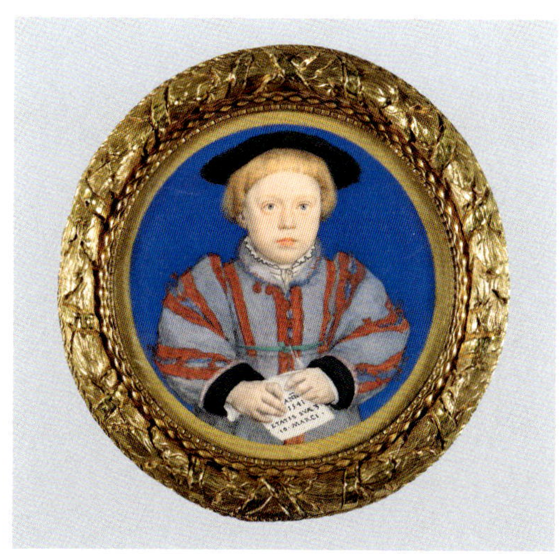

Katherine Brandon,
Duchess of Suffolk (1519–80)
1541?
Black and coloured chalks with black ink
on pink prepared paper
28.9 × 20.9 cm
RCIN 912194

Katherine, Duchess of Suffolk, was the daughter and heir of William Willoughby, Baron Willoughby de Eresby, and his Spanish wife Maria de Salinas, who probably travelled to England with Katherine of Aragon in 1501.[191] Her father died in 1526, and in 1529 Katherine became the ward of Charles Brandon, 1st Duke of Suffolk (*c.*1484–1545), who sought to expand his East Anglian power base by acquiring her extensive Lincolnshire lands. To this end, after the death of his wife Mary in 1533, Brandon took the 14-year-old Katherine as his fourth wife. As Duchess of Suffolk, Katherine was the mother of Brandon's two sons, Henry and Charles (p. 131).

During the 1540s, the duchess increasingly moved towards Protestantism, becoming a patron of such reformers as Hugh Latimer and Martin Bucer.[192] She encouraged the placement of Protestant priests in Lincolnshire parishes, sponsored scholars at Cambridge, was the dedicatee of evangelical texts, and encouraged Katherine Parr, who with her brother William was a close friend, to publish *The Lamentacion of a Sinner* (1547).[193] Such was her dedication to reform that she and her second husband, Richard Bertie, went into exile when Catholicism was reintroduced under Queen Mary, only returning after the accession of Elizabeth I.

This drawing was probably made in 1541, when Katherine was 22 years old. In the same year, Holbein painted miniatures of her two young sons, and it is possible that this work was also preparatory for a miniature. The commission may have come from the duke of Suffolk, for whom Holbein drew a design for a seal sometime after 1537.[194] Alongside the duchess's torso and face, Holbein has carefully recorded the details of her hood, noting the patterns of the different bands and the presence of the colour red. He has used a brush and a pen to apply ink in different ways. An inscription at the bottom notes her gown is made of damask. The drawing has been trimmed at the lower edge, but the duchess appears to have a tie knotted at her waist, similar to that seen in the portrait of Anne Cresacre (p. 45). A later miniature by an unknown artist, also said to show the duchess, remains at her residence of Grimsthorpe Castle.[195]

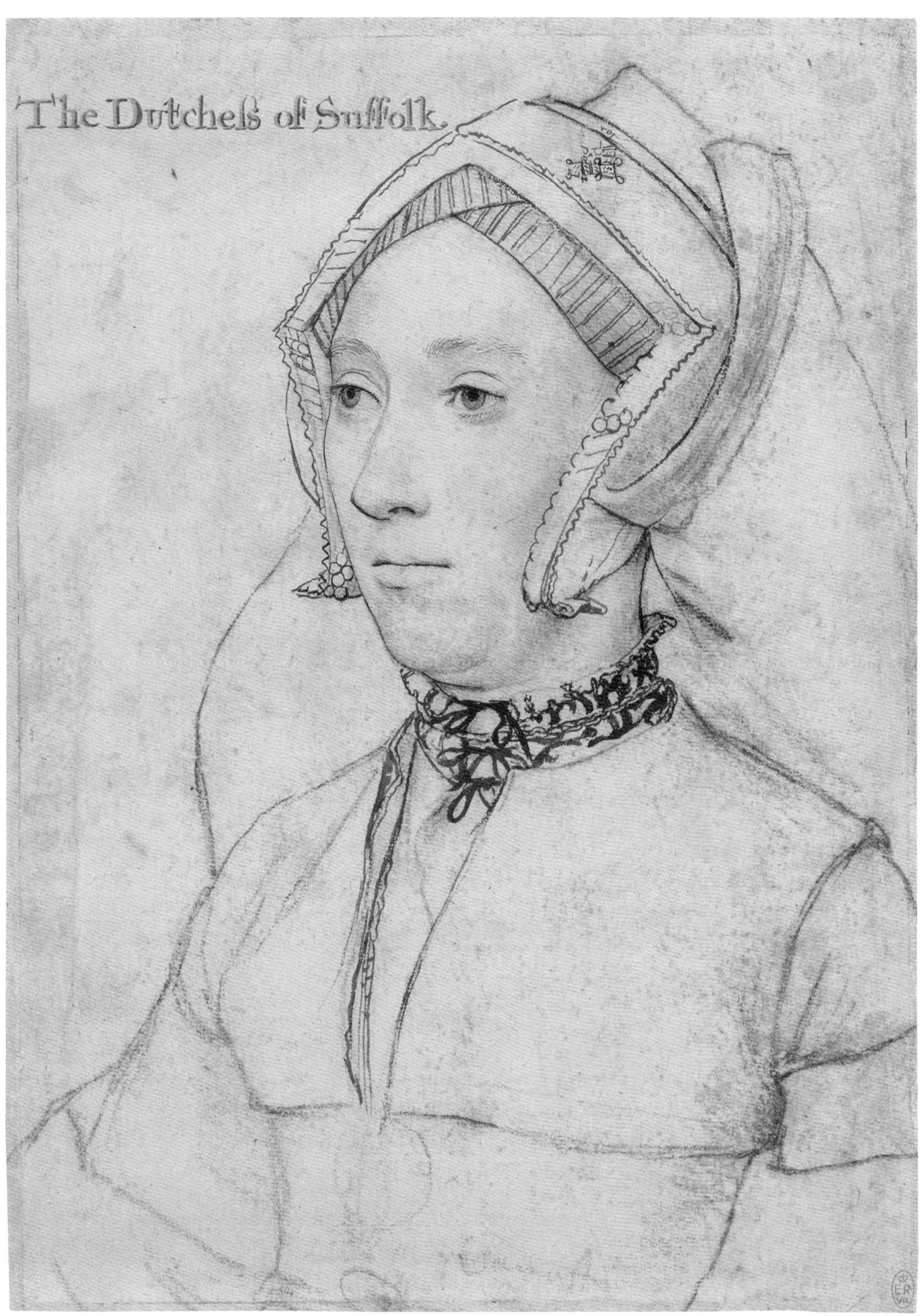
The Dutchess of Suffolk

Unidentified man, perhaps George Cornwall

*c.*1543?
Black and coloured chalks with black and brown inks on pink prepared paper
27.9 × 19.1 cm
RCIN 912208

The subject of this striking drawing, and the resulting painting (Fig. 51), remains a mystery. Although traditionally identified as 'Simon George of Cornwall', there are no traces of a contemporary of that name and the eighteenth-century inscription on which the identification is based may be a mistranscription, as it is on the portrait of Charles Wingfield (p. 120).[196] George Vertue, who recorded the drawings when they were hanging at Kensington Palace in 1743, listed this sitter as 'Sir George Cornwall', and he may be the naval commander of that name who was knighted in 1544 and died in 1562.[197]

Holbein portrays his sitter in profile to the left. He started with a light sketch in coloured chalks and metalpoint, which he worked up heavily in black inks, concentrating on the sitter's face and hat. Yellow chalk gives a brownish tone to the moustache and beard, and a greyer ink indicates the depth of the eye socket.[198] The costume is very lightly drawn. Some of the outlines have been traced over with a stylus for transfer to the panel.[199] The finished painting is a roundel and, although the main contours follow the drawing, it portrays the sitter with a full beard, which is absent from the preparatory study, and with differing dress. This appears to be a late change: X-rays have revealed that the sitter was originally depicted with facial hair as seen in the drawing.[200] The reason for the alteration is not known: it seems likely to have been at the request, or at least with the agreement, of the subject. He wears a hat badge showing Leda and the Swan, into which is tucked a sprig of pansies, sometimes a symbol of remembrance.[201] As he holds a carnation in his right hand, it has been suggested that this is a marriage portrait.[202] If the tentative identification of the sitter as George Cornwall is correct, then the portrait would be one of the latest in Holbein's oeuvre, since Cornwall, who was born in around 1509, married Mary Brydges, who appears to have been his first wife, in 1543.[203]

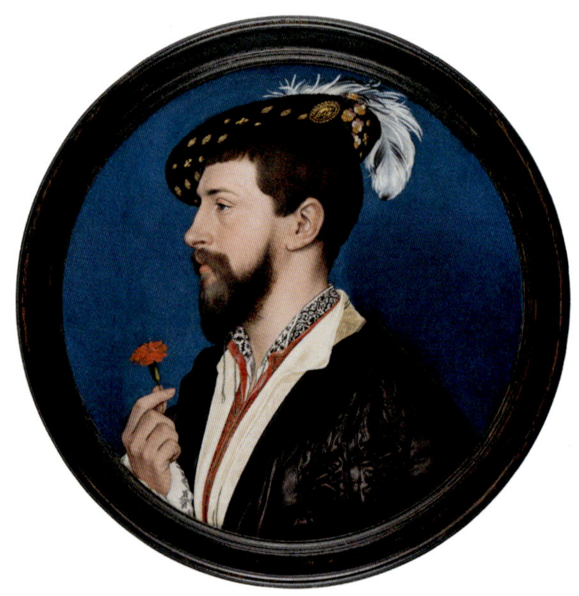

Fig. 51 **Hans Holbein, *Unidentified man, perhaps George Cornwall*, 1543?, oil on panel**
Städel Museum, Frankfurt, 1065

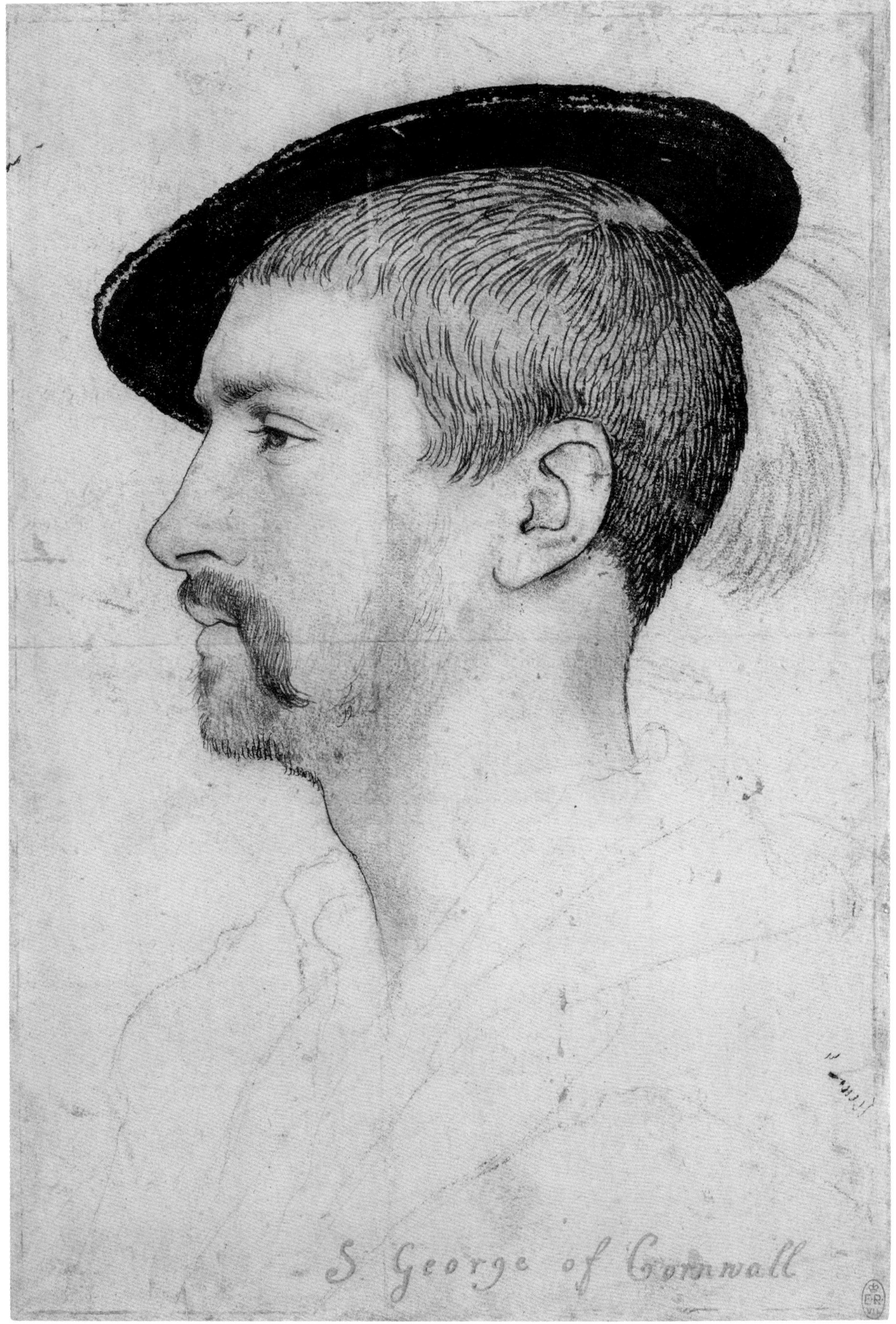
S George of Cornwall

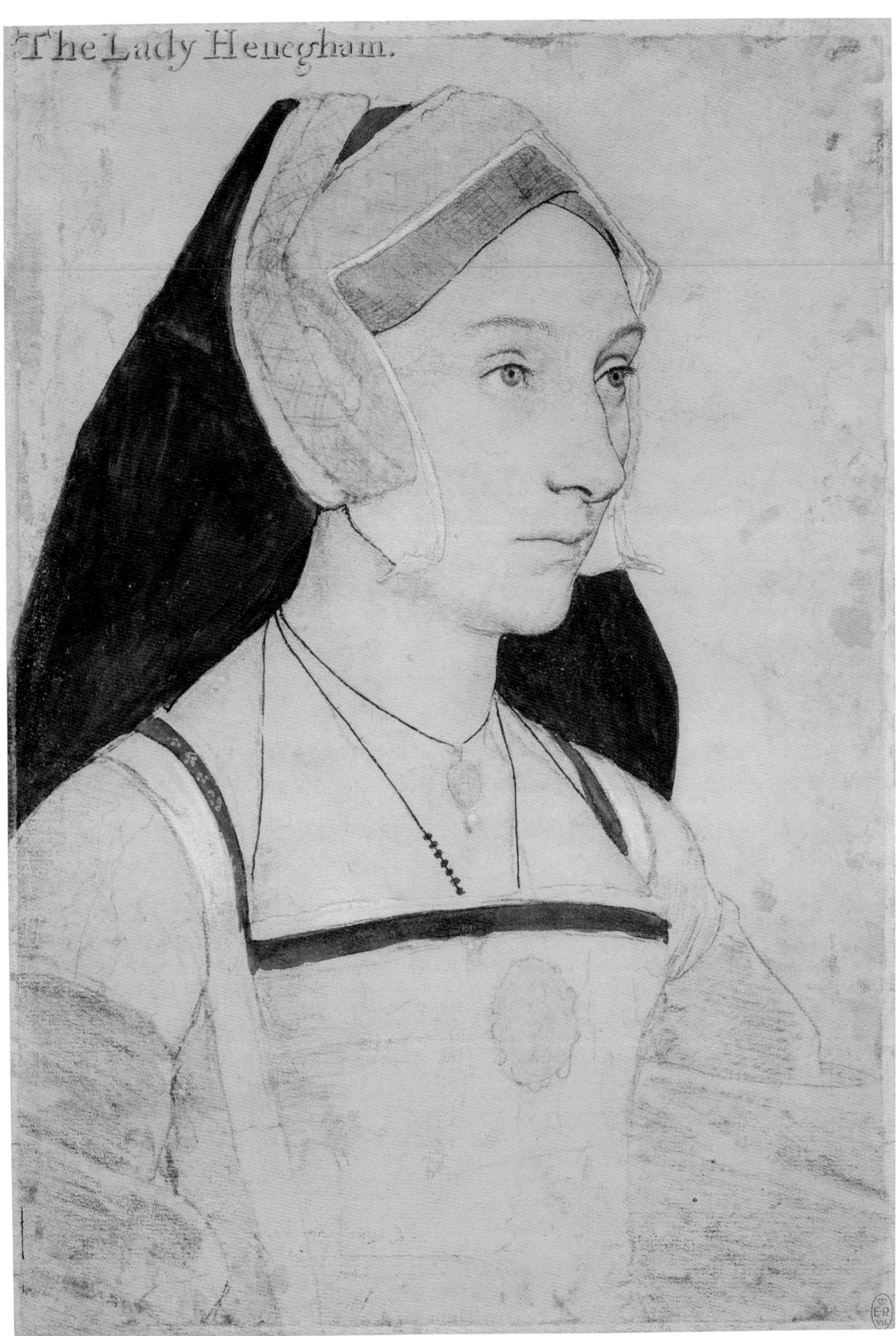
The Lady Henegham.

Mary Shelton,
later Lady Heveningham (1510/15–70/1)
*c.*1543?
Black and coloured chalks with black and brown inks and white heightening on pink prepared paper
30.3 × 21.1 cm
RCIN 912227

Mary Shelton was a cousin of Anne Boleyn. She was one of the courtiers in the queen's circle, among them Henry Howard, Earl of Surrey (p. 84), and his sister Mary, Duchess of Richmond and Somerset (p. 90).[204] She was engaged to Surrey's esquire, Thomas Clere, until Clere's death in 1545 from a wound sustained in France, and afterwards acted as one of his two executors, becoming involved in a number of legal proceedings to settle his estate.[205] By October 1546 she had married Sir Anthony Heveningham, the name by which she is identified in the inscription on the drawing. So close was Shelton to the Earl of Surrey that on his arrest for treason in 1546, Richard Southwell (p. 94) suggested she should be interrogated, noting that 'yt ys thowght that menye secrettes hathe passed betwen them before her maryag & sethens [since]'.[206]

Something of the exuberant character of the group of young men and women to which Shelton belonged is seen in a deposition of 1543 in which it was described how:

> about Candlemas last passed my lord of Surrey, Thomas Cleer, yong Wiat, Shelley my lord of Surreys servant, and young Pickering, with other their servants … went out of [the] house after ix of the clok with iiij stone bowes, and taryed furth tyl after midnight and the next daye after there was a greate clamor of the breaking of glass windows, both of houses and churches, and showtinge at men that night in the streets.[207]

It was this group that was the source of the courtly love poems in the Devonshire Manuscript, which was compiled by Mary Shelton, Mary, Duchess of Richmond and Somerset, and Lady Margaret Douglas in the 1530s and early 1540s (see p. 92).[208] Shelton was the recipient of one of the poems, 'Suffryng in sorow in hope to attayn', in which the line openings spell SHELTVN. In the margins of the manuscript, she discusses the poem's merits with Lady Margaret. Shelton also inscribed verses in the volume, perhaps of her own composition.[209]

This is one of the most meticulously worked of Holbein's drawings. Particular care has been taken with the delineation of the features, with tiny lines indicating the modelling of the nose, in an approach similar to that adopted by Holbein in his drawing of John Godsalve (p. 138). White is used to bring out Shelton's eyes and the pearl on the pendant at her neck. A date of around 1543, when Shelton was in her late twenties or early thirties, would make sense for this sheet, as it would for that of Godsalve, since it would coincide with the period when Shelton was engaged to Clere. It is tempting to see in the care and time that Holbein spent on the drawing a suggestion of the compelling nature of the sitter, whose beauty was matched by the strength of character captured in her measured gaze.

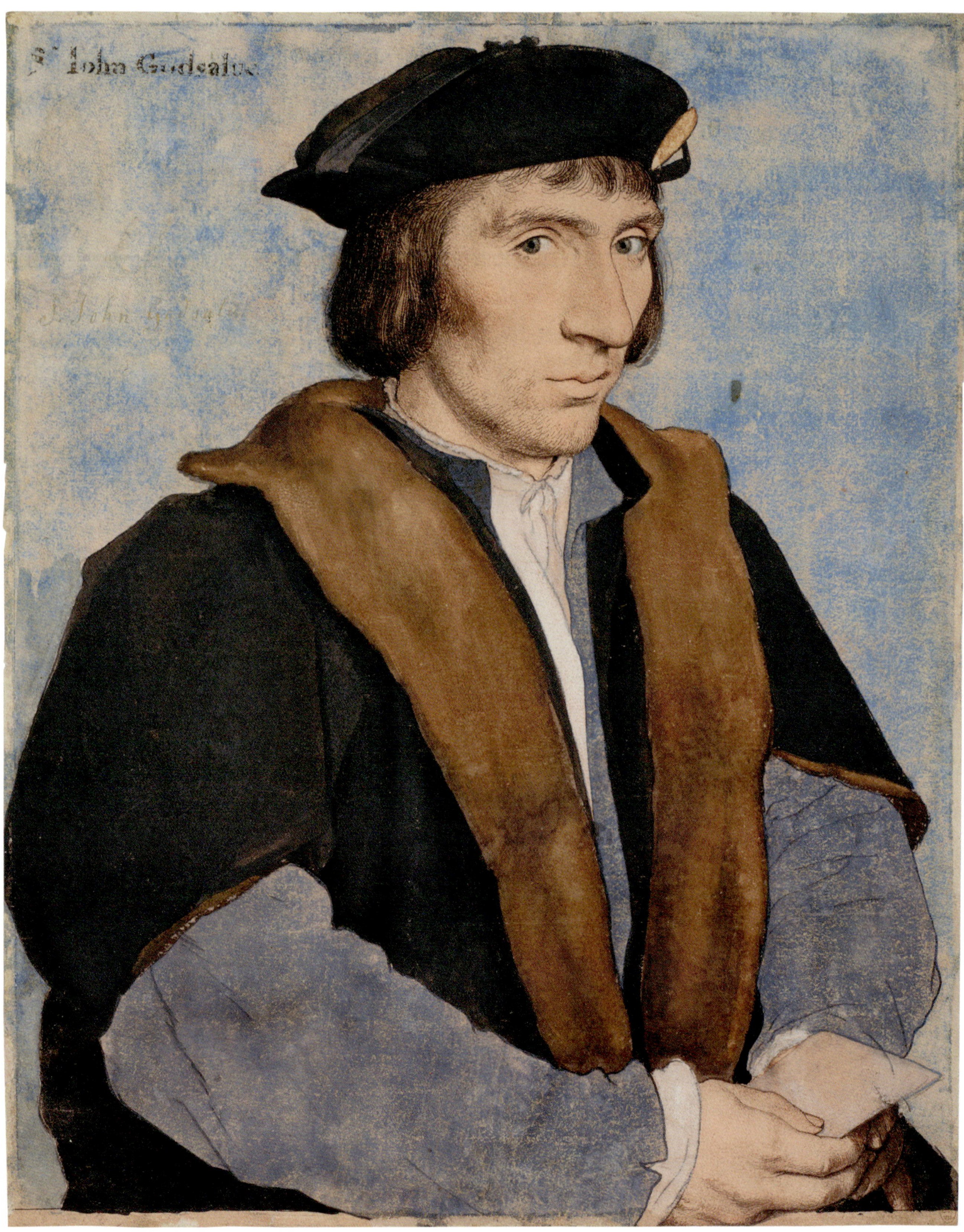
Sr Iohn Godsalve

John Godsalve (*c*.1505–56)
c.1543?
Black and coloured chalks with watercolour, black and brown inks on pink prepared paper
36.2 × 29.2 cm
RCIN 912265

Holbein's depiction of John Godsalve is among the most beautiful and unusual of his portrait drawings, and has been heavily worked up in colours. The background blue is azurite, which Holbein also used in his miniatures and oil paintings.[210] Godsalve's face and hands are carefully modelled in pen and ink and a subtle black chalk, which creates the shadow to the left of the sitter's nose. His fur-lined black gown and bonnet have been painted with dense ink. The whole is on a pink ground, comparable not only to many of Holbein's portrait drawings, but also to his paintings.[211]

The purpose of this drawing is unclear, although it seems that it was always intended to be coloured.[212] It has been suggested that the sheet was to be attached to a panel for display in a similar manner to a painting and the relatively large size of the paper may support this idea. Holbein certainly used paper as a support for a number of other works, among them the portrait of his wife Elsbeth and their two children and his depiction of Erasmus writing, both of which were painted in oil on paper glued to a panel, while the portrait of Anne of Cleves at the Musée du Louvre is on vellum attached to panel.[213] If this was the intention, it was never achieved, and the drawing was presumably among those remaining in Holbein's studio at his death, since there is no indication that it joined the group at a later date.

There is no reason to think that Holbein retained the drawing due to any dissatisfaction on the part of the sitter. Godsalve had previously been depicted by the artist and it is hard to see a reason for a rejection of this sensitive and flattering portrait. The preservation of the drawing among Holbein's studio effects may simply be due to an accident of timing: the artist may have been working on it at his death in 1543, since there are a number of indications that the sheet is not finished, such as the lack of modelling on the sleeves and white shirt and the additional layer of blue watercolour that has been started at the lower left.[214] We might also expect a finished work to have a motif on the hat badge, which is left blank. At this date, Godsalve, in his late thirties, was a successful MP and administrator, who would receive the Freedom of the City of Norwich the following year.

The Godsalves were among Holbein's earliest patrons in England: a double portrait of John and his father Thomas, dated 1528, is now in Dresden. Resident in Norwich, the Godsalves were part of the East Anglian circle who provided Holbein with early commissions. Thomas Godsalve, a public notary, was clearly interested in the latest cultural developments, forming a collection of books that included recent publications such as the Nuremberg Bible.[215] John inherited his father's interests in art and artistic novelty. In May 1533 he wrote to the Clerk of Works at Hampton Court asking him to help the letter's bearer 'into the spicery for to have an antique which I left ther wherof he bringeth the kaye.'[216] That Godsalve left his 'antique' in the spicery, which would have been kept securely locked, may indicate that it was of monetary as well as aesthetic value.

Access to and interest in such material also may have been enabled by Godsalve's senior administrative position as Clerk of the Signet from at least 1531 to 1545 and his holding of the office of the Common Metre of Cloth of Silver and Gold from November 1532. At the Office of the Common Metre, where the measurement of imported fabric was regulated, he would have encountered the Italian merchants who brought expensive and luxurious cloths to England for sale. His surviving register as Clerk of the Signet, dating from 1541 to 1543, includes a copy of Lucas Horenbout's 1534 letter of denization, which Godsalve transcribed at the beginning of his manuscript as a model to follow (suggesting he may have issued the original warrant in 1534, but if so, this is not recorded).[217] Among the warrants that came across his desk at the Signet, and which he recorded meticulously, were payments to the goldsmiths Morgan Wolf and Cornelis Hayes, and the armourer Erasmus Kyrkenar, and licences to Italian merchants such as Antonio Landi of Florence, a close acquaintance of the Italian goldsmith Benvenuto Cellini.[218] He issued grants of denization to those who came from across Europe to work on Henry VIII's magnificent Renaissance palace at Nonsuch, and the king's planned tomb at Westminster.[219] The warrant for the workers at Nonsuch was handed by Godsalve to William Kendall, one of the craftsmen responsible for the stuccowork at the palace.[220] He arranged for money to be provided to the printer Thomas Berthelet, for payments to the Serjeant-Painter Andrew Wright and for the annuity of £100 a year paid to the Italian artist and engineer Girolamo da Treviso.[221] As Clerk, Godsalve was the administrator of, rather than the moving force behind, each of these warrants, but his register records in each instance to whom he handed the document and shows that his position gave him contact with the leading artists and artisans at court, as well as the many men and women who sat to Holbein who appear in his lists.

After Henry VIII's death, Godsalve's career continued to flourish and he was among those knighted at the coronation of Edward VI. Godsalve made his will in November 1556, 'knowing and remembring that this worlde is transitory, and that deathe is most certayn, and that the hower therof moost uncertayne, and mynding to leave all thinges in quyet ordre'.[222] He asked to be buried in the parish church of St Stephen's in Norwich, next to his father's tomb, and left charitable bequests as well as provision for his family and servants, and rings for his friends who were to administer the will, each engraved with the words 'J.G. I am goone and you must follow'.

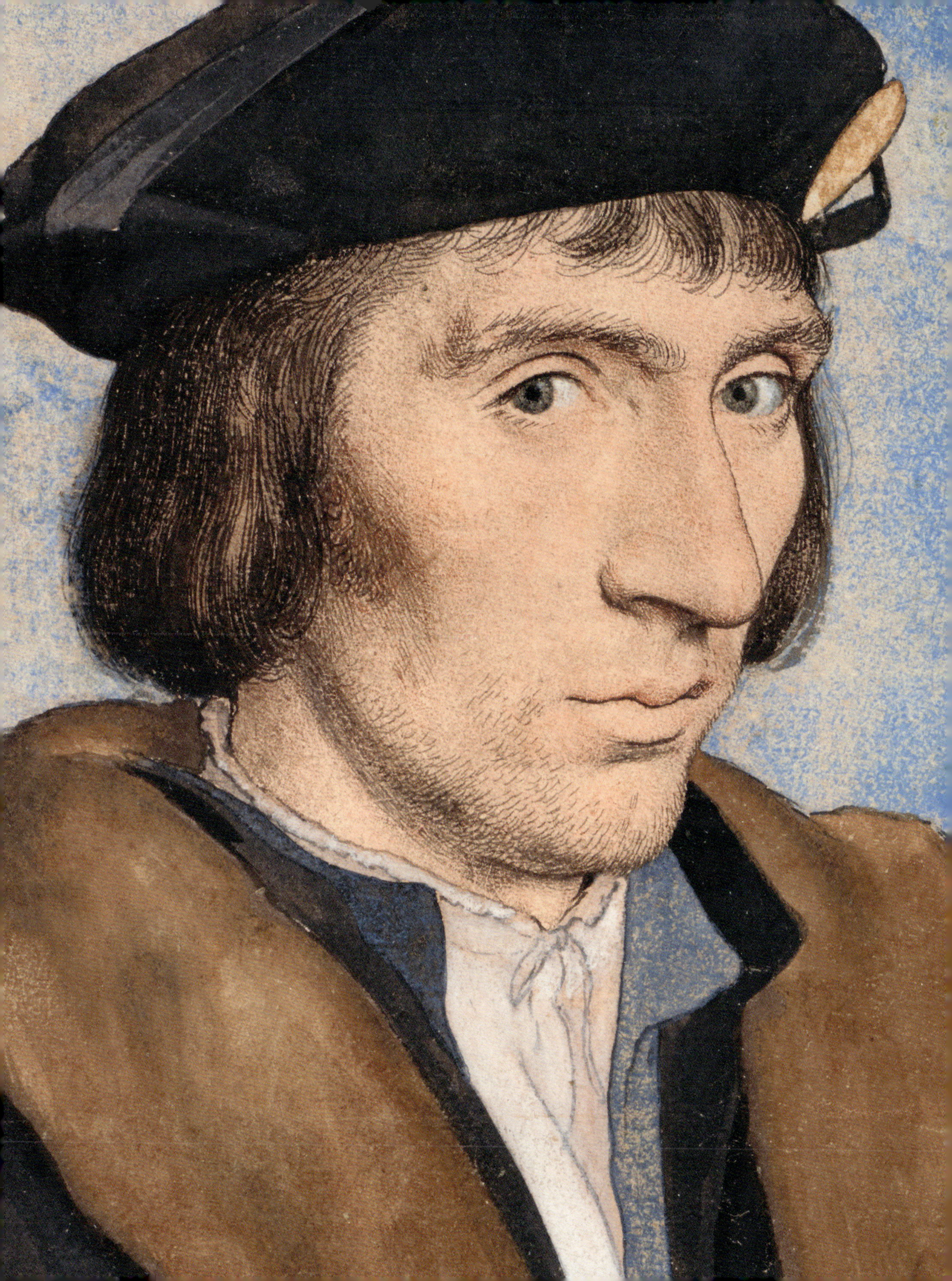

Notes

Portrait Artist at the Tudor Court

1. Mackelaitė 2021, pp. 46–7.
2. CWE, no. 1740; Woltmann 1872, p. 288; Christensen 1973, p. 210.
3. Cox-Rearick 1995, pp. 97, 135, 161–5.
4. CWE, no. 1452.
5. Among others, Reinhardt 1982, p. 260; Bätschmann 2001, p. 37; Buck 2003, p. 19.
6. Woltmann 1872, pp. 88–9; Button 2013, p. 128; Buck 1997, pp. 173–4; Buck 2003, p. 12; Mackelaitė 2021, p. 43.
7. Foister 1983a, p. 27; Roberts 1993, p. 16.
8. CWE, no. 1740.
9. Quoted in Dowling 1986, p. 142.
10. CWE, no. 1770.
11. Foister 2001.
12. Ibid., pp. 110–11.
13. Foister 2004, p. 3.
14. Buck 2003, p. 18.
15. S. Foister, 'Holbein, Hans, the younger (1497/8–1543)', *ODNB*, online edn, 2009, https://www.oxforddnb.com/view/article/13478 (accessed 18 Feb. 2023).
16. CWE, no. 2788.
17. Markow 1978; Holman 1979; Petter 2002.
18. Foister 2004, pp. 130–7.
19. Ibid., p. 104.
20. Parker 1983, p. 24.
21. Brigden 2012, pp. 116–18.
22. Foister 1983a, p. 33; Foister 2004, p. 33.
23. Foister 2004, p. 29.
24. Mackelaitė 2021.
25. Ibid., p. 41.
26. Foister 2004, p. 226.
27. Buck 2003, p. 28; Foister 2004, pp. 58, 226; Foister 2006, p. 41.
28. Ainsworth 1990; Foister 2004, pp. 59–61.
29. Ainsworth 1990.
30. Roy and Wyld 2001, pp. 99–100.
31. Buck and Sander 2003, nos 7, 36.
32. Roberts 1993, pp. 84–5.
33. Foister 2004, p. 98.
34. Ibid., p. 95.
35. CWE, no. 1488.
36. Foister 2006, p. 30.
37. Foister 1991; Foister 2004, p. 65; Plender and Saltmarsh 2014.
38. Buck 2003, p. 28.
39. S. Foister, 'Holbein, Hans, the younger (1497/8–1543)', *ODNB*, online edn, 2009, https://www.oxforddnb.com/view/article/13478 (accessed 18 Feb. 2023).
40. LPFD, XIII, part 2, no. 1280.
41. Buck 1997, pp. 103–93; Foister 2004, pp. 175–91.
42. Buck 1997, pp. 82–94.
43. Ibid., pp. 336–7; Foister 2004, pp. 187–91, 264–5.
44. Quoted in Hand 1993, p. 86.
45. Reinhardt 1982, p. 266.
46. LPFD, XIV, part 1, no. 920.
47. BL, MS Cotton Vitellius C/XVI, fol. 265v.
48. R. Lang (ed.), 'Two Tudor subsidy rolls for the City of London, 1541 and 1582', *British History Online*, 1993, http://www.british-history.ac.uk/london-record-soc/vol29 (accessed 18 Feb. 2023).
49. Calabi and Keene 2007, p. 341.
50. TNA, DL 42/133, fols 137v, 258v.
51. Foister 2004, pp. 11, 271 n. 19.
52. Dodgson 1938–9; Foister 2004, pp. 159–69.
53. Foister 2004, pp. 154–9.
54. Ibid., pp. 137–47; Horbatsch 2021.
55. Rowlands 1993, I, no. 328.
56. Black 1863; Black and Franks 1863.
57. Parker 1983, p. 8; Rowlands 1993, I, pp. 152–76.
58. Foister 1983a, p. 13.
59. Parker 1983, pp. 10–20; Foister 1983a, pp. 4–12.
60. Milner 1904, p. 334.
61. Huygens 1876, p. 227.
62. William Sanderson in 1658, quoted in Parker 1983, p. 28.
63. Egmont 1923, II, p. 190.
64. Foister 1983a; Oliver *et al.* 2006.
65. Foister 1983a, p. 9.
66. Foister 2004, p. 67.
67. Goldring 2002.
68. Van Mander 1994, I, p. 150.

Catalogue

1. CWE, no. 1770.
2. Müller and Kemperdick 2006, pp. 370–7.
3. Foister 2006, no. 23.
4. Roberts 1987, p. 32.
5. Button 2013, p. 258.
6. Mantel and Salomon 2018.
7. Ainsworth 1990, p. 177; Foister 2006, p. 35.
8. Rowlands 1985, pp. 71–2, 132–3, Mantel and Salomon 2018, p. 54.
9. Mantel and Salomon 2018, p. 59.
10. J.J. Scarisbrick, 'Warham, William (1450?–1532)', *ODNB*, online edn, 2015, https://www.oxforddnb.com/view/article/28741 (accessed 18 Feb. 2023).
11. CSP Spain, III, part 2, no. 69.
12. Button 2013, p. 135.
13. Ibid., p. 218.
14. Rowlands 1985, pp.133–4.
15. Foister 1983a, p. 2.
16. TNA, SP 1/83, fols 157–162; SP 1/93, fols 106–111.
17. Cleland and Eaker 2022, no. 76; Heard 2004, pp. 196–7.
18. Queen's Gallery 1978, no. 15; Button 2013, p. 104.
19. Parker 1983, pp. 39–40.
20. Roberts 1993, p. 42.
21. Scott 1890; Prospero 1988, p. 120; Foister 1991, p. 120.
22. Hearn 1996, no. 98; Foister 2004, p. 68.
23. Kunstmuseum, Basel (inv. 314).
24. Foister 2004, p. 245.
25. TNA, SP 1/78, fol. 57v.
26. Petter 2002; Woollett 2021, pp. 15–17.
27. Foister 2004, p. 206.
28. Holman 1979.
29. Foister 2004, p. 37.
30. Chorley 2018, pp. 335–6.
31. Holman 1979, pp. 141–2. Gemäldegalerie, Berlin (Gisze); Kunsthistorisches Museum, Vienna (Tybis).
32. Chorley 2018, p. 335.
33. Ibid.
34. Wubs-Mrozewicz and Jenks 2022, p. 130; TNA, PROB 11/25/178.
35. Buck and Sander 2003, no. 17; Foister 2004, pp. 206–7; Heard and Whitaker 2011, p. 166.
36. Ian Tyers, dendrochronological report, 2010.
37. I am very grateful to Nicola Christie, Head of Paintings Conservation, Royal Collection Trust, for the following, which comes from her close examination of the panel over many months.
38. Heard and Whitaker 2011, p. 166.
39. Vredveld 2013, p. 557.
40. Heard and Whitaker 2011, p. 167.
41. A. Hawkyard, 'John Poyntz (*c*.1485–1544)' in 'Poyntz, Sir Robert (*b*. late 1440s, *d*. 1520)', *ODNB*, online edn, 2015, https://www.oxforddnb.com/view/article/70796 (accessed 18 Feb. 2023).
42. Armstrong 1990, p. 185.
43. Roberts 1993, no. 23.
44. Foister 1983a, p. 36.
45. Brigden 2012.
46. Ibid., p. 243.
47. C.1536-8, collection of the Duke of Northumberland.
48. Holbein's *Ambassadors* was once believed to show Wyatt and his secretary (Woltmann 1872, pp. 361–3).
49. RCIN 912251.
50. Rowlands and Starkey 1983; Hayward 2007, p. 169.
51. Hayward 2007, p. 169.
52. Foister 2004, p. 55.
53. E.W. Ives, 'Anne [Anne Boleyn] (*c*.1500–1536)', *ODNB*, online edn, 2004, https://www.oxforddnb.com/view/article/557 (accessed 18 Feb. 2023).
54. Rowlands 1993, I, nos 350 (d), 351 (c) and (d); Rowlands and Starkey 1983, p. 92; LPFD, VII, no. 1668; Foister 2004, p. 12.
55. Buck 1998.
56. Foister 2004, p. 154.
57. Buck 1998.
58. King 1994, p. 78.
59. Ibid., p. 88; Roberts 1993, p. 86; Foister 2004, p. 154.
60. Buck 1998.
61. BL, MS Royal 2 A XVI.
62. Foister 2004, p. 154.
63. Holbein's drawing of Richard Rich is in the Royal Collection (RCIN 912238).
64. Roberts 1993, p. 86.
65. A. Hawkyard, 'Sir Nicholas Poyntz (*b*. in or before 1510, *d*. 1556)' in 'Poyntz, Sir Robert (*b*. late 1440s, *d*. 1520)', *ODNB*, online edn, 2015, https://www.oxforddnb.com/view/article/70796 (accessed 18 Feb. 2023).
66. For the copies, see Rowlands 1985, no. R24.
67. R. Bell, in Starkey 1991, pp. 120–5.
68. Ibid.; Rodwell 2003.
69. See n. 65.
70. Foister 2004, pp. 102, 108–9.
71. I am grateful to Dr Martin Henig for his help with the identification of this intaglio.
72. Plender and Saltmarsh 2014.
73. Foister 2004, p. 227.
74. Lehmberg 1960; S. Lehmberg, 'Elyot, Sir Thomas (*c*.1490–1546)', *ODNB*, online edn, 2008, https://www.oxforddnb.com/view/article/8782 (accessed 18 Feb. 2023).
75. S. Lehmberg, 'Elyot, Sir Thomas (*c*.1490–1546)', *ODNB*, online edn, 2008, https://www.oxforddnb.com/view/article/8782 (accessed 18 Feb. 2023).
76. Foister 2004, pp. 240–1. The others are Henry Wyatt and Brian Tuke. Anne of Cleves also wears a jewelled crucifix in both Holbein's painting and miniature.
77. Lehmberg 1960, pp. 166–7.
78. Quoted in ibid., p. 175.
79. Det 1909; Ives 1998; E.W. Ives, 'Bourbon, Nicholas (*c*.1503–1549/50)', *ODNB*, online edn, 2004, https://www.oxforddnb.com/view/article/70782 (accessed 18 Feb. 2023); Marr 2021.
80. Foister 2006, p. 53.
81. *Nugae Libri* VI, no. XII; Foister 2006, p. 53; Marr 2021, p. 107.
82. Ainsworth 1990, pp. 182–3.
83. Gray 2000; G. Phillips, 'Sadler, Sir Ralph (1507–1587)', *ODNB*, online edn, 2008, https://www.oxforddnb.com/view/article/24462 (accessed 18 Feb. 2023).

84. Anstruther 1953, pp. 3–69; H.R. Woudhuysen, 'Vaux, Thomas, second Baron Vaux (1509–1556)', *ODNB*, online edn, 2008, https://www.oxforddnb.com/view/article/28163 (accessed 18 Feb. 2023).
85. TNA, SP 1/103, fol. 184.
86. Published in Edwards 1576, p. 80.
87. This paper has a distinctive pattern of chain lines.
88. Roberts 1987, p. 64.
89. Foister 1983a, p. 35; Roberts 1987, p. 78; Roberts 1993 (exh. cat.), no. 12; the profile portrait is on the same paper as that used by Holbein for Lady Lister (RCIN 912219; see Fig. 18) and an unidentified woman who may be the earl's sister, Mary Fitzroy (RCIN 912190; see p. 90).
90. Brigden 1994; Brigden, 'Howard, Henry, earl of Surrey (1516/17–1547)', *ODNB*, online edn, 2008, https://www.oxforddnb.com/view/article/13905 (accessed 18 Feb. 2023).
91. LPFD, I, part 1, no. 1426.
92. LPFD, XVIII, part 2, no. 401.
93. LPFD, V, no. 941.
94. Dowling 1986, p. 147.
95. Button 2013, p. 230.
96. Parker 1983, pp. 40–1; TNA, LR 2/115, 2/116, 2/117.
97. TNA, LR 2/117, fol. 119.
98. BL MS Cotton Vespasian F/XIII, fol. 144; TNA, SP 1/114, fol. 48.
99. TNA, SP 1/227, fols 82–83.
100. Ibid.
101. TNA, LR 2/116.
102. TNA, SP 1/227, fol. 223v.
103. Buck and Sander 2003, p. 104.
104. Calabi and Keene 2007, p. 341.
105. TNA, PROB 11/47/231, fol. 149v.
106. CSP Spain, XIII, appendix: miscellaneous 1558.
107. Queen's Gallery 1978 (exh. cat.), no. 64; Parker 1983, pp. 41, 155.
108. Parker 1983, p. 41.
109. Rowlands 1993, I, no. 319; Hayward 2007, p. 171.
110. NRO, LEST supplementary 26/1, nos 1, 28.
111. Kimbell Museum, Fort Worth; Pillsbury and Jordan 1985.
112. NRO, LEST supplementary 26/1, no. 2.
113. Oestmann 1994.
114. Foister 1983a, p. 33; Foister 2004, p. 33.
115. Richards 2005, p. 16.
116. Oestmann 1994, p. 21.
117. Foister 2006, no. 161.
118. Roberts 1993, p. 19; Button 2013, p. 249. The other drawings are RCINS 912235, 912248, 912207 and 912243.
119. Foister 2004, pp. 26–7.
120. Ibid.; Roberts 1993, no. 27; Queen's Gallery 1978, no. 45.
121. For Mistress Souch, see Brigden 1994, p. 524.
122. Foister 2004, p. 184.
123. Roberts 1987, p. 88.
124. Foister 2004, pp. 65, 184–7.
125. Foister 2006, p. 87.
126. Roberts 1993, p. 56.
127. Button 2013, p. 271.
128. Rica Jones, 2006, analysis of the painting in an unpublished report, Royal Collection conservation file.
129. Button 2013, p. 259.
130. Parker 1983, p. 44.
131. LPFD, IV, no. 1939/10; LPFD, XXI, part 1, no. 1165/91.
132. LPFD, V, no. 1598; LPFD, XIII, part 1, no. 384/99; LPFD, XVIII, part 2, no. 327/6.
133. Clapham 1912.
134. TNA, C 1/668/3, Reskimer v. Vyvoll, *c.*1530–2.
135. TNA, E 40/13229.
136. TNA, PROB 11/47/226.
137. Roberts 1987, p. 72; Foister 2006, p. 42.
138. Parker 1983, pp. 22, 48; Grosvenor 2007, p. 61.
139. A. Weikel, 'Mary I (1516–1558)', *ODNB*, online edn, 2008, https://www.oxforddnb.com/view/article/18245 (accessed 18 Feb. 2023).
140. Ibid.
141. Madden 1831, p. 20.
142. Foister 2004, p. 198.
143. Parker 1983, p. 44.
144. Holbein has also annotated the clothing with an 's', perhaps standing for 'samet' (velvet) or 'schwarz' (black).
145. Roberts 1993, p. 58.
146. Ibid.
147. Starkey 1981.
148. Ibid.
149. Brewer and Bullen 1867–73, I, p. 40; D. Edwards, 'Butler [Bocach], James, ninth earl of Ormond and second earl of Ossory (*b.* in or after 1496, *d.* 1546)', *ODNB*, online edn, 2006, https://www.oxforddnb.com/view/article/4189 (accessed 18 Feb. 2023).
150. Hand 1993, pp. 83–91.
151. Foister 2004, p. 196; Button 2013, p. 302.
152. Foister 2006, p. 101.
153. Hearn 1996, p. 41.
154. Foister 2004, p. 23.
155. Roberts 1987, p. 21.
156. L.L. Ford, 'Audley, Thomas, Baron Audley of Walden (1487/8–1544)', *ODNB*, online edn, 2004, https://www.oxforddnb.com/view/article/896 (accessed 18 Feb. 2023).
157. LPFD, XIV, part 2, no. 775; Lehmberg 1972, p. 8.
158. Buck and Sander 2003, p. 127.
159. Ibid.
160. M.L. Robertson, 'Wingfield, Sir Richard (*b.* in or before 1469, *d.* 1525)', *ODNB*, online edn, 2008, https://www.oxforddnb.com/view/article/29739 (accessed 18 Feb. 2023).
161. BL, MS Harley 69, fol. 18r.
162. Foister 1983a, p. 9.
163. Christie 1796, no. 4.
164. C.S. Knighton, 'Brooke, George, ninth Baron Cobham (*c.*1497–1558)', *ODNB*, online edn, 2008, https://www.oxforddnb.com/view/article/70783 (accessed 18 Feb. 2023).
165. TNA, SP 1/137, fol. 128.
166. TNA, SP 1/166, fol. 65v.
167. Byrne 1981, VI, pp. 31–2; TNA, PROB 11/43/628.
168. BL, MS Harley 283, fol. 305.
169. Roberts 1993, p. 68; Hearn 1996, p. 22 and no. 9; Foister 2004, pp. 55, 69.

170. TNA, E 178/3521, inquisition into the goods of Henry Brooke, Lord Cobham, 1603.
171. Camden quoted in Powell 2016, p. 218; S.E. James, 'Parr, William, marquess of Northampton (1513–1571)', *ODNB*, online edn, 2008, https://www.oxforddnb.com/view/article/21405 (accessed 18 Feb. 2023).
172. LPFD, XVIII, part 1, no. 918.
173. TNA, E 101/520/9, fols 7, 7v, 11.
174. S.E. James, 'Parr, William, marquess of Northampton (1513–1571)', *ODNB*, online edn, 2008, https://www.oxforddnb.com/view/article/21405 (accessed 18 Feb. 2023); TNA, E 101/520/9, fol. 8v, DL 42/133, fol. 164.
175. Mackelaitė 2021, p. 52.
176. Foister 2006, p. 80. The stall plate is now in the British Museum: BM 1855,0130.1.
177. CSP Venetian, IV, part 1, no. 694.
178. Heard and Whitaker 2011, p. 178.
179. TNA, LR 2/115, fol. 1v.
180. CSP Spain, VIII, nos 364, 365.
181. Hayward 2009, p. 174.
182. TNA, LR 2/117, fol. 64; LR 2/115, fol. 44v.
183. Foister 2004, p. 95; TNA, LR 2/117, fol. 119.
184. Reynolds 1999, pp. 51–2.
185. Ibid., p. 51; James 1998; Moyle 2021, pp. 495–6.
186. Victoria and Albert Museum 1980–1, nos P5, P6; Reynolds 1999, p. 52.
187. Hayward 2009, pp. 165, 29.
188. Reynolds 1999, p. 52; Remington in Heard and Whitaker 2011, p. 185.
189. Reynolds 1999, p. 53.
190. Foister 2004, p. 228.
191. S. Wabuda, 'Bertie [*née* Willoughby; *other married name* Brandon], Katherine, duchess of Suffolk (1519–1580)', *ODNB*, online edn, 2008, https://www.oxforddnb.com/view/article/2273 (accessed 18 Feb. 2023); Harkrider 2008.
192. Harkrider 2008.
193. Ibid., pp. 48–50.
194. Rowlands 1993, I, no. 356; Foister 2004, p. 145.
195. Rowlands 1993, I, p. 181.
196. A 'Simon George' of 'Quotoule' (perhaps Cothele) recorded in a 1620 visitation of Cornwall has been offered as a candidate, but since his granddaughters were aged 6, 4 and 2 in 1620, he is unlikely to be the sitter here. See Foister 1983b, p. 156; Vivian 1887, p. 174.
197. Savile and Reade 1908, pp. 79–84; A.J. Edwards, 'Cornwall, George', *History of Parliament Online*, http://www.historyofparliamentonline.org/volume/1509-1558/member/cornwall-george-1509-62 (accessed 19 Feb. 2023); TNA, PROB 11/46/137 (will of 1563), In August 1545 he was listed as the captain of the ship *The Swepestake* (SP 1/445, fol. 23).
198. Button 2013, pp. 292–3.
199. Ibid., p. 211.
200. Götz 1932, pp. 116–17; Ainsworth 1990, p. 180.
201. Foister 2004, pp. 232, 238.
202. Ainsworth 1990, p. 180.
203. Savile and Reade 1908, p. 80.
204. E. Heale, 'Shelton, Mary [*married names* Mary Heveningham, Lady Heveningham; Mary Appleyard] (1510–15–1570/71)', *ODNB*, online edn, 2004, https://www.oxforddnb.com/view/article/68085 (accessed 18 Feb. 2023); Baron 1994, pp. 333–4; Heale 1995, p. 299; Remley 1994.
205. TNA, PROB 11/30/376, C 1/1190/1-2 and C 1/1156/33.
206. TNA, SP 1/233, fol. 36.
207. TNA, SP 1/176, fol. 141; Brigden 1994, p. 517.
208. BL, MS Add 17492; Baron 1994; Heale 1995.
209. Heale 1995, p. 301.
210. Button 2013, p. 189.
211. Ibid., p. 181.
212. Roberts 1993, p. 18; Button 2013, pp. 190–2.
213. Roberts 1993, p. 52.
214. Buck and Sander 2003, p. 84.
215. Moore and Crawley 1992, no. 4; Harrap 2016.
216. TNA, SP 1/76, fol. 128.
217. TNA, DL 42/133, fols 4–5.
218. TNA, DL 42/133, fols 27, 38, 40, 143, 187, 201.
219. TNA, DL 42/133, fols 53, 73, 84, 223.
220. Biddle 1984.
221. TNA, DL 42/133, fols 76, 280, 135v, 142, 87.
222. TNA, PROB 11/40/161.

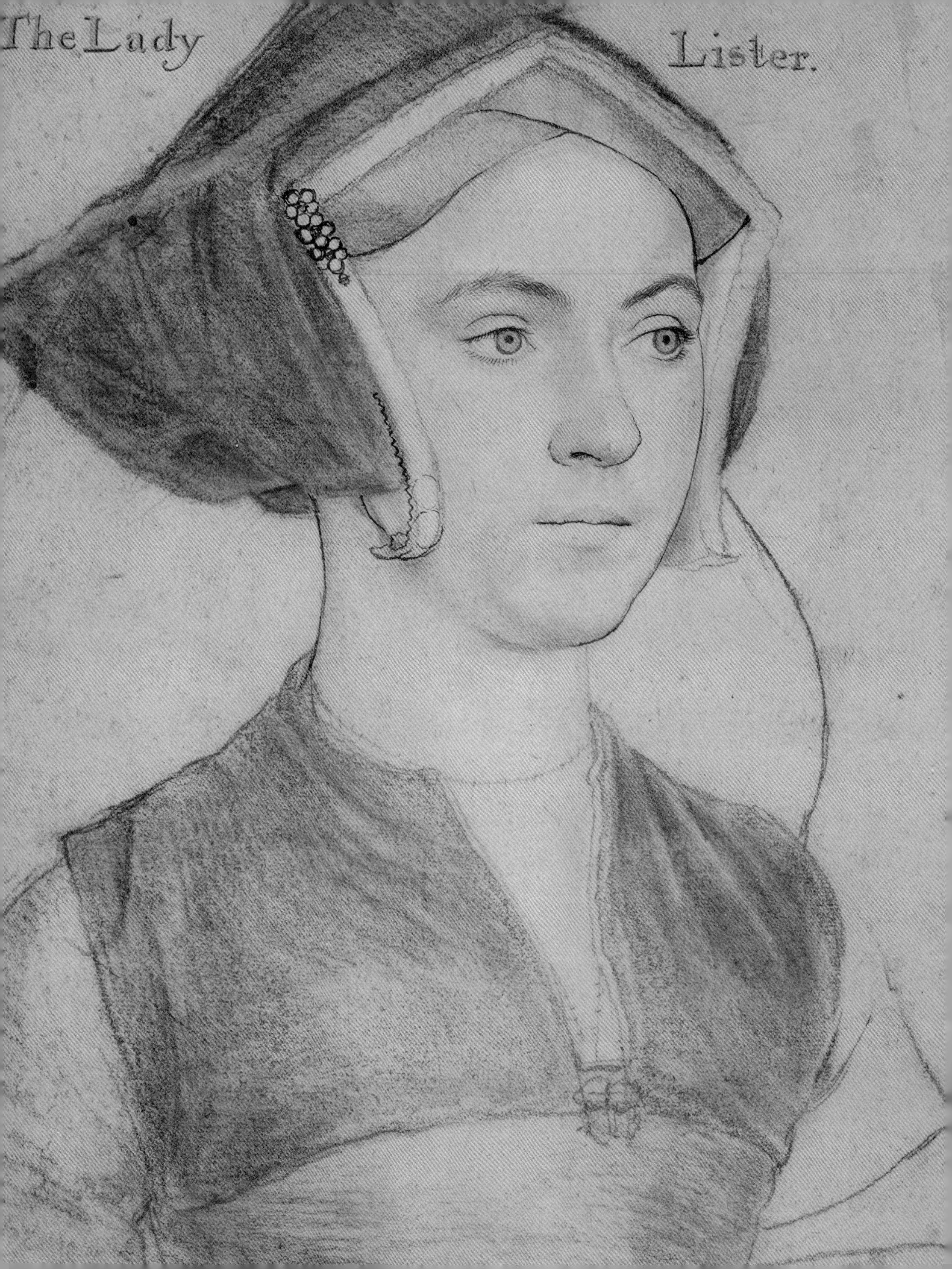
The Lady
Lister.

Abbreviations and bibliography

BL
British Library, London

CSP Spain
Calendar of State Papers, Spain

CSP Venetian
Calendar of State Papers, Venetian

CWE
The Collected Works of Erasmus, Toronto, 1974–present

LPFD
Letters and Papers, Foreign and Domestic, Henry VIII

NRO
Norfolk Record Office

ODNB
Oxford Dictionary of National Biography, online edition

RCIN
Royal Collection Inventory Number

TNA
National Archives, Kew

Ainsworth 1990
M. Ainsworth, '"Paternes for Phiosioneamye": Holbein's portraiture reconsidered', *Burlington Magazine*, 132 (no. 1044), March 1990, pp. 173–86

Anstruther 1953
G. Anstruther, *Vaux of Harrowden: A Recusant Family*, Newport

Armstrong 1990
E. Armstrong, *Before Copyright: The French Book-Privilege System, 1498–1526*, Cambridge

Baron 1994
H. Baron, 'Mary (Howard) Fitzroy's hand in the Devonshire Manuscript', *Review of English Studies*, XLV (no. 179), Aug. 1994, pp. 318–35

Bätschmann 2001
O. Bätschmann, 'Holbein and Italian art', in Roskill and Hand 2001, pp. 37–53

Bell 1991
R. Bell, 'The royal visit to Acton Court in 1535', in Starkey 1991, pp. 120–5

Biddle 1984
M. Biddle, 'The stuccoes of Nonsuch', *Burlington Magazine*, 126 (no. 976), July 1984, pp. 411–17

Black 1863
W.H. Black, 'On the date and other circumstances of the death of the painter Hans Holbein, as disclosed by the discovery of his will', *Archaeologia*, 33:1, pp. 272–6

Black and Franks 1863
W.H. Black and A.W. Franks, 'Discovery of the will of Hans Holbein', *Archaeologia*, 39:1, pp. 1–18

Brewer and Bullen 1867–73
J.S. Brewer and W. Bullen (eds), *Calendar of the Carew Manuscripts Preserved in the Archiepiscopal Library at Lambeth, 1515–1574*, 6 vols, London

Brigden 1994
S. Brigden, 'Henry Howard, Earl of Surrey, and the "Conjured League"', *Historical Journal*, September, 37:3, pp. 507–37

Brigden 2012
S. Brigden, *Thomas Wyatt: The Heart's Forest*, London

Buck 1997
S. Buck, *Holbein am Hofe Henrichs VIII*, Berlin

Buck 1998
S. Buck, 'Text versus Bild: Holbeins Interpretation Heinrichs VIII. Am Beispiel der "Salomo-Miniatur"', *Zeitschrift für Schweizerische Archäologie und Kunstgeschichte*, LV, pp. 281–92

Buck 2003
S. Buck, 'Hans Holbein the Younger: portraitist of the Renaissance', in Buck and Sander 2003, pp. 11–33

Buck and Sander 2003
S. Buck and J. Sander (eds), *Hans Holbein the Younger: Painter at the Court of Henry VIII*, exh. cat., The Mauritshuis, The Hague

Button 2013
V. Button, 'The portrait drawings of Hans Holbein the Younger: function and use explored through material and techniques', unpublished PhD thesis, Royal College of Art, London

Byrne 1981
M. St C. Byrne (ed.), *The Lisle Letters*, 6 vols, Chicago and London

Calabi and Keene 2007
D. Calabi and D. Keene, 'Merchants' lodgings and cultural exchange', in D. Calabi and S.T. Christensen (eds), *Cultural Exchange in Early Modern Europe*. II: *Cities and Cultural Exchange in Europe, 1400–1700*, Cambridge, pp. 315–49

Chorley 2018
C. Chorley, 'Hans Holbein, *Hans of Antwerp*: findings from the recent examination, cleaning and restoration', in T.-H. Borchert, J. Couvert and A. Dubois (eds), *Technical Studies of Paintings: Problems of Attribution (15th–17th Centuries). Papers Presented at the Nineteenth Symposium for the Study of Underdrawing and Technology in Painting Held in Bruges, 11–13 September 2014*, Leuven, pp. 326–37

Christensen 1973
C.C. Christensen, 'The Reformation and the decline of German art', *Central European History*, VI: 3, September, pp. 207–32

Christie 1796
A Catalogue of the Genuine, Capital, and Valuable Collection of Pictures ... Selected by that Eminent Artist and Esteemed Connoisseur Benjamin Van Der Gucht, Esq ... which Will be Sold ... by Mr Christie ... on Friday, March 11th, 1796, London

Clapham 1912
A.W. Clapham, 'On the topography of the Dominican Priory of London', *Archaeologia*, 63, pp. 57–84

Cleland and Eaker 2022
E. Cleland and A. Eaker, *The Tudors. Art and Majesty in Renaissance England*, exh. cat., Metropolitan Museum of Art, New York

Cox-Rearick 1995
J. Cox-Rearick, *The Collection of Francis I: Royal Treasures*, Antwerp and New York

Det 1909
A.-S. Det, 'Hans Holbein et Nicolas Bourbon, de Vendeuvre', *Mémoires de la Société Académique d'Agriculture, des Sciences, Arts et Belles-Lettres, du Département de l'Aube*, 3rd series, XLVI, pp. 47–77

Dodgson 1938–9
C. Dodgson, 'Woodcuts designed by Holbein for English printers', *Walpole Society*, 28, pp. 1–11

Dowling 1986
M. Dowling, *Humanism in the Age of Henry VIII*, London

Edwards 1576
R. Edwards (compiler), *The Paradise of Daintie Deuises*, London

Egmont 1923
Diary of the First Earl of Egmont (Viscount Percival), Historical Manuscripts Commission, 3 vols, London 1920–3

Foister 1983a
S. Foister, 'Introduction and catalogue', in *Drawings by Holbein from the Royal Library Windsor Castle*, London and New York, pp. 1–47

Foister 1983b
S. Foister, 'Appendix', in Parker 1983, pp. 153–8

Foister 1991
S. Foister, 'Workshop or followers? Underdrawing in some portraits associated with Hans Holbein the Younger', in *Proceedings of the 9th Louvain-la-Neuve Colloque sur le dessin sous-jacent dans la peinture*, Collège Érasme, Louvain-la-Neuve, 12–14 September, pp. 113–24

Foister 2001
S. Foister, 'Holbein's paintings on canvas: the Greenwich festivities of 1527', in Roskill and Hand 2001, pp. 109–23

Foister 2004
S. Foister, *Holbein and England*, New Haven and London

Foister 2006
S. Foister, *Holbein in England*, exh. cat., Tate, London

Goldring 2002
E. Goldring, 'An important early picture collection: the Earl of Pembroke's 1561/62 inventory and the provenance of Holbein's "Christina of Denmark"', *Burlington Magazine*, 144 (no. 1188), March 2002, pp. 157–60

Götz 1932
O. Götz, 'Holbeins Bildnis des Simon George of Quocoute: Ein Beitrag zur Geschichte des Rundbildes in der Renaissance', *Städel-Jahrbuch*, VII–VIII, pp. 116–48

Gray 2000
M. Gray, 'Sadleir of Sutton House and Standon Lordship: an iconography', *Hackney History*, VI, unpaginated

Grosvenor 2007
B. Grosvenor (ed.), *Lost Faces: Identity and Discovery in Tudor Royal Portraiture*, exh. cat., Philip Mould Ltd, London

Hand 1993
J.O. Hand, *German Paintings of the Fifteenth through Seventeenth Centuries: The Collections of the National Gallery of Art, Systematic Catalogue*, Washington 1983

Harkrider 2008
M.F. Harkrider, *Women, Reform and Community in Early Modern England: Katherine Willoughby, Duchess of Suffolk, and Lincolnshire's Godly Aristocracy, 1519–1580*, Woodbridge

Harrap 2016
D.A. Harrap, 'The phenomena of prayer: the reception of the *Imitatio Christi* in England (1438–*c*.1600), unpublished PhD thesis, University of London

Hayward 2007
M. Hayward, *Dress at the Court of King Henry VIII*, Leeds

Hayward 2009
M. Hayward, *Rich Apparel: Clothing and the Law in Henry VIII's England*, Farnham

Heale 1995
E. Heale, 'Women and the courtly love lyric: the Devonshire MS (BL Additional 17492)', *Modern Language Review*, XC:2, April, pp. 296–313

Heard 2004
K. Heard, 'Episcopal patronage of the visual arts in England, 1450–1550', unpublished PhD thesis, University of Cambridge

Heard and Whitaker 2011
K. Heard and L. Whitaker (eds), *The Northern Renaissance: Durer to Holbein*, exh. cat., The Queen's Galleries, Edinburgh and London

Hearn 1996
K. Hearn (ed.), *Dynasties: Painting in Tudor and Jacobean England, 1530–1630*, exh. cat., Tate, London

Herman 1994
P.C. Herman (ed.), *Rethinking the Henrician Era: Essays on Early Tudor Texts and Contexts*, Urbana and Chicago

Holman 1979
T.S. Holman, 'Holbein's portraits of the Steelyard Merchants: an investigation', *Metropolitan Museum Journal*, XIV, pp. 139–58

Horbatsch 2021
O. Horbatsch, 'Hans Holbein the Younger as designer for goldsmiths in Tudor England', in T. Schroder and D. Thornton (eds), *A Royal Renaissance Treasure and its Afterlives: The Royal Clock Salt*, London, pp. 77–89

Huygens 1876
'Journal van Constantijn Huygens, den zoon, van 21 October 1688 tot. 2 Sept. 1696', *Werken van Het Historisch Genootschap Gevestid te Utrecht*, n.s. XXIII

Ives 1998
E.W. Ives, 'A Frenchman at the court of Anne Boleyn', *History Today*, XLVIII:8, Aug. 1998, pp. 21–6

James 1998
S.E. James, 'Lady Margaret Douglas and Sir Thomas Seymour by Holbein: two miniatures re-identified', *Apollo*, CXLVII (no. 435), May 1998, pp. 15–20

King 1994
J.N. King 'Henry VIII as David: the king's image and Reformation politics', in Herman 1994, pp. 78–92

Lehmberg 1960
S.E. Lehmberg, *Sir Thomas Elyot: Tudor Humanist*, Austin

Lehmberg 1972
S.E. Lehmberg, 'Sir Thomas Audley: a soul as black as marble?', in A.J. Slavin (ed.), *Tudor Men and Institutions: Studies in English Law and Government*, Baton Rouge, pp. 3–31

Mackelaitė 2021
A. Mackelaitė, 'Hans Holbein the Younger as portrait draftsman', in Woollett 2021, pp. 39–53

Madden 1831
F. Madden, *Privy Purse Expenses of the Princess Mary, Daughter of King Henry the Eighth, afterwards Queen Mary*, London

Mantel and Salomon 2018
H. Mantel and X.F. Salomon, *Holbein's Sir Thomas More*, New York and London

Markow 1978
D. Markow, 'Hans Holbein's Steelyard portraits, reconsidered', *Wallraf-Richartz-Jahrbuch*, XL, pp. 39–43

Marr 2021
A. Marr, 'Holbein's second portrait of Nicolas Bourbon', *Bibliothèque d'Humanisme et Renaissance*, LXXXIV:1, pp. 105–13

Milner 1904
E. Milner, *Records of the Lumleys of Lumley Castle*, London

Moore and Crawley 1992
A. Moore and C. Crawley, *Family & Friends: A Regional Survey of British Portraiture*, London

Moyle 2021
F. Moyle, *The King's Painter: The Life and Times of Hans Holbein*, London

Müller and Kemperdick 2006
C. Müller and S. Kemperdick, *Hans Holbein the Younger. The Years in Basel, 1515–1532*, exh. cat., Kunstmuseum, Basel

Oestmann 1994
C. Oestmann, *Lordship and Community: The Lestrange Family and the Village of Hunstanton, Norfolk, in the First Half of the Sixteenth Century*, Woodbridge

Oliver *et al.* 2006
L. Oliver, V. Button, A. Derbyshire, N. Frayling and R. Withnall, 'New evidence towards an attribution to Holbein of a drawing in the Victoria and Albert Museum', *Burlington Magazine*, 148 (NO. 1236), March 2006, pp. 168–72

Parker 1983
K.T. Parker, *The Drawings of Hans Holbein in the Collection of His Majesty The King at Windsor Castle*, rev. edn with an appendix by Susan Foister, London

Petter 2002
K. Petter, '"Add but the Voice and you have Derich himself, ..." Sleuthing for clues on the Steelyard portraits of Hans Holbein the Younger', *Belvedere. Zeitschrift für bildende Kunst*, I, pp. 74–9

Pillsbury and Jordan 1985
E. Pillsbury and W. Jordan, 'Recent painting acquisitions – II: the Kimbell Art Museum', *Burlington Magazine*, 127 (no. 987), June 1985, pp. 409–18

Plender and Saltmarsh 2014
S. Plender and P. Saltmarsh, 'Copies and versions: discussing Holbein's legacy in England. Technical examination of copies of Holbein portraits at the National Portrait Gallery', in E. Hermens (ed.), *European Paintings 15th–18th Century: Copying, Replicating and Emulating*, London, pp. 50–7

Powell 2016
J. Powell, 'The network behind "Tottel's" Miscellany', *English Literary Renaissance*, XLVI, 2, Spring, pp. 193–224

Prospero 1988
A. Prospero, 'Clerics and laymen in the work of Carlo Borromeo', in J.M. Headley and J.B. Tomaro (eds), *San Carlo Borromeo: Catholic Reform and Ecclesiastical Politics in the Second Half of the Sixteenth Century*, Washington, pp. 112–38

Queen's Gallery 1978
Holbein and the Court of Henry VIII, exh. cat., The Queen's Gallery, London

Reinhardt 1982
H. Reinhardt, 'Nachrichten über das Leben Hans Holbeins des Jüngeren', *Zeitschrift für schweizerische Archäologie und Kunstgeschichte*, XXXIX, pp. 253–76

Remley 1994
P.G. Remley, 'Mary Shelton and her Tudor literary milieu', in Herman 1994, pp. 40–77

Reynolds 1999
G. Reynolds, *The Sixteenth and Seventeenth-Century Miniatures in the Collection of Her Majesty The Queen*, London

Richards 2005
P. Richards, 'The hinterland and overseas trade of King's Lynn 1205–1537: an introduction', in K. Friedland and P. Richards (eds), *Essays in Hanseatic History: The King's Lynn Symposium 1998*, Dereham, Norfolk, pp. 10–21

Roberts 1987
J. Roberts, *Drawings by Holbein from the Court of Henry VIII: Fifty Drawings from the Collection of Her Majesty Queen Elizabeth II, Windsor Castle*, exh. cat., Houston

Roberts 1993
J. Roberts, *Holbein and the Court of Henry VIII: Drawings and Miniatures from The Royal Library, Windsor Castle*, exh. cat., National Galleries of Scotland, Edinburgh, Fitzwilliam Museum, Cambridge, and National Portrait Gallery, London

Rodwell 2003
K. Rodwell, 'Nicholas Poyntz and Acton Court: a reformer's architecture', in D. Gaimster and R. Gilchrist (eds), *The Archaeology of Reformation 1480–1580*, Leeds, pp. 159–74

Roskill and Hand 2001
M. Roskill and J.O. Hand (eds), *Studies in the History of Art*, 60, *Hans Holbein: Paintings, Prints and Reception*, Center for Advanced Study in the Visual Arts, National Gallery of Art, Washington DC, New Haven and London

Rowlands 1985
J. Rowlands, *Holbein: The Paintings of Hans Holbein the Younger,* Oxford

Rowlands 1993
J. Rowlands, *Drawings by German Artists and Artists from German-Speaking Regions of Europe in the Department of Prints and Drawings in the British Museum*, 2 vols, London

Rowlands and Starkey 1983
J. Rowlands and D. Starkey, 'An old tradition reasserted: Holbein's portrait of Anne Boleyn', *Burlington Magazine*, 125 (NO. 968), Feb. 1983, pp. 90–2

Roy and Wyld 2001
A. Roy and M. Wyld, '*The Ambassadors* and Holbein's techniques for painting on panel', in Roskill and Hand 2001, pp. 97–107

Savile and Reade 1908
C.G. Savile and C. Reade, *The House of Cornewall*, Hereford

Scott 1890
[?] Scott, 'The portraits of Bishop Fisher', *The Eagle*, XVI, pp. 325–36

Starkey 1981
D. Starkey, 'Holbein's Irish sitter?', *Burlington Magazine*, 123 (no. 938), May 1981, pp. 300–1

Starkey 1991
D. Starkey (ed.), *Henry VIII: A European Court in England*, exh. cat., National Museums Greenwich

Strong 1967
R. Strong, *Holbein and Henry VIII*, London

Van Mander 1994
K. van Mander, *The Lives of the Illustrious Netherlandish and German Painters, from the First Edition of the Schilder-boeck (1603–1604)*, with an introduction and translation, H. Miedema (ed.), 6 vols, Doornspijk

Victoria and Albert Museum 1980–1
Princely Magnificence: Court Jewels of the Renaissance, 1500–1630, exh. cat., Victoria and Albert Museum, London

Vivian 1887
J.L. Vivian, *The Visitations of Cornwall, Comprising the Heralds' Visitations of 1530, 1573 & 1620*, Exeter

Vredveld 2013
H. Vredveld, '"Lend a Voice": the humanistic portrait epigraph in the age of Erasmus and Dürer', *Renaissance Quarterly*, LXVI:2, Summer, pp. 509–67

Woltmann 1872
A. Woltmann, *Holbein and his Time*, F.E. Burnett (trans.), London

Woollett 2021
A. Woollett (ed.), *Holbein: Capturing Character*, exh. cat., J. Paul Getty Museum, Los Angeles, and the Morgan Library and Museum, New York

Wubs-Mrozewicz and Jenks 2022
J. Wubs-Mrozewicz and S. Jenks (eds), *Message in a Bottle: Merchants' Letters, Merchants' Marks and Conflict Management in 1533–34. A Source Edition*, Turnhout

Acknowledgements

I first discovered the Tudors as an A-level student. As I was preparing for my exams, the Royal Collection mounted a touring exhibition of Holbein's portrait drawings, and my local museum was among the venues. Encountering the drawings for the first time was magical. Not only were these the faces of the men and women I was reading about in my textbooks, but the works were beautiful. They remained stuck in my mind and, as postcards, to endless student pinboards, and spurred an enduring curiosity about the visual culture of England in the sixteenth century.

It has therefore been a joy to work with many colleagues, within Royal Collection Trust and beyond, on this book and the exhibition that accompanies it. I am particularly grateful to Victoria Button, Nicola Christie, Martin Clayton, Stella Panayotova, Lucy Peter, Alice de Quidt and Richard Williams, all of whom read sections or all of the draft text and provided very helpful comments and feedback, and to Anjali Bulley, Polly Fellows, Nicola King, Kate Owen, Ocky Murray, Linda Schofield and Sarah Tucker, who have improved that text immeasurably since it was submitted to them. For help, support and encouragement while I was writing this book I am also indebted to Piers Baker-Bates, Quentin Buvelot, Claire Chorley, Jonathan Conlin, Nicole DeSantis, Adam Eaker, Elizabeth Goldring, Caroline de Guitaut, Diane, Guy and Justine Heard, Martin Henig, Olenka Horbatsch, Kathryn Jones, Karen Lawson, Isabella Manning, Alexander Marr, Simon Metcalf, Amy Parrish, Daniel Partridge, Lauren Porter, Rosie Razzall, Anna Reynolds, Bridget Riley, Rosanna de Sancha, Claire Shepherd, Rachael Smith, Emma Stuart, Joanna Thomas, Tung Tsim Lam, Madeleine Whicheloe, Rhian Wong, Bridget Wright, Emma Challinor, Archivist at Longleat, Ariane Mensger and her colleagues in the Basel Kupferstichkabinett, Johanna Lange and her colleagues at the Berlin Kupferstichkabinett, Hebe Halstead and her colleagues at the British Museum Prints and Drawings Study Room, Denise Görlich and her colleagues at the Dresden Kupferstichkabinett, the staff of the National Archives, and the staff of the Norfolk and East Sussex Record Offices.

The exhibition I saw as a teenager was curated by Jane Roberts, Librarian and Curator of the Print Room. The book that she wrote to accompany the tour is permanently on my desk. It has been a daily source of wisdom and guidance, as was Janie from the moment I came to work at Windsor in 2007. My last and most important debt of thanks therefore is to Janie herself, for giving me the chance to work with this wonderful collection and showing me so brilliantly how it should be done.

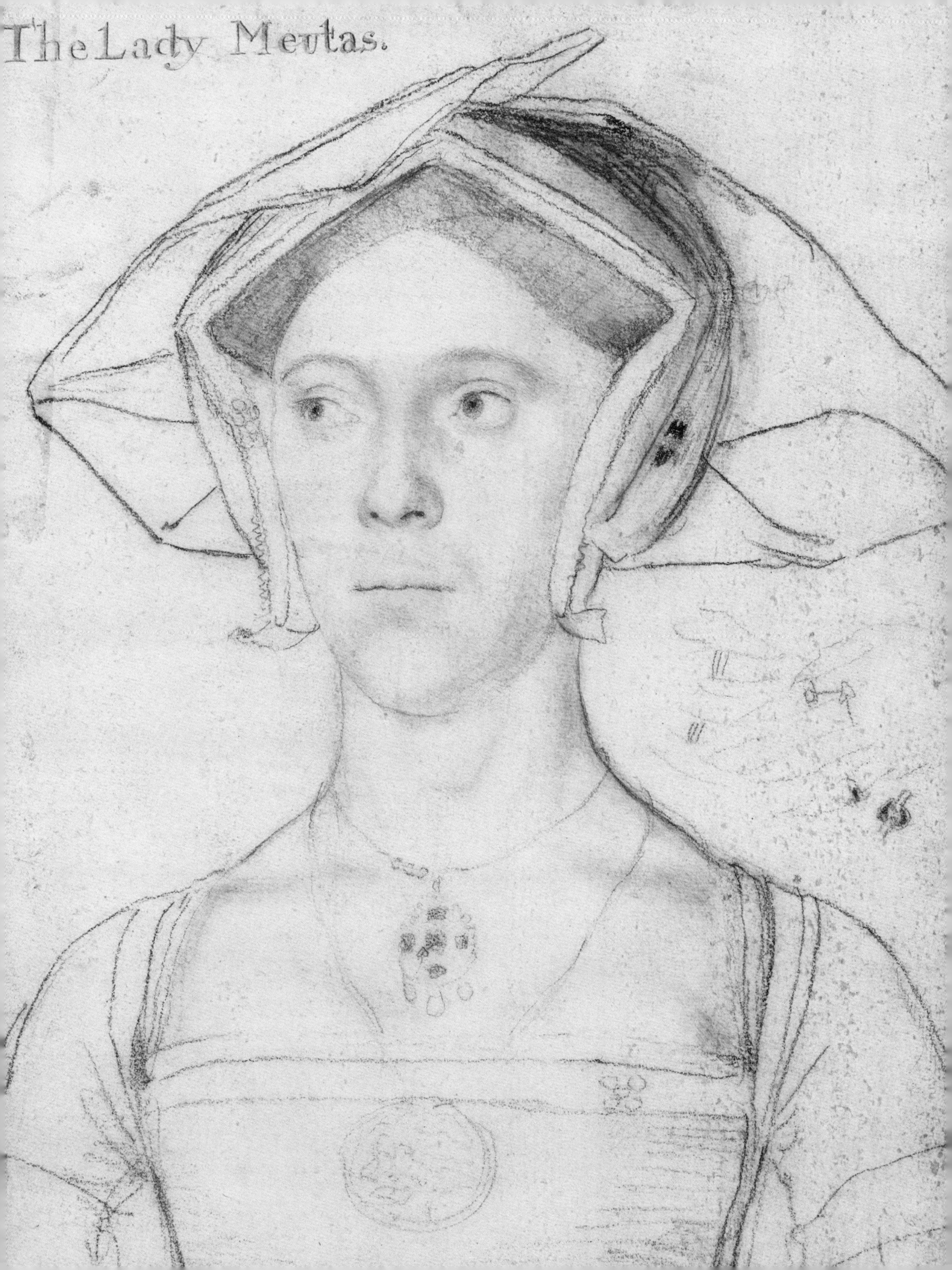
The Lady Meutas.

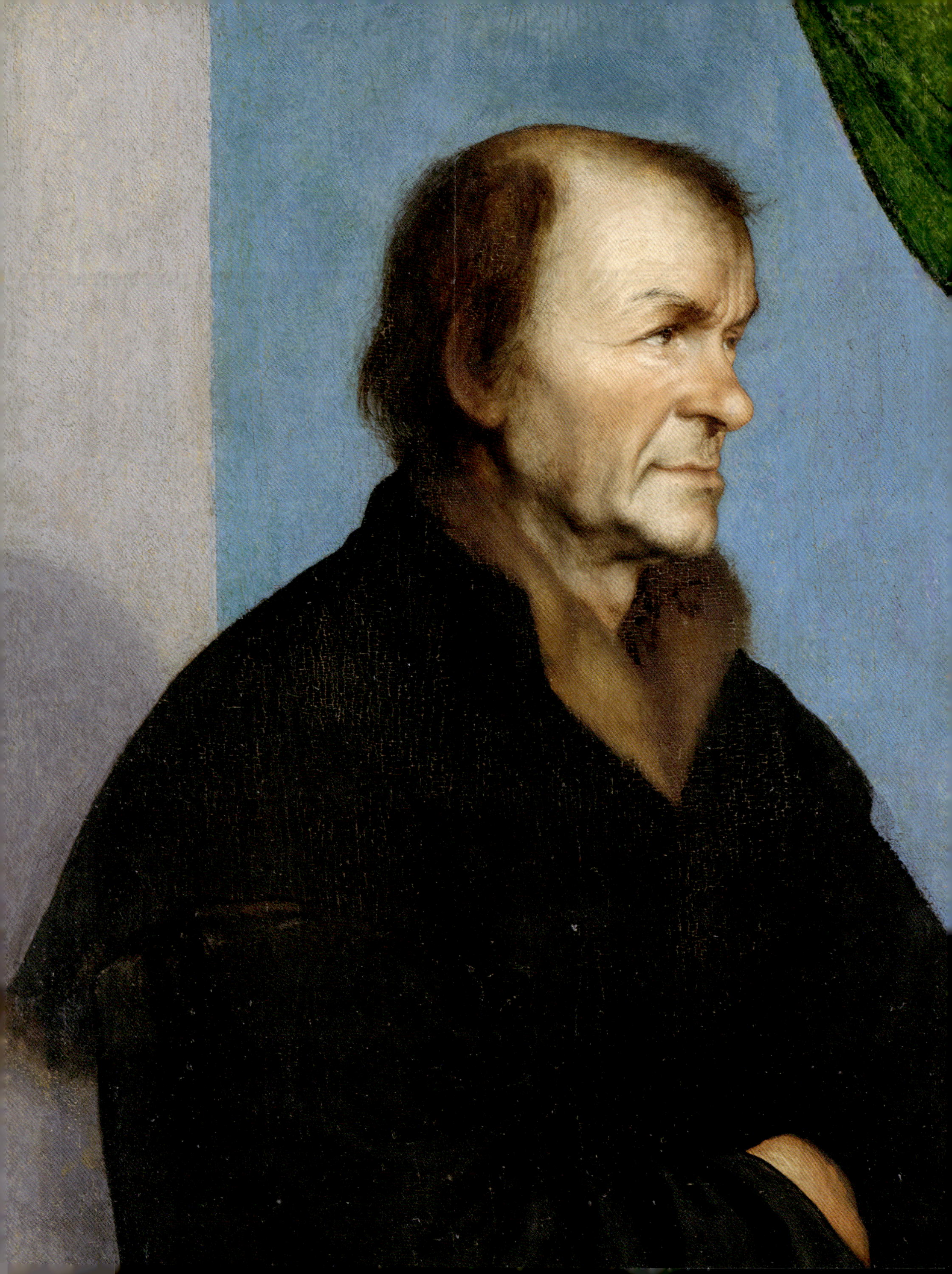

Picture credits

All images are Royal Collection Trust / © His Majesty King Charles III 2023 unless otherwise indicated below.

Bibliothèque nationale de France: Fig. 42

© The Trustees of the British Museum. All rights reserved: Fig. 29

Courtesy of East Sussex Record Office: Fig. 40

© Frick Collection: Figs 15, 35

Gabinetto Fotografico delle Gallerie degli Uffizi: Figs 1, 47

Kunstmuseum Basel: Figs 4, 7, 13, 14, 33, 37

Kunsthistorisches Museum, Wien: Fig. 48

Mauritshuis, The Hague: Fig. 16

Metropolitan Museum of Art, New York / The Jules Bache Collection, 1949: Fig. 43

© Museo Thyssen-Bornemisza, Madrid: Fig. 23

© The National Gallery, London: Figs 11, 17, 24

Courtesy National Gallery of Art, Washington DC / Andrew W. Mellon Collection: Fig. 50

© National Portrait Gallery, London: Fig. 41

National Galleries Scotland. Purchased by Private Treaty with the aid of the National Heritage Memorial Fund and the National Heritage Purchase Grant (Scotland) 1981: Fig 28

© National Trust Images / Nostell Priory: Fig. 34

Rijksmuseum Amsterdam / Creative Commons (CCO): Fig. 5

Photo RMN-Grand Palais (domaine de Chantilly) Réne-Gabriel Ojeda: Fig 6

© RMN-Grand Palais (Musée du Louvre) / Tony Querrec: Fig. 36

Saint Louis Art Museum / Museum Purchase 1:1943: Fig. 38

Städel Museum, Frankfurt am Main: Fig. 51

© Victoria and Albert Museum, London: Fig. 26

Würth Collection/Photo Volker Naumann: Fig. 8

Every effort has been made to trace and credit all known copyright or reproduction rights holders; the publishers apologise for any errors or omissions and welcome these being brought to their attention.

Index

Page numbers in *italic* font denote illustrations.

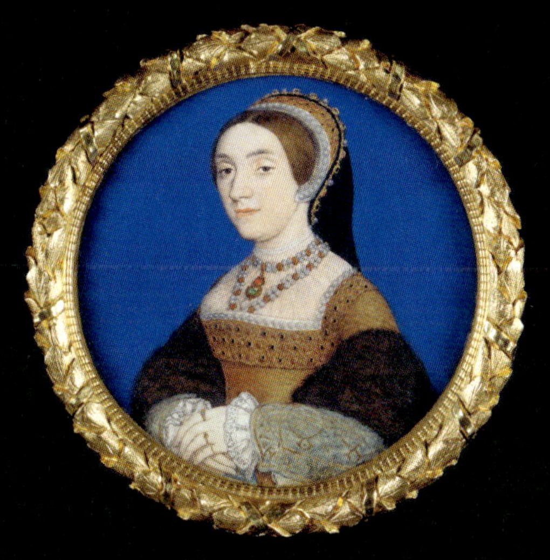

First published 2023 by Royal Collection Trust
York House
St James's Palace
London SW1A 1BQ

Reprinted 2024 (twice)

Published on the occasion of the exhibition *Holbein at the Tudor Court* at The Queen's Gallery, Buckingham Palace, London, in 2023.

ISBN 978 1 909741 87 4
SKU 103781
10 9 8 7 6 5 4 3

A catalogue record for this book is available from the British Library.

Publisher: Kate Owen
Project Managers: Polly Fellows and Anjali Bulley
Edited by Linda Schofield
Index by Nicola King
Design by Ocky Murray
Production management by Sarah Tucker
Typeset in le Monde Livre
Colour reproduction by Alta Image, London
Printed on Magno Volume 150gsm
Printed and bound in Wales by Gomer Press

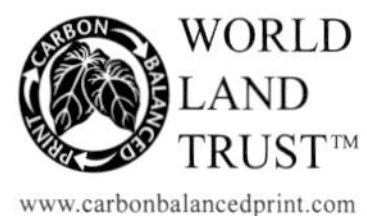

www.carbonbalancedprint.com
CBP2275

Front cover: William Reskimer (see p. 109)
Back cover: William Reskimer (see p. 107)
Page 2: Mary Shelton, later Lady Heveningham (see p. 136)
Page 4: John Godsalve (see p. 138)
Page 36: Derich Born (see p. 58)
Page 159: Katherine Howard (see p. 130)